A Swansea
Anthology

For brother John and for Sophie and Daniel,
who were born here

A Swansea Anthology

Edited by
James A. Davies

seren

Seren is the book imprint of
Poetry Wales Press Ltd,
57 Nolton Street, Bridgend,
CF31 1AE, Wales

First Edition Editorial and Preface © James A. Davies, 1996
Second Edition Editorial and Preface © James A. Davies, 2006

For individual contributions see Acknowledgements pages

Reprinted 1998
Second Edition 2006

A CIP record for this title is available
from the British Library CIP Office

ISBN 1-85411-175-4484

The publisher acknowledges the financial support of the
Welsh Books Council

Cover photography by David Palmer
davidphoto78@aol.co.uk

Printed by Cromwell Press Ltd, Trowbridge

Contents

1188 SWEYNSEI
1234 SWEINESHEIE
1278 SWEYNESHEIE
1313 SWEYNESEYE
1433 SWEYNESEY
1463 SWAYNESEY
1553 SWAUNESEY
1569 SWANESEY
1585 SWANSEY, or SWANZEY
1738 SWANSEA

from *The Swansea Guide*, by John Lewis (1851)

Preface 2006

The ten years since this anthology first appeared have been a traumatic period for Swansea, though less so for Gower. The city has had problems, most evident in the decline of its commercial and retail centre in the face of large and vibrant out-of-town shopping areas. The closure of its Leisure Centre, once a top tourist attraction, the removal of Swansea City from the Vetch Field and the end of first-class rugby at St Helen's, the perceived failure of the Maritime Quarter to sustain a viable community much beyond rentals and property investment, the inability of the once famous Swansea Music Festival to attract many top-line performers, the rise and rise of yobbery that dominates too much of the city centre on too many nights of each week, changed the city's ambience and not for the better.

But the times, and the city, are a-changing once again. Though the city centre remains a major problem - the Leisure Centre is being refurbished, the arrival of the National Waterfront Museum and the Wales National Pool is giving Swansea a higher profile, a modern sports stadium has been built at Landore - a success story for Swansea City, though less so for the Ospreys, the regional rugby club dominated by Neath and which has failed to draw much committed support from the city - and SA1, the old dock area on the eastern side of the river, is being developed as a residential and commercial area. And if one adds to this the success of Gower, though besieged by summer visitors, in resisting over-development and maintaining clean beaches, then, possibly, the area is about to undergo one of its periodic improving transformations.

The one continuing and undoubted positive is Swansea and Gower writing. The richest literary history in English of any place in Wales and surpassed by few in Britain outside London and Edinburgh, shows no sign of diminishing. This editor's necessary watchwords have been selectivity and new names. There has been little attempt (a Barbara Hardy poem is the only exception) to illustrate later writing by those already represented in the 1996 volume. Rather, nineteen new writers who satisfy the anthology's criteria have been added.

Here is Swansea's literary history mainly in English. Heini Gruffudd's anthology, *Cerddi Abertawe a'r Cwm* (2002), has done the business for Swansea poetry in Welsh, and this extension to *A Swansea Anthology* does no more than nod at the Welsh language tradition by including three poems in translation. Two are a song lyric by performer Neil Rosser and Mari George's romantic poem on Swansea

Bay. The third, by Tudur Hallam, on rugby at St Helen's, points up tensions between the city and its western approaches (and perhaps only in Wales - or Llanelli - would living less than an hour from one's favourite rugby ground be regarded as exile).

There are three fine Swansea novelists: Paul Ferris, Russell Celyn Jones, and Stevie Davies, with Martin Amis contributing extracts from his autobiography. Alun Richards and Jo Mazelis continue a short-story tradition founded by Dylan Thomas. Non-fictional prose is rarely without some reference to social problems: Robert Minhinnick's essay on Townhill's Paradise Park, in a deprived area of the city, is a superb example of compassionate reporting; Mervyn Matthews preserves a disturbing instance of labour history in his account of work in the docks.

The new poetry can still celebrate a Swansea upbringing, following Dylan Thomas, Harri Webb, *et al.*, but rarely gives itself wholly to celebration; there is no modern equivalent of Vernon Watkins's "Ode to Swansea". Rather, there is a general edginess evident even in the Gower poems: Michael Lenihan touches on the problems of crowds and litter, William Greenway looks behind a bay's beauty to find remnants of a past atrocity. In Swansea itself Kathryn Gray dramatises street life, with its moments of violence, seeming danger, and strange glamour.

Many of the new writers included in this edition are exiles or returnees, viewing Swansea with attempted but uneasy objectivity, no longer quite sure what to make of the place. Such uncertainty reflects the city's own: perhaps on the cusp of new dynamic development, perhaps facing further decline as Cardiff's tourniquet tightens. Yet, for old hands and new names the inspirational force of Swansea and Gower is as strong as ever. These places continue to fascinate writers, and can still, so often, to repeat a line from the 1996 Introduction, "take a hold on the heart".

Preface 1996

This book is an anthology of writings about Swansea and Gower. The sole criterion for inclusion is that each author, whatever his or her origin, should have written about either place – the borough or the peninsula – in an interesting and lively way. In the event, many contributors achieve much more than this. Further, those chosen have, where necessary, been given plenty of space, which might seem appropriate for responses to an area of fine views and long vistas. As a consequence this anthology is selective; fully comprehensive coverage, as they say in another context, is not the aim. Here is the editor's personal choice of poetry and prose reflecting his sense of a part of the world with which he has long had connections and which, for many years, has been his home.

★   ★   ★

Swansea has been compared to Rome, both, it is said, having been built on seven hills; die-hard Swansea Jacks continue to believe Rome comes out badly from the comparison. Landor, that famous eccentric, preferred, or seemed to prefer, Swansea's bay to that of Naples, confirming his eccentricity by citing the climate. Swansea itself rises above such exotic links as a city of contrasts, both internal and with its surroundings. It remains an "ugly-lovely town', crammed between hills and the magnificent bay, its east side still industrial, its western suburbs often filling the leafy grounds of old mansions. Once it was a frontier town where mainly English-speaking South Wales met the Welsh-speaking heartlands of Dyfed and the Swansea Valley, and did so in the mild (and damp) seaside climate – milder still on Gower – favoured by Landor, and which was usually different from the cold (and damp) Welsh uplands

Though named by and for a Viking, Swansea was essentially a Norman creation, part of the Marcher Lordship of Gower. When Gerald of Wales visited in 1188 and stayed at "the castle of Sweynsei", the town – which, to judge from his *Itinerary*, reduced him almost to silence – was firmly established as a regional capital and a place of strategic importance. Thereafter it developed as a port and as a market town (it did not become a city until 1969), with a few small local industries and coal mines.

In the late eighteenth and early nineteenth centuries – the time of Ann Hatton, Landor, and Bowdler – Swansea tried to be a resort, "the

Brighton of Wales". That ambition literally went up in smoke as the works, factories, and docks of the Victorian town created "Copperopolis", the metallurgical capital of the world. The dynamic rise of urban, industrial, and sea-faring Swansea, its subsequent decline, its one-time legacy of pollution – admired by some locals for creating the greatest tips in the western world – and general devastation, have continued to exert their own fascination.

Before World War II Swansea had its cultural golden age, when Dylan Thomas and Vernon Watkins became the most famous of a circle of gifted writers, artists and musicians, who met at the Kardomah Café. Fortunately for them they had gone their separate ways when, in 1941, German bombs destroyed both café and most of central Swansea, a catastrophe explored so movingly by John Ormond and echoing through much later writing. The rebuilt city found its first mordant remembrancer in Kingsley Amis. His numerous successors have explored and celebrated Swansea's often strangely-accented modern urban world of street, work, and club, of cultural and sporting life.

Since the Middle Ages, when Dafydd y Coed and Lewys Glyn Cothi praised the virtues of Gower gentry – demonstrating as they did so a concern for books, and a more developed interest in French wine and foreign food that still characterises many Gower residents – the peninsula has remained mainly unspoilt though not, of course, unchanged. It resisted the railway – which gave up in Penclawdd – and repelled industry and wholesale development. This beautiful and mysterious area, with its spectacular coastline and ancient monuments, has continued to draw writers. Those attracted to Rhossili, in particular, could almost fill its car-park, as well as a separate anthology.

In Glanmor Williams's words, "Of all the cities and towns of Wales, Swansea has a history unsurpassed in length, importance, variety, and interest". Perhaps those contrasts and that history have fostered literature. Perhaps it is the salt in the air. Whatever the reason, the area has a literary history unsurpassed in Wales. And though, for some, Swansea is always 'Abertawe' and Welsh-speakers a substantial presence, that literary history is mainly in English, for in Swansea, certainly since the eighteenth century, English has been the dominant language, as George Borrow noted, and Gower remains almost wholly an "Englishry".

Most writing about Swansea covers the period from the eighteenth century to the 1990s, during which it has grown greatly in size and importance, whilst Gower, for the most part, has maintained a rurality often more genteel than bucolic. The area has sometimes been called "the graveyard of ambition", though rewards for living here are more positive than that doleful phrase suggests. That it can take a hold on the heart is evident from this anthology; strong affection for place is so often the sub-text. Edward Thomas got it right: three years before his death on the Western Front he confessed "I cannot understand: that some people should be ... indifferent to Swansea". Or to Gower, one might add. This anthology is a compelling reason for that incomprehension, as is the certainty that a future edition will have to be extended.

James A. Davies

David Jones
The Sleeping Lord

And is his bed wide
                  is his bed deep on the folded strata
is his bed long
            where is his bed and
            where has he lain him
from north of Llanfair-ym-Muallt
                (a name of double *gladius*-piercings)
south to the carboniferous vaultings of Gẁyr
                (where in the sea-slope chamber
they shovelled aside the shards & breccia
            the domestic litter and man-squalor
of gnawed marrowbones and hearth-ash
with utile shovels fashioned of clavicle-bones
            of warm-felled great fauna.
Donated the life-signa:
            the crocked viatic meal
            the flint-worked ivory agalma
the sacral sea-shell trinkets
            posited with care the vivific amulets
of gleam-white rodded ivory
            and, with oxide of iron
ochred life-red the cerements
            of the strong limbs
of the young *nobilis*
            the first of the sleepers of
Pritenia, *pars dextralis*, O! aeons & aeons
            before we were insular'd.)

Note: the passage refers to the headless human skeleton,
dyed with red ochre and now known to be of a Stone Age
man, found in 1823 in one of Gower's Paviland Caves.
'Llanfair-ym-Muallt' is Builth Wells.

from *The Sleeping Lord and Other Fragments* (1974)

Lewys Glyn Cothi
His Boast of Siôn ap Dafydd and His Wife, Maud

We'll to the Gower tomorrow!
As we did yesterday, go
To those mansions by seaway –
Two days back, yea, every day.
I'll go tonight, for Siôn's sake,
Ap Dafydd, before daybreak,
To the ends of Gower, his shoot springs,
To the sky reach his saplings,
And full of leaf, a vineyard
Splendid at his house, is Maud.
Spear-shatterer Dafydd's son,
Siôn of the seed of Lleision;
Maud, in the canon, a limb,
Of Morgan, line of Gwilym.
In one love, two companions –
Dewi and one God keep one!

God, in God's image, two people
Made for him, they please us well,
Twin stocks, like Eve and Adam,
Well-rooted the two of them.
The fields of Llysnewydd's lord
Are as Damasen's greensward,
Where God made the first humans
As he made Meilig and Non.
Siôn and Maud, rose of degree,
(Twofold root of nobility),
All the parents of Gower shall grow,
Each two, each three, to follow.
To Isaac was born Jacob
And from him and his wife a son.
So, in Hebrew and Greek, we're told
In time Israel was peopled.
From Siôn's sons and their progenies
Pears will ripen on grown trees;
Burgeoning glades Gower will fill with
From this weft of Llysnewydd.
Wine (more than enough) has he

In his house by the Tawy.
Ingle where red Llywelyn,
The harper, gets floods of drink.
After him, to play and rhyme
I've place there, for a lifetime.
In Cilfái there's no less mead
Than all the booze in Gwynedd –
Long life to them, who physic
With Rhône wine the poor and weak!
Their table, while they live, is
Rich with exotic dainties.
Bread breathes frankincense upon
Us, out of Spain or Lisbon,
Pomegranate, ten quarts per pair,
And, between courses, Bon-sucre –
Another name – a red wine
Shipped in. The other's whitewine.

On three homes, then, my blessing,
And the land from which they spring.
Loud in my paternoster
God, Siôn and Maud fill my prayer.
Even if my old age ceases
To sing of faith and the Cross,
Still shall my praise be uttered,
Voice and heart, for Siôn and Maud.

Note: Siôn ap Dafydd (fl. fifteenth century), gentleman,
lived at Llysnewydd, in the Parish of Llangyfelach, in the
lordship of Gower and Kilvey ('Cilfái'). The latter (Kilvey)
is now part of east Swansea.

from *Gwaith Lewys Glyn Cothi*, ed. Dafydd Johnston (1995).
Trans. Tony Conran

Dafydd y Coed
In Praise of Hopkin ap Thomas

Noble Hopkin, bright court of drink,
Double dispensing defender, abundant gift giver
               and striker in battle;
Moneyed hand, there is at his court,
Foremost warrior, the Elucidarium
And the Grail and the Annals,
And authority of every law and its grace.

Its grace was bestowed upon the man,
And the praise of the most worthy Ifor;
Blessed noble defender,
Sweet, honest, wise, auburn-haired lord,
Fine second Gwalchmai son of Gwyar,
And the spear and shield of Gower.

Gower's protector, flourishing like Fin,
His song I'll know as long as I live;
Great lord, good chief of four battles,
Mighty and fine leader of the wise,
Hawk who loves the noble and the weak.
Mighty Hopkin dispenses green clothes.

Note: Hopkin ap Thomas (circa 1330 - after 1403), gentleman, of Ynystawe in the lordship of Gower and Kilvey, was
known for his generous patronage of the bards. He was also
known for his fine library, some volumes of which are listed
in stanza 1.

Translated into 'lined prose' by Lowri Lloyd, from the longer
poem in *The Myverian Archaiology of Wales* (1870)

Daniel Defoe
'a very thriving place'

The south part of this country is a pleasant and agreeable place, and is very populous; 'tis also a very good, fertile, and rich soil, and the low grounds are so well cover'd with grass, and stock'd with cattle, that they supply the city of Bristol with butter in very great quantities salted and barrell'd up, just as Suffolk does the city of London.

The chief sea port is Swanzey, a very considerable town for trade, and has a very good harbour: Here is also a very great trade for coals, and culmn, which they export to all the ports of Sommerset, Devon, and Cornwal, and also to Ireland itself; so that one sometimes sees a hundred sail of ships at a time loading coals here; which greatly enriches the country, and particularly this town of Swanzey, which is really a very thriving place; it stands on the River Tawye, or Taw: 'Tis very remarkable, that most of the rivers in this county chime upon the letters *T*, and *Y*, as Taaf, Tawy, Tuy, Towy, Tyevy.

There are lately mineral waters found out at Swanzy, which are reported to be of great efficacy in fluxes, and Haemorrhages of all sorts. Consumptions, if not too far gone, diabetes, palsies, rheumatisms, dropsies, and other distempers, are said to fall before these styptick and restorative waters. They certainly have very good effects in many difficult cases; but it is doing an injury to the reputation of any medicine in the world, to make it a Catholicon, and good for everything.

from *A Tour Through the Whole Island of Great Britain* (1724-6)

Anon.
On Havod, Near Swansea

Delightful Havod, most serene abode!
Thou sweet retreat, fit mansion for a god!
Dame nature, lavish of her gifts we see,
And Paradise again restored in thee.
Unrivall'd thou beneath the radiant sun;
Sketty and *Forest* own themselves outdone.
Thy verdant fields, which wide extended lie,
For ever please, for ever charm the eye:
Thy shady groves afford a safe retreat

From falling show'rs, and summer's scorching heat:
Thy stately oaks to heav'n aspiring rise,
And with their utmost tops salute the skies;
While lowlier shrubs amidst thy lawns are seen,
All clad in liv'ries of the loveliest green:
From ev'ry bush the feather'd tribe we hear,
Who ravish with their warbling notes the ear.
  But what compleats the beauty of the whole,
And has with raptures often filled my soul,
Here *Swansea* virgins ev'ry morn repair,
To range the fields and breathe in purer air;
And soon as *Phoebus* ushers in the day,
Regale themselves with salutary whey.
Here lovely M–s charming nymph is seen,
Fair as an angel, graceful as a queen:
Here H–n too the flow'ry pasture treads,
Whom none in beauty, none in wit exceeds:
Here R– comes, for ever brisk and gay,
Who steals insensibly our hearts away;
Her killing eyes a frozen priest would move,
The youth who sees her, cannot chuse but love.
Here *Rosalinda* does uncensured go,
To meet her swain, and cares not who shall know;
For what ill-natur'd tongue will dare to say
She came to meet him, when she came for whey?
S–s, W–r, W–s hither all resort,
Nymphs that would grace the greatest monarch's court;
So sweet, so charming, so divinely fair,
You'd swear a train of goddesses were there.
Here oft they pass their blissful hours away
In pleasant chat, or else in sportive play;
Or sometimes in harmonious concert sing,
While neighbouring groves with sweetest echoes ring:
The birds are hush'd, and all amaz'd appear,
Sounds more melodious than their own to hear:
Hard by old *Taway* gentle glides along,
And stays his stream to listen to their song;
While t'other side a distant brook we hear,
Run murm'ring, 'cause he can't approach the fair.
  O happy place! the world I'd freely give,
That I might always at my *Havod* live:
My *Havod* should in deathless pages shine,

Were I, like *Pope*, a fav'rite of the nine:
Or on *Kilvay*, or *Kevenbrin* they dwell,
Or in *Coomboorla's* unfrequented vale:
Would they propitious but inspire my lays,
The world should ring with charming *Havod's* praise.
    But oh! the muses deign not to inspire,
My bosom burns not with poetic fire;
I then must cease and lay aside my quill,
Lest I eclipse thy fame, by praising ill.

Note: unlikely though it may seem, and despite the spelling, this is a poem about 'the Hafod' when it was a favourite walk and beauty spot.
    The poem was composed in 1737 and is sometimes attributed to Richard Savage. He did not, however, arrive in Swansea until 1739. George Grant Francis, who served as librarian of the Royal Institution of South Wales during the nineteenth century, and who reprinted the poem in *The Cambrian*, makes the sensible point that the poem contains too much topographic and personal detail for a stranger to have mastered in the short time that Savage was here.

from *The Cambrian* (11 August 1865)

John Wesley
'a plain, simple people, right willing to hear'

August 1758

SUNDAY, 27. We reached Swansea at seven and were met by one who conducted us to his house and thence to a kind of castle in which was a green court surrounded by high old walls. A large congregation assembled soon and behaved with the utmost decency. A very uncommon blessing was among them, as used to be among them that are simple of heart. The congregation was considerably more than doubled at five in the afternoon. Many gay and well-dressed persons were among them, but they were as serious as the poorest.

MONDAY, 28. I scarce ever saw such rain in Europe as we had for a considerable part of this morning. In one of the main streets the water ran with a stream capable of turning a mill. However, having appointed to preach at Newton, about six miles from Swansea, I was determined not to break my word though I supposed but few would attend. But I was mistaken; such a number of people came together as no house in the town could contain. A barn was soon prepared, and it pleased God to send a gracious rain upon their hearts.

After preaching in Swansea in the evening, I met those who desired to join in society and explained to them the nature and design of it, with which they were quite unacquainted.

July 1764

TUESDAY, 31. We set out for Glamorgan and rode up and down steep and stony mountains for about five hours to Laugharne. Having procured a pretty ready passage there, we went on to Llanstephan ferry where we were in some danger of being swallowed up in the mud before we could reach the water. Between one and two we reached Kidwelly, having been more than seven hours on horseback, in which time we could have rode round by Carmarthen with more ease both to man and beast. I have therefore taken my leave of these ferries, considering we save no time by crossing them (not even when we have a ready passage) and so have all the trouble, danger and expense clear gains. I wonder that any man of common sense who has once made the experiment should ever ride from Pembroke to Swansea any other way than by Carmarthen.

An honest man at Kidwelly told us there was no difficulty in riding the sands, so we rode on. In ten minutes one overtook us who used to guide persons over them, and it was well he did, or in all probability we had been swallowed up. The whole sands are at least ten miles over, with many streams of quicksands intermixed. But our guide was thoroughly acquainted with them and with the road on the other side. By his help, between five and six, we came well tired to Oxwich in Gower.

Gower is a large tract of land, bounded by [Glamorgan] on the north-east, the sea on the south-west and rivers on the other sides. Here all the people talk English and are in general the most plain, loving people in Wales. It is therefore no wonder that they receive the word with all readiness of mind.

Knowing that they were scattered up and down, I had sent two persons on Sunday, that they might be there early on Monday and so sent notice of my coming all over the country. But they came to Oxwich scarce a quarter of an hour before me, so that the poor people had no notice at all. Nor was there any to take us in, the person with whom the preacher used to lodge being three miles out of town. After I had stayed a while in the street (for there was no public house), a poor woman gave me houseroom. Having had nothing since breakfast I was very willing to eat or drink, but she simply told me she had nothing in the house but a dram of gin. However, I afterwards procured a dish of tea at another house and was much refreshed. About seven I preached to a little company, and again in the morning. They were all attention, so that even for the sake of this handful of people I did not regret my labour.

August 1768

MONDAY, 8. I rode to Llanelli and preached to a small, earnest company on "Ye are saved through faith". Thence we found a kind of way to Oxwich where I pressed the one thing needful on a plain, simple people, right willing to hear, with great enlargement of heart.

TUESDAY, 9. I took a full view of the castle, situated at the top of a steep hill and commanding a various and extensive prospect both by sea and land. The building itself is far the loftiest which I have seen in Wales. What a taste had they who removed from hence to bury themselves in the hole at Margam!

> Note: 9 August 1768 - Wesley is referring to Oxwich Castle and to the Mansels, who moved from Oxwich at the Dissolution.

from *John Wesley in Wales 1739-1790* (1971)

Ruth Bidgood
Catherine at Stouthall

It must be the yellowest house in Wales!
What would John Lucas, who made it grow
in Palladian dignity from the old
farmhouse of his kin, think of this
mustard ostentation? No sure answer; he had
his quirks and whims. Yet this insistent colour
would not suit Catherine, daughter of shadow,
his dark-haired wife with melancholy eyes.
Could her Gower neighbours have met the bride
without a whisper in the mind, 'Glanareth'?
without a sickened scenting of her father's
spilt blood in that old house in hills to the north?
(And what had the delectable mother known? –
gone with her lover, and dragging two daughters
on her dubious journeying?) Perhaps

this dark girl kept a distance, let the quiet
of her coastland home, the structure of affection
and obligation, measured progress through
a given life, work on her mind. Or perhaps
that other mansion and its mayhem seemed
a half-heard story, not her own at all,
and neighbours' speculations were hardly noticed,
powerless to break the calm.

Her pictured face
is unreadable. It is hard to hold
the thought of her together with today's
exuberance of colour. She is more akin
to black water, deep grass, the dark of trees
swaying in winds not always off the sea,
but reaching out from far-off northern hills.

Note: Stouthall was repainted in 1992, and is no longer
yellow.

from *The Fluent Moment* (1996)

Henry Skrine
'all the resources of polished society'

[...] after visiting the imperfect remains of Neath abbey, crossed a hill
to reach those numerous collieries and copper-works, which, occupying an immense tract of country towards the north of Swansea, blast
the soil all around with their sulphureous influence, destroying the
appearance of verdure, and preventing cultivation. These works,
formed by several spirited proprietors, are chiefly conducted by Mr
Morris, whose handsome seat of Clasemont overlooks the whole territory; all the hills around are covered with their buildings, and the
principal assemblage of houses, formed into regular streets with a
church and wharfs, bears the title of Morristown. – Through this
curious place, and amidst all that train of villas and abundant popula-
tion which indicate the prosperity arising from successful enterprise,
we approached the walls of Swansea, now swelled into a port of great
importance, from its neighbouring manufactures.

Swansea, both in its extent, the width of its streets, and the aspect
of its buildings, far exceeds all the towns in South Wales: it has of late

been greatly improved; and, though its principal consequence is derived from its increasing commerce, it owes much to the mildness of its climate, and the singular beauty of the bay it commands. These advantages, together with a commodious shore for sea bathing, have made it the summer resort of that gay tribe of company which embellishes the public places on the coast of England, as well as the winter residence of many families from the less frequented parts of South Wales. A theatre and an assembly-room contribute to the general amusement, and all the resources of polished society are here at times to be found, amidst the noise of manufactures, and the buzz of incessant commerce. – The remains of Swansea castle consist chiefly of one massy tower with a curious light parapet upon Gothic arches; this castle and that of Oystermouth were built by Henry Beaumont, Earl of Warwick, in the reign of king Henry I. Oystermouth is a very fine ruin on the coast, at the distance of about four miles from Swansea, near the promontory of the Mumbles-head, which terminating in high hills, and stretching out far into the bay, affords a safe anchorage to ships passing up or down the channel.

This head-land of the Mumbles forms a point of the peninsula of Gower, which extends in a long and narrow isthmus between the two great bays of Glamorgan and Caermarthenshire; this is in general a rocky and uninteresting district, except where the sea views enliven it; yet has fancy, or some other cause of predilection, disposed Mr Talbot to create a highly-ornamented villa, with all its luxurious appendages, at Penrice, near the extremity of this tract, where the castles of Penrice and Pennarth, built soon after the conquest, distinguish the bay of Oxwich. The house is an elegant modern structure, and the diversities of lawn, wood, and water, introduced with much taste and design, strongly contrast the asperities of the surrounding district, and surprise a stranger with a degree of refinement he could little expect in such a tract.

–Yet may an observer, without too critic an eye, deem the trim aspect of this park, and its smooth sheet of water, inconsonant with the rough outline of the coast and country, and censure that design which has introduced the principal approach through the fictitious fragments of a modern ruin, within sight of an ancient castle, whose ivied walls overhanging the beach, seem to frown defiance at this newly created rival. Still more must he wonder, that its owner should desert the noble seat of Margam, in the midst of a populous and plentiful country, to form a fairy palace in a dreary and desolate wild, far from the usual haunts of men, and near the extremity of a bleak peninsula.

from *Two Successive Tours Throughout the Whole of Wales* (1798)

Ann Julia Hatton ('Ann Of Swansea')
Swansea Bay

In vain by various grief opprest
I vagrant roam devoid of rest
With aching heart, still ling'ring stray
Around the shores of Swansea Bay.

The restless waves that lave the shore
Joining the tide's tumultuous roar;
In hollow murmurs seems to say
Peace is not found at Swansea Bay.

The meek-eyed morning's lucid beam
The pensive moon's pale shadowy gleam,
Still ceaseless urge – why this delay?
Go, hapless wretch, from Swansea Bay.

'Tis not for me the snowy sail
Swells joyous in the balmy gale:
Nor cuts the boat with frolic play,
For me the waves of Swansea Bay.

The glow of health that tints each cheek,
The eyes that sweet contentment speak;
To mock my woes their charms display
And bid me fly from Swansea Bay.

Haste, smiling nymphs, your beauties lave
And sport beneath the sparkling wave,
While I pursue my lonely way,
Along the shores of Swansea Bay.

The foaming mountain's awful sweep
The rocks that beetle o'er the deep
The winds that round their summits play
All bid me fly from Swansea Bay.

Then Kilvey Hill, a long adieu
I drag my sorrows hence from you:
Misfortune, with imperious sway,
Impels me far from Swansea Bay.

from *Poetic Trifles* (1811)

Walter Savage Landor
'give me Swansea'

At Swansea in [1796] he had made the acquaintance of some ladies of Lord Aylmer's family, one of whom, regarded by him always with a very tender sentiment, went shortly afterwards to India and died suddenly while yet very young.

> Ah, what avails the sceptred race,
> Ah, what the form divine!
> What every virtue, every grace!
> Rose Aylmer, all were thine.
> Rose Aylmer, whom these wakeful eyes
> May weep, but never see,
> A night of memories and of sighs
> I consecrate to thee.

[...] Later in [1826] there is much in Landor's letters to his mother of the gaieties in Florence, of Lord and Lady Normanby's private theatricals, of the Duchess of Hamilton's parties, and of the enjoyment all these had given to his children. In December, noticing her mention of a visit of his sisters to Swansea, following her usual adjuration to him to return to live again among them, he says that the streak of black along that most beautiful coast in the universe had never succeeded in rendering him quite indifferent to Swansea. How beautiful did he think the seashore covered with low roses, yellow snapdragons, and thousands of other plants, nineteen years ago.

> Two years afterwards the detestable tramroad was made along it. Would to God there was no trade upon earth! Besides, before this, thousands of small vessels covered the bay, laden with lime, and whatever else is now carried with those train wagons. The gulf of Salerno, I hear, is much finer than Naples; but give me Swansea for scenery and climate. I prefer good apples to bad peaches. If ever it should be my fortune, which I cannot expect and do not much hope, to return as you wish to England, I pass the remainder of my days in the neighbourhood of Swansea between that place and the Mumbles. Nothing but the education and settlement of my children would make me at all desirous of seeing England again.

from *Walter Savage Landor,* by John Forster (1869).
For 'Rose Aylmer', see Landor, *Works* (1846)

A letter from Bath, November 17, 1839

I am not surprised at hearing that Trelawney has retired from society. He possesses a strong and philosophical mind, and we have only the choice of living quite alone or with scoundrels. He might perhaps have taken the alternative if these had any genius or even any pleasantry. I could be well content in solitude as deep as his. Never were my spirits better than in my thirtieth year when I wrote *Gebir*, and did not exchange twelve sentences with men. I lived among woods, which are now killed with copper works, and took my walk over sandy sea-coast deserts, then covered with low roses and thousands of nameless flowers and plants, trodden by the naked feet of the Welsh peasantry, and trackless. These creatures were somewhat between me and the animals, and were as useful to the landscape as masses of weed or stranded boats.

Note: Landor wrote *Gebir* in Swansea in 1798, when he was twenty-three.

from *The Literary Life and Correspondence of the Countess of Blessington*, by R.R. Madden (1855)

Abertawy

It was no dull tho' lonely strand
Where thyme ran o'er the solid sand,
Where snapdragons with yellow eyes
Lookt down on crowds that could not rise,
Where Spring had fill'd with dew the moss
In winding dells two strides across.
There tiniest thorniest roses grew
To their full size, nor shared the dew:
Acute and jealous, they took care
That none their softer seat should share;
A weary maid was not to stay
Without one for such churls as they.
I tugg'd and lugg'd with all my might
To tear them from their roots outright;
At last I did it ... eight or ten ...
We both were snugly seated then;
But then she saw a half-round bead,

And cried, *Good gracious! how you bleed!*
Gently she wiped it off, and bound
With timorous touch that dreadful wound.
To lift it from its nurse's knee
I fear'd, and quite as much fear'd she,
For might it not increase the pain,
And make the wound burst out again?
She coaxt it to lie quiet there
With a low tune I bent to hear;
How close I bent I quite forget,
I only know I hear it yet.
Where is she now? Call'd far away,
By one she dared not disobey,
To those proud halls, for youth unfit,
Where princes stand and judges sit.
    Where Ganges rolls his widest wave
She dropt her blossom in the grave;
Her noble name she never changed,
Nor was her nobler heart estranged.

from *Heroic Idylls* (1863)

Thomas Bowdler (nephew)
Thomas Bowdler in Swansea

On his return from Malta he fixed his residence at the Rhyddings, near
Swansea, in a small house situated on the rising ground immediately
above the sea, and commanding a view of that beautiful bay. The neighbourhood of the sea was to him an object of particular attention, as it
secured to him a mild climate, and the benefit of sea bathing during
some months of the year. Here, therefore, during the fourteen succeed-
ing years of his life, his winter was regularly spent; and from hence in
the summer months he made excursions to England and Scotland, for
the sake of visiting his friends and relatives, or into foreign parts, either
with the same object, or for the benefit of his health. [...]
    A literary object of a very different nature, but undertaken chiefly
with a view to the moral improvement of society, now engaged Mr T.
Bowdler's attention. This was no less than presenting the plays of
Shakspeare to the public, purified from every thing that could offend
the most delicate eye or ear. Upon this subject two opinions have pre-

vailed in extreme opposition to each other. While some ardent admirers of our poet have refused to part with a syllable of his works lest the beauty of the whole should be diminished, others have desired to exclude him from their shelves, lest they who read him should be contaminated. Extremes are generally faulty, and happily in this case a middle course could be adopted with less difficulty than could have been imagined till the trial was made; which would leave entire and untouched all that is really valuable, removing only that which is indecent and offensive; which would take away the impurities that have gathered upon the surface, and thereby show to greater advantage the beauty and uniformity of the work. This was attempted some years since by one of Mr T. Bowdler's nearest relatives in respect of twenty of the best plays. He himself afterwards carried into execution the same plan with regard to the whole number, and in the year 1818 published *The Family Shakspeare* in ten volumes, "in which nothing is added to the original text, but those words and expressions are omitted, which cannot with propriety be read aloud in a family."[...]

The near approach of his latter end was continually in his view, and he marked his strength gradually decline, without dismay or discontent; expressing no fear, unless it were that he might outlive the use of his faculties, and thereby become a burthen to those around him. This evil, if such it be, and all the inconveniences and discomforts of protracted sickness, were averted by a premature dissolution, if at the age of threescore years and ten, it could be called premature. Being detained at Swansea by transacting some distressing business, he caught a cold, which, falling upon the lungs, in a few days terminated his life.[...]

[...] His remains were deposited in a spot which he had marked out in the churchyard of the parish of Oystermouth, near the western extremity of the bay of Swansea; attended by a considerable number of the gentlemen resident in the neighbourhood, who were anxious to testify their sense of his merits, and their regret at the loss which they had individually sustained. These feelings were not confined to the bosom of intimate friends, or to the common language of every day. The sigh of regret was universal; all could tell that one stream of bounty to the poor was cut off, and one powerful stimulus to active exertion and to the support of sound principles, was suddenly checked. [...]

By his will Mr T. Bowdler, mindful of the blessings which he had enjoyed, and the source from which they came, bequeathed twenty-five pounds to the poor of the parishes of Swansea and Oystermouth, and of Box, in which he was born; and a like sum to be given to poor persons within three miles of St Boniface, adding these words::

I consider these last four bequests as humble marks of my gratitude to almighty God, for the happiness which he graciously permitted me to enjoy during a considerable portion of my life in the undisturbed tranquillity of these retired, but friendly abodes of peace, and religious, but cheerful meditation.

To the church of Swansea he also bequeathed a favourite picture, painted by Sasse Ferrati[...]

from *Memoir of the Late John Bowdler*, [with a note on Thomas Bowdler] (1825)

George Borrow
'it's no use speaking Welsh'

I continued my way to Swansea. Arrived at a place called Glandwr, about two miles from Swansea, I found that I was splashed from top to toe, for the roads were frightfully miry, and was sorry to perceive that my boots had given way at the soles, large pieces of which were sticking out. I must, however, do the poor things the justice to say, that it was no wonder that they were in this dilapidated condition, for in those boots I had walked at least two hundred miles, over all kinds of paths, since I had got them soled at Llangollen. "Well", said I to myself, "it won't do to show myself at Swansea in this condition, more especially as I shall go to the best hotel; I must try and get myself made a little decent here." Seeing a little inn, on my right, I entered it, and addressing myself to a neat comfortable landlady, who was standing within the bar, I said:
"Please to let me have a glass of ale! – and hearkee; as I have been walking along the road, I should be glad of the services of the 'boots'."
"Very good, sir," said the landlady with a curtsey.
Then showing me into a nice little sanded parlour, she brought me the glass of ale, and presently sent in a lad with a bootjack to minister to me. O, what can't a little money effect? For sixpence in that small nice inn, I had a glass of ale, my boots cleaned and the excrescences cut off, my clothes wiped with a dwile, and then passed over with a brush, and was myself thanked over and over again. Starting again with all the spirited confidence of one who has just cast off his slough, I soon found myself in the suburbs of Swansea. As I passed under what appeared to be a railroad bridge I inquired in Welsh of an ancient-looking man, in coaly habiliments, if it was one. He answered in the same language that it was, then instantly added in English:

"You have taken your last farewell of Wales, sir; it's no use speaking Welsh farther on."

I passed some immense edifices, probably manufactories, and was soon convinced that, whether I was in Wales or not, I was no longer amongst Welsh. The people whom I met did not look like Welsh. They were taller and bulkier than the Cambrians, and were speaking a dissonant English jargon. The women had much the appearance of Dutch fisherwomen; some of them were carrying huge loads on their heads. I spoke in Welsh to two or three whom I overtook.

"No Welsh, sir!"

"Why don't you speak Welsh?" said I.

"Because we never learnt it. We are not Welsh."

"Who are you then?"

"English – some calls us Flemings."

"Ah, ah!" said I to myself; "I had forgot."

Presently I entered the town, a large, bustling, dirty, gloomy place, and inquiring for the first hotel was directed to the 'Mackworth Arms', in Wine Street. As soon as I was shown into the parlour I summoned the 'boots', and on his making his appearance I said in a stern voice: "My boots want soling; let them be done by to-morrow morning."

"Can't be, sir; it's now Saturday afternoon, and the shoe-maker couldn't begin them to-night!"

"But you must make him!" said I; "and look here, I shall give him a shilling extra, and you an extra shilling for seeing after him."

"Yes, sir; I'll see after him – they shall be done, sir. Bring you your slippers instantly. Glad to see you again in Swansea, sir, looking so well."

Swansea is called by the Welsh Abertawé, which signifies the mouth of the Tawy. Aber, as I have more than once had occasion to observe, signifies the place where a river enters into the sea or joins another. It's a Gaelic as well as a Cumric word, being found in the Gaelic names Aberdeen and Lochaber, and there is good reason for supposing that the word harbour is derived from it. Swansea or Swansey is a compound word of Scandinavian origin, which may mean either a river abounding with swans, or the river of Swan, the name of some northern adventurer who settled down at its mouth. The final ea or ey is a Norwegian aa, which signifies a running water; it is of frequent occurrence in the names of rivers in Norway, and is often found, similarly modified, in those of other countries where the adventurous Norwegians formed settlements.

Swansea first became a place of some importance shortly after the beginning of the twelfth century. In the year 1108 the greater part of Flanders having been submerged by the sea an immense number of Flemings came over to England, and entreated of Henry the First, the king then occupying the throne, that he would allot to them lands in which they might settle. The king sent them to various parts of Wales which had been conquered by his barons or those of his predecessors: a considerable number occupied Swansea and the neighbourhood; but far the greater part went to Dyfed, generally but improperly called Pembroke, the south-eastern part of which, by far the most fertile, they entirely took possession of, leaving to the Welsh the rest which is very mountainous and barren.

I have already said that the people of Swansea stand out in broad distinctness from the Cumry, differing from them in stature, language, dress, and manners, and wish to observe that the same thing may be said of the inhabitants of every part of Wales which the Flemings colonized in any considerable numbers.

I found the accommodation very good at the 'Mackworth Arms'; I passed the Saturday evening very agreeably, and slept well throughout the night. The next morning to my great joy I found my boots, capitally repaired, awaiting me before my chamber door. Oh, the mighty effect of a little money! After breakfast I put them on, and as it was Sunday went out in order to go to church. The streets were thronged with people; a new mayor had just been elected, and his worship, attended by a number of halbert and javelin men, was going to church too. I followed the procession, which moved with great dignity and of course very slowly. The church had a high square tower and looked a very fine edifice on the outside and no less so within, for the nave was lofty with noble pillars on each side. I stood during the whole of the service as did many others, for the congregation was so great that it was impossible to accommodate all with seats. The ritual was performed in a very satisfactory manner and was followed by an excellent sermon. I am ashamed to say that I have forgot the text, but I remember a good deal of the discourse. The preacher said amongst other things that the Gospel was not preached in vain, and that he very much doubted whether a sermon was ever delivered which did not do some good. On the conclusion of the services I strolled about in order to see the town and what pertained to it. The town is of considerable size, with some remarkable edifices, spacious and convenient quays, and a commodious harbour into which the river Tawy flowing from the north empties itself. The town and harbour are overhung on the side of the east by a lofty green mountain with a Welsh name, no doubt exceedingly appropriate, but which I regret to say has escaped my memory.

After having seen all that I wished I returned to my inn and discharged all my obligations. I then departed [...]

from *Wild Wales* (1862)

William Thomas ('Islwyn')
Swansea

Old Abertawe, you are to me
The Jerusalem of memory.
Your estuary is in my heart,
Your waves' music, and will not part
But follows (though I've wandered far)
Like a cherub's song, dropped from a star
An age, a golden age ago
Before I started to know woe
Or whistle of an impudent train
Drowned the sweet anthem of the main –
Sound of the Tawe in my breast
And your waves' music, always blest.

from *Cymru* (no date). Trans. Tony Conran

The Dream

O if that blissful dream had lasted!
    I dreamt that on the seashore I
Was with her, and the darling breeze
    Scented from gardens beyond the sea
Merrily whistled, like an echo
Of a celestial choir on high.

I looked at her. O, how lovely
    She blushed! And how gentle a glance
The look she turned upon the poet,
    Her poet, Islwyn ...
In her manner guilelessness,
While pictured in her eye was peace.

We looked about us in that place –
    For us the spot was dear,
Sacred to all the happiness
    That we remembered here.
This appropriate scene's chief grace
Being our first meeting-place!

Treading O so lightly, I turned to the sea
And so, with an understanding smile, turned she
And the two of us our thanksgiving made
To the waves.

We thanked them
For visiting our beloved place, keeping it pure
And with a thousand myriad small white rocks
Mending its floor.

With a gentle smile she said,
'Islwyn, love, sing a tune to me.'
And sing we did, of Calvary.

And she herself swelled the praise,
Until the assembly of the birds
in the church of the green glade
Was silenced by the greater magic
our mild voices made
As they sang, sang of Calvary ...

But Oh, it was too dear to last,
All too soon the joy was past.
A thousand times too sweet
For this earth was that gentle song.
A thousand times too full
Of magic to continue long.
I woke. The dear dream fled from me
And with the dream's sweetness, She!

Then, with the shadow of her, fled
All my gladness. The sweet song
Turned to a bitter lament,
Our mild anthem for ever dead.
No image to worship, no feature ...
And look, Islwyn lonely.

from *Islwyn*, ed. T.H. Parry Williams (1948).
Trans. Tony Conran

Francis Kilvert
'the cleanest coast I ever saw'

April 1872

TUESDAY, 16. After breakfast we set out to drive to Llan Madoc, over high commons, then through pretty lanes, catching glimpses of the Carmarthenshire coast, Pembrey, Bury Port, and the smoke of Llanelly, across the sands and blue water of the arm of Carmarthen Bay called the Bury River.

A sharp pull up a steep hill brought us to Llan Madoc on the brow of a windy bare hill looking out on Carmarthen Bay. Westhorp and Mrs Westhorp went into the bare unfinished ugly barrack of a Rectory while I minded Bob and the wagonette. Presently they came out with the Vicar, Mr Davies, who looked like a Roman priest, close shaven and shorn, dressed in seedy black, a long coat and broad shovel hat. He took us into the Churchyard, but let us find our own way into the Church which was beautifully finished and adorned but fitted up in the high ritualistic style. The Vicar said that when he came to the place the Church was meaner than the meanest hovel in the village.

The Vicar invited us to join him at his luncheon to which we added the contents of our own picnic basket. He had a very good pie to which we did justice for we were all very hungry with the sea air. We were waited on by a tall clean old woman with a severe and full cap border who waits on Mr Davies and is so clean that she washes the kitchen four times a day. She used to wash her master's bedroom floor as often till he caught a cold which frightened her and she desisted.

We suggested that she might be of Flemish blood which would account for her cleanliness. The idea had never occurred to Mr Davies and he was much struck by it. The house was thoroughly untidy and bachelorlike and full of quaint odds and ends. The rigging of a boat stood in the hall for the Vicar is a great sailor and sails Carmarthen Bay in a boat built by himself. A quantity of pretty wood fretwork and carved work also stood about in the hall and the rooms, and miniature bookcases and cabinets for drawing room tables made by himself and sold for the benefit of Cheriton Church Restoration Fund. He is very clever and can turn his hand to anything. Besides which he seemed to me an uncommonly kind good fellow, a truly simple-minded, single-hearted man.

The Vicar showed us what he called his newest toy – a machine almost exactly like a sewing machine – for sawing out the pattern in his wood carving. He promised to make me a little 10/- bookcase.

We came back by another road from Cheriton, round the southern side of Cefn Bryn, past Penrice Castle and beautiful views of the coast, the sea and cliffs and Oxwich Bay with the old ruins of Penrice Castle standing grandly up in the foreground. Between Penmayne and Kilvrough we turned off the road into some fields to visit the 'Graves of the Unknown' – the "graves of the children of the people".

These graves consist of four chambers, each chamber formed by four rude stones from two to three feet high set on end and enclosing a square space about three feet square. A narrow space separates the chambers from each other and two of the chambers are on one side and two on the other of a narrow passage or gangway running the whole length of the place of burial. At either end of this gangway there is a threshold step made by a low stone set up edgewise. These graves were uncovered a few years ago and there were found in some of them skeletons sitting upright, for they were not large enough to admit a skeleton lying down.

In one of the chambers of death grew this cowslip. It was a strange weird place – how old, no one could tell – and no one knew who was buried there.

No man knoweth anything about their sepulchres unto this day.

The place of graves lies in a narrow green meadow shut in by lofty wooded banks and precipices of grey rock peeping through the trees. High up among the rocks on one bank is a large bone cavern.

When we reached home Louisa Sheldon came out to carry the wraps and things in from the carriage. "We're home in good time, are we not, Sheldon?" said Westhorp. "Pretty well to-day, Sir," answered the admirable Sheldon, smiling. She is a capital girl, housemaid, parlourmaid, butler, footman, valet, and the mainstay of the family. The Vicar of Sketty, Mr Bonley, and his sister Miss Brown walked over to dine and sleep. He has for some unknown reason taken the name of Bonley, because he disliked the name of Brown. I think while I was about it I would have taken a better name than Bonley which does not seem to me a bit better than Brown. We sat up till 1 o'clock disputing about the Athanasian Creed, Bonley taking the High Church ground and Westhorp and I the liberal view. Of course we left off exactly where we began, and no one was convinced. I hate arguing.

WEDNESDAY, 17. This is the cleanest coast I ever saw – no seaweed, no pebbles, hardly a shell – not a speck for miles along the shining sand, and scarcely even any scent of the sea. But the rocks were covered with millions of barnacles, mussels, limpets, and sea snails, and there were sea anemones in the little pools along the rocks.

As we lay on the high cliff moor above Oxwich Bay sheltered by some gorse bushes there was no sound except the light surges of the sea beneath us and the sighing of the wind through the gorse and dry heather. "They heard the voice of the Lord God walking in the garden in the cool of the day." The white gulls were flying about among the low black rocks. Some of them sat upon the rocks round the Three Cleeves and some were floating tranquilly upon the sea, rising and falling with the waves.

When we reached home we heard there had been an accident in the coal mine at Killay. The water had burst into the pit and drowned two men and a pony. A brave fellow had volunteered to go down the pit to look after them but with characteristic recklessness he had gone with a naked light and was blown up by firedamp and fearfully burnt though not killed. They say it will be three weeks before the water will be sufficiently pumped out of the pit to allow of the bodies being found.

THURSDAY, 18. This morning we drove to the Mumbles, the Westhorps, Miss Brown and myself. As we went through lovely Sketty where Welby was Vicar for fourteen years we stopped to look at the Church and Churchyard. The Church is nice but the lychgate is desecrated by the names of all the snobs of Swansea.

A tramway runs along the road side from Swansea to the Mumbles, upon which ply railway carriages drawn by horses.

Oystermouth Castle stands nobly upon a hill overlooking the town and bay. The lurid copper smoke hung in a dense cloud over Swansea, and the great fleet of oyster boats under the cliff was heaving in the greenest sea I ever saw. We had luncheon upon the Cliffs overlooking the white lighthouse tower upon the most seaward of the Mumbles. A shepherd was holloing and driving the sheep of the pasture furiously down a steep place into the sea, and a school of boys came running down the steep green slope, one of them playing 'Rosalie the Prairie Flower' on an accordion as he ran. A steam tug shot out of Swansea Harbour to meet a heavily laden schooner under full press of canvass in the bay and towed her into port, and the great fleet of oyster boats which had been out dredging was coming in round the lighthouse point with every shade of white and amber sails gay in the afternoon sun as they ran each into her moorings under the shelter of the great harbour cliff. As we went along the narrow Cliff path among the gorse towards Langland and Caswell Bay, a flock of strange and beautiful black and white birds flew along the rock faces below us towards the lighthouse piping mournfully. They were I suppose a small kind of gull but they seemed to me like the spirits of the shipwrecked folk seeking and mourning for their bodies. Among the sighing of the gorse came upon a lift of the wind a faint and solemn tolling of a deep bell from seaward. It was the tolling of the buoy bell moored off the Mumbles, a solemn awful sound, for the bell seemed to be tolling for the souls of those who had gone down at sea and warning the living off their graves.

When we came down from the cliff and were going through the town to our inn a furious whirlwind of dust arose and everything was hidden in the dense white cloud. People were obliged to grope for the walls of the houses and cry out to carriages which they could hear but not see not to drive over them.

SATURDAY, 20. Left dear hospitable Ilston Rectory at 8.15 and drove to Killay Station with Mr and Mrs Westhorp and Henry. There I bade them all Goodbye sadly and they drove on to Swansea. As I was taking my ticket Hughes, Rector of Bryngwyn, clapped me on the back. He was going to Hay so out of politeness I was obliged to go third class with him though I had paid for a second class ticket. I had much rather have gone alone for I hate talking while travelling by railway.

from Kilvert's Diary (1938-40)

Clement Scott
The Women of Mumbles Head

Bring novelists, your notebook! bring, dramatists, your pen!
And I'll tell you a simple story of what women do for men.
It's only a tale of a lifeboat, of the dying and the dead,
Of a terrible storm and shipwreck, that happened off
      Mumbles Head.
Maybe you have travelled in Wales, sir, and know it north
      and south;

Maybe you are friends with the natives that dwell at
      Oystermouth;
It happened, no doubt, that from Bristol you've crossed in a
      casual way
And have sailed your yacht in the summer, in the blue of
      Swansea Bay.

Well, it isn't like that in the winter, when the lighthouse
stands alone,
In the teeth of Atlantic breakers, that foam on its face of stone,
It wasn't like that when the hurricane blew, and the storm
bell tolled or when

There was news of a wreck, and the life-boat, and a desperate
cry for men.
When in the work did the coxswain shirk? a brave old salt
was he!
Proud to the bone of as four strong lads as ever had tasted
the sea,
Welshmen all to the lungs and loins, who, about that coast
'twas said,
Had saved some hundred lives a piece – at a shilling or so
a head!

It didn't go well with the lifeboat! 'twas a terrible storm that
blew,
And it snapped the rope in a second that was flung to the
drowning crew;
And then the anchor parted – 'twas a tussle to keep afloat!
But the father stuck to the rudder, and the boys to the brave
old boat.

Then at last on the poor doom'd lifeboat a wave broke
mountains high!
'God help us now!' said the father, 'it's over my lads goodbye.'
Half of the crew swam shoreward! half to the sheltered caves,
But father and sons were fighting death in the foam of the
angry waves.

Up at the lighthouse window two women beheld the storm,
And saw in the boiling breakers a figure – a fighting form,
It might be a grey haired father, then the women held their
breath,
It might be a fair haired brother, who was having a round
with death;
It might be a lover, a husband whose kisses were on the lips
Of the women whose love is the life of men, going down to
the sea in ships:
They had seen the launch of the lifeboat, they had seen the worst
and more;

Then kissing each other, these women went down from the
    lighthouse straight to the shore.

There by the rocks on the breakers these sisters, hand in hand,
Beheld once more that desperate man who struggled to reach
    the land.
'Twas only aid he wanted to help him across the wave
But what are a couple of women with only a man to save?
What are a couple of women? well more than three craven men
Who stood by the shore with chattering teeth refusing to stir
    – and then
Off went the women's shawls, sir, in a second they're torn
    and rent,
Then knotting them into a rope of love, straight into the sea
    they went!

'Come back!' cried the lighthouse keeper, 'For God's sake,
    girls, come back!'
As they caught the waves on their foreheads, resisting the
    fierce attack.
'Come back!' moaned the greyhaired mother, as she stood by
    the angry sea,
'If the waves take you, my darlings, there's nobody left to me.'
'Come back!' said the three strong soldiers, who still stood
    faint and pale,
'You'll drown in the face of the breakers! You will fall if you
    brave the gale!'

'Come back!' said the girls, 'we will not! go tell it to all the
    town
We'll lose our lives, God willing, before that man shall
    drown.'
'Give one more knot to the shawls, Bess! Give one strong clutch
    of your hand!
Just follow me, brave, to the shingle, and we'll bring him safe
    to land!
Wait for the next wave, darling, only a minute more,
And I'll have him safe in my arms, dear, and we'll drag him
    safe to the shore.'
Up to the arms in water, fighting it breast to breast,
They caught and saved a brother alive! God bless us we know
    the rest –

Well many a heart beats stronger, and many a tear was shed,
And many a glass was tossed right off to the Women of
    Mumbles Head.

from *The Women of Mumbles Head* (1883)

Maura Dooley
The Women of Mumbles Head

The moon is sixpence,
a pillar of salt or
a shoal of herring.
but on such a night,
wild as the wet wind,
larger than life,
she cast a long line
over the slippery sea.
and the women of Mumbles Head
are one, long line
over the slippery sea.
wet clothes clog them,
heavy ropes tire them,
but the women of Mumbles Head
are one, long line,
over the slippery sea.
and under white beams
their strong arms glisten,
like silver, like salt,
like a shoal of herring,
under the slippery sea.
and they haul
for their dear ones,
and they call
for their dear ones,
casting a long line
over the slippery sea.
But the mounting waves
draw from them,
the mountain waves
draw from them,

the bodies of their dear ones,
O, the bodies of their dear ones,
drawn under the slippery sea.
In a chain of shawls
they hook one in,
fish-wet, moonlit,
they've plucked him back
from under the slippery sea.
For the moon is sixpence,
a pillar of salt
or a shoal of herring,
and the women of Mumbles Head
are one, a long line
over the slippery sea.

from *Sound Barrier Poems 1982-2002* (2002)

E. Howard Harris
The Phantom Fleet

The evening twilight shimmers on the blue of Swansea Bay,
The lighthouse leaps with sudden light before the close of day,
And in this hour of magic round headland sailing free
The Cuba copper clippers glide as phantoms o'er the sea.
From Cuba and Iquique, from 'Frisco, Callao,
Creep in the old-time clippers from the days of long ago.

The schooner and the brigantine and many craft beside
Are homing to the harbour and floating with the tide,
With their cargoes of salt-petre and their freights of copper
            ore,
The fleet of old windjammers as they sailed in days of yore.
From Cuba and Iquique, from 'Frisco, Callao,
Creep in the old-time clippers from the days of long ago.

They are brave with sails and pennons as they move across
                    the sea,
And the sea blood in my body fills the joyous heart of me,
For they did a work for Swansea, though they never come
                    again

Save as phantoms on the water from the distant Spanish main.
From Cuba and Iquique, from 'Frisco, Callao,
Creep in the old-time clippers from the days of long ago.

They battled with the breezes and breakers of the Horn,
With a cheer amid the tumult for the place where they were
born,
And jury-rigged they often had to make the nearest port,
But with singing and with swearing they kept the ship afloat.
From Cuba and Iquique, from 'Frisco, Callao,
Creep in the old-time clippers from the days of long ago.

There is nothing more majestic than a vessel in full sail,
So the phantom fleet returning with a joyous cry I hail,
As the fine old Swansea seamen hail that homeland Mumbles
Head,
The children they have cherished, and the wives that they
have wed.
From Cuba and Iquique, from 'Frisco, Callao,
The shadow of the Ranzo boys lost in the long ago.

from *The Singing Seas* (1926)

Sea Shanty (19th century)
Old Swansea Town Once More

Oh, the lord made the bees, an' the bees did make the honey,
But the Divil sent the woman for to rob us of our money,
An' around Cape Horn we'll go!
An' when me money's all spent ol' gal, we'll go 'round Cape
Horn for more, ol' gal, ol' gal!
You're the one I do adore,
An' all I'm livin' in hopes to see
is ol' Swansea Town once
more, ol' gal, ol' gal!
You're the one I do adore,
So take me ropes and make me fast,
In ol' Swansea Town once more!

Now we're outward bound around Cape Horn, to 'Frisco an'
      around,
I'll send you letters when we get there, an' you'll know
      I'm homeward bound, ol' gal, ol' gal!
Now when we're homeward bound, my dear,
I'll bring you silks galore,
I'll bring you jewels an' rings an' things,
An' ye won't wear the weeds no more, old gal, old gal!
   *Chorus:*You're the one I do adore,
     An' all I'm livin' in hopes to see,
     Is ol' Swansea Town once more, old gal, old gal!
     You're the one I do adore,
     So take me ropes an' make me fast
     In ol' Swansea Town once more!

Now when we're leavin' 'Frisco Town,
Outside of the Golden Gate,
I'll write my last letter to you, me dear,
Then ye won't have so long to wait, old gal, old gal!
   *Chorus.*You're the one, etc.

An' when we're leavin' the old Fallerones,
Bound for my ol' Swansea,
I know ye'll pull, gal, on the string,
For to haul me in from sea, old gal, old gal!

An' then when we've rounded old Cape Horn,
Climbin' the hill for home,
Passed the Western Islands into the Bay,
We'll have no further for to roam, old gal, old gal!

An' then when we up Channel do sail,
I'll pray that you'll be there,
To wait, me dear, on Swansea pier,
My lovely presents for to share, old gal, old gal!

When Swansea Town we're off once more,
We'll see the lights so clear,
I know that's Megan down on the pier,
In her dimity apron dear, old gal, old gal!

from Shanties from the Seven Seas (1961)

E.A. Dillwyn
'if ever you should find yourself at Swansea'

Do not people's natures, more or less, take after the places where they are born and pass their lives? And is not a man much more likely to be rough and wild if he has been brought up in an exposed cottage whose walls rock and shake with every blast of wind, than he would have been if he had lived in some snug valley home, sheltered on all sides by hills and trees, and never had any further acquaintance with bad weather but what I may call an accidental one – that is to say, only knowing about it when he was out of doors – instead of being always in the midst of it, both indoors and out, and compelled to feel and know what it was like wherever he might be? If I am right in this idea, it will account for the Upper Killay folk being a rather rough set; for Upper Killay stands just at the edge of Fairwood moor, which is a place where you feel the whole force of every wind that blows, and where there always is some air stirring even though there may be none anywhere else, and where a hailstorm beats against you as if each stone wanted to make a hole through, and come out on the other side. [...]

[...] As for the traitor, Pugh Morgan, I have heard what became of him through letters and newspapers which have reached me at various times from some of my old friends.

You may remember how Martha was struck with the idea that Pugh might have betrayed us through jealousy of Tom, and how I sent her to communicate her suspicions to Jenkin Thomas – I being at that moment starting on my flight, and having no time to see him myself. When she had told Jenkin he spoke about it to one or two other Rebeccas, and then they began to make secret inquiries, which revealed that Pugh had certainly been in Swansea on the day of the fight at Pontardulais 'pike; and furthermore, that on the same day, a man answering to his description, specially noticeable by reason of his squeaky voice, had been closeted with the head of the police, and had not left his house till next day.

This was fatal to Morgan. [...]

I have already mentioned Clyne Wood, which is close to Killay and runs down to the sea. Well, this wood is full of deep pits, where workings for coal have been begun and then deserted because of the coal failing; and as these old pits are generally overgrown with brambles and long grass and bushes at the mouth, it is a hard matter to see them; and being usually more or less full of water, they are very nasty places for any living creature to get into, and many a dog has been lost in them when taken there by gentlemen out shooting. It happened that a gentleman was one day leaning over one of these deserted coal-pits, and trying to look into it, when the gun he was holding slipped out of his hand and fell in; and as he set great store by this gun, he took a good deal of trouble to get it back again. To accomplish this he had to get ropes and ladders, and send someone down into the pit; and at the bottom was found the remains of a man's body. A thick cord fastened the hands and feet together, and proved that he must have been thrown in by someone else, and had not fallen in by accident. The face was quite unrecognisable, as the flesh had been almost all eaten away from the bones by rats; but on dragging the mud and slime at the bottom of the pit, a tin box was discovered bearing Pugh Morgan's name upon it, and also a knife that was known to have belonged to him, and it was generally believed that the body must have been his.

How he came there was never known, but I think I can make a pretty good guess at it. The men who had been betrayed by Pugh Morgan at Pontardulais, and who had sworn to be revenged on the traitor if ever they should discover him, were men with fierce passions who would not fail to keep their oath of vengeance. I can imagine that a party of these men may have got hold of Pugh in some out-of-the-way place, or possibly may have seized him at night in his own cottage, have stifled his cries for help, tied him hand and foot, carried him gagged and helpless to Clyne Wood, flung him down the coal-pit, and there left him to drown if it should be full of water, or, if it should be dry, to linger on half smashed by the fall till he died of hunger, as a fitting reward for his treachery. Whether it were really so or not I cannot tell; but at all events nothing more was ever seen or heard of Pugh Morgan – and no man may expect to live securely and die in peace who has betrayed to prison and death those who trusted in him.

And now the story of the life of my old self is ended, and I trust you to tell it to Miss Gwenllian for me if ever you have the opportunity. And if ever you should find yourself at Swansea, and if you go to the top of one of the hills to the west of the town, and see the view from there – looking across the bright blue sea to Devonshire in one direction, and seeing, as you turn round, Lundy Island, and Cefn Bryn, and the distant mountains in Pembrokeshire, Carmarthenshire, Breconshire, and the Swansea valley, and the coast beyond Neath, and across to the Dunraven cliffs – then perhaps you will be able to understand why I have so pined and longed for my own home and country ever since I have been here, and why it grieves me that I cannot see it again just once more before I die; for I have never seen any other place that has seemed to me so beautiful.

from *The Rebecca Rioter: A Story of Killay Life* (1880)

John Beynon
An old lie out

(Reaching out under Swansea Bay from Blackpill are the workings of a colliery drowned when the sea broke through into the galleries. The owners denied that certain men had lost their lives and refused the families compensation. Years later high tides caused the water level to rise up the old shaft in Clyne Valley.)

We had no time to pray
Who shared poverty and were brave:
A row of faces, hung balloons,
In the darkness as the roof split
Lengthwise, squashed under its hammer,
A soft melon to the forged wall
Of water we could not see
But had, unwillingly, to obey:
We rolled unconscious, already drowned.

They closed the pit and a mile inland
Seventy years later the sea rose up
The crumbled shaft and burst
Over the long grass and lay
Our bones in homage under a drying sun,
To kindle, not disown:
How we would have laughed to see
The flash of windscreens and curious eyes
As we were spat out, one by one,
The rank earth repelling all their lies
And our voiceless anger gloriously sown.

from *Green Horse* (1978)

Samuel Clearstone Gamwell ('Pierre Claire')
'Don't Joe; Don't!'

At the Uplands Park
Ere leaf and bark
Are bidden from sight in the Night's black cowl
You may often hear

In the tree-tops near
The whirring notes of the Spinner Owl.
Its purring noise
The heart decoys,
Like the chanting of Pussy at evening meal,
Or a homely rhyme
Of the olden time
When the maidens sat plying the busy wheel.
But I've sometimes heard an odder bird
Sing: 'No – I – won't!'
(Then, after a rustle, as if of a tussle):
'Don't Joe; don't!'

'Tis a lovely spot,
Not soon forgot,
With sweet walks winding around the hill;
In its leafy bowers
Lurk the scent of flowers
And the silvery voice of a laughing rill.
Through the summer day,
When the children play,
Delightful to hear is their merry shout,
As they meet and disperse,
While the smiling nurse
Leads over the greensward the frolic rout.
But the echoes around oft catch a sound
Like: 'No – I – won't!'
(Then, after a squealing, these accents appealing):
'Oh, don't, Joe; don't!'

'Tis said that a ghost,
Or a phantom host,
Inhabit the deeps of Cwmdonkyn lake;
That the voices of those
Long gone to repose
Come back after sunset our nerves to shake.
And the credulous hold
That a Baker bold,
While taking that way his belated bread,
Was startled to hear,
On the night air clear,
Mysterious murmurs of import dread,

That seemed to say, in a petulant way,
    'No – I – won't!'
(Then, after a hissing, that sounded like kissing),
    'Don't, Joe; don't!'

    I've consulted books
    Of forbidding looks
On the science of natural history,
    In hope to find
    What name and kind
This bird of strange omen and cry might be;
    There are jays and daws,
    There's the rook that caws
Round the homes of the aristocracy.
    There's the whip-poor-will,
    And the wee cross-bill,
And the 'peeker that peeks in the old oak tree';
But none of the list its song can twist
    Into 'No–I–won't!'
(Then, after a ruffle, suggesting a scuffle),
    'Don't, Joe; don't!'

    In vain I've sought
    With careful thought
To fathom this marvellous mystery;
    No clue is found
    To the kissing sound
In the study of ornithology.
    But the wish to glean
    What the noise may mean
Brings to Uplands at twilight a multitude;
    Nor is it rare
    That maidens fair
Hear the mystical music with fortitude.
And while they listen, their bright eyes glisten
    A 'No – I – won't!'
But when he sitting by them, would pacify them,
    'Tis 'Don't, Joe; don't!'

from *Some 'Pierre Claire' Poems* (1897)

[from] At Singleton

A Memory of June 4th, 1887

The leafy park of sea-side Singleton
Lay in the sunlight of as fair a sky
As ever wooed the unreluctant earth
And won her answering smile. Below, the beach –
A semi-circle of some twenty miles
Of yellow sand dunes and grey limestone rocks,
Rugged and bold – with outstretched arms embraced
That beauteous Bay which not unfitly claims
To share the palm that favoured Naples holds.
Behind, the shelt'ring ridge of Sketty Hills
Preserved the semblance of old beacon fires
In flames of golden gorse; while all the woods,
Gay in the tints of tardy summertide,
Rolled up the fringes of their serried crests
Against the dome of blue. Through verdant glades,
Down dusky avenues of oaks and elms,
And through rare rifts of leafage, could be caught
Glimpses of sunlit landscapes far away;
Elsewhere the lines of tall ancestral trees,
Standing like sentinels around the walls,
Confined the view to Singleton itself,
So full of nature's sweetest, softest charms –
For worshippers a temple wide enough.

Upon a central space, where terraced banks,
With flowers enamelled rise to velvet lawns,
The pleasant mansion of the Vivians stands,
Its weathered stonework marked by many a stain
Of grey and yellow lichen; and its face,
Like a shy damsel's, hid behind a veil
Of dark green creepers, dotted here and there
With pendant blossoms, purple, cream and red.
Not built for ostentation, but delight,
Not lifting up to heaven a Babel-tower,
Nor spreading over acres, like a town,
It stands a monument of happy art,
In harmony with nature's sweetest self,
The home and heirloom of a favoured race.

from *Some 'Pierre Claire' Poems* (1897)

The Sketty Chimes

(No one can live in, or pass through, Sketty without being
pleasantly startled and lingeringly held by the sweet music
or the chimes. These emanate from beneath the tapering
spire of the Church belfry, which is so charmingly half-
hidden on its eminence by trees almost as high as itself. The
bells have been long in their place, but the clock and the
mechanism connected with the chimes were added recently
by the Hon. Aubrey Vivian, who used for this purpose the
money bequeathed to him by an old servant of the family
of the Vivians, of Singleton, the head of which is now raised
to the Peerage under the name of Lord Swansea.)

The sweet, soft air of early even-fall
    Thrills to the dulcet music of the Chimes –
Where Sketty lifts to heaven her tree-tops tall,
And the slant sun shoots red rays over all –
      Like long-remembered love-touched rhymes.

White lie the roads in dust; the distant Town
    Looms on the backward vision like a hill
Mantled in mist, now white, now grey, now brown,
    Mottled with vapours by the Vale sent down;
      But, here, the sky is blue and still.

Fair was the fertile thought and kind the hand
    That, reverent, set on high these tuneful bells
To mark with melody the dwindling sand
Of Life's dear hour-glass in this leafy land,
      Where whispering Sea Wind lulls and swells.

'Tis said the Handmaid of a rich, proud race,
    Who long had served them for a servant's wage,
Dying, bethought her dearly of a grace
That she might do her master – e'en to place
      His son in her small heritage.

Her humble hoard, thus lovingly bequeathed
    To one who loved sweet things of olden times
Lo, that poor Handmaid's memory now is wreathed
Forever with the landscape where she breathed,
      In these sweet-sounding Sketty Chimes!

Thus may it be hereafter more and more:
Thus may We – Servants – live that, when we die,
We may hand down our large or little store
Of wealth or worth to beautify the Door
Of Life for people yet to be.

from *Some 'Pierre Claire' Poems* (1897)

David Smith and Gareth Williams
Wales v. England (7 January 1899)

This was the first international at St Helen's since 1895. The ground, magnificently situated on the curve of Swansea Bay, would alternate with the Arms Park until 1954. Its international tradition reached back seventeen years in 1899 to the first home international with England in 1882, so neither the expected crowds nor the importance of this game would overawe the jostling town of winding streets that mediated their commercial way between the pressing hills and open sea. There were five Swansea men in the side. The ever-present W.J. Bancroft as captain had kept away, as he always did, from "the fragrant weed" for a week before the match, and was confident the return of Evan and David James would ensure victory, though if they were too closely penalised by sterner refereeing he might swing it himself. A twenty-nine year-old veteran of 328 first class games, Bancroft had already that season converted 43 goals, dropped 2 goals, kicked 3 penalties and scored 5 tries. His play was reported to be as vigorous as ever, still enlivened by a readiness to throw the ball to himself from line-outs and to run from behind his own goal (in the Irish game that March an encroaching crowd would limit his space for manoeuvre and hundreds of forwards, some of them Welsh, would cheer to hear the Swansea imp had gone down). The Jameses were opposed by the skilful Livesay of Blackheath and the captain, Arthur Rotherham of Richmond, who would complain of their play during the game. The Swansea forwards were the new caps, Fred Scrines, a fast spoiling forward (3 caps in all, the last in 1901) and Parker (both caps that year), who were part of a formidable All Whites team that would sweep the Welsh honours for that season. [...]
    [...] The now customary brass band blared away before the first international match on Welsh soil for two full years started promptly at 2.45 p.m. The crowd had been pouring into Swansea all day. The

G.W.R. alone was running fifteen day excursion trips from Cardiff to Swansea, leaving at 10.00 a.m. to return at 6.00 p.m., their usual fare of 7s. 7d. slashed to 3 shillings; the Taff Vale Railway Company had joined forces with the Rhondda and Swansea Bay Company, whose trains rattled through the mountain wall that had once blocked off the top of the Rhondda, to offer a day trip for half a crown and with a later start for morning workers. Over 20,000 people were expected. The gate receipts totalled £1,500, which made it the largest crowd at a Welsh international. The newly-wed Walter Rees (now on the Neath School Board and to be Mayor in 1905) was much pleased, though less so by those other entrants on the rugby scene, the ticket touts, who were selling three shilling tickets for a sovereign.

From the railway station in the town, disgorged from carriages where they had been packed in up to twenty at a time, grey-white engine smoke billowing around them before blowing up to join the white pall of the copper works, the rugby fans hired horse cabs or caught a tram or, more often, walked the couple of miles to the ground in a jostling, chattering, stream of bowlers and ulsters, cloth caps and mufflers, brown polished brogues and black shiny lace-up boots with clattering nails for long wear. It was a scene that was already taking on the shape of familiarity for participants and onlookers. Old friends, favourite eating-houses, a bagful of chestnuts so hot they burned your frozen fingers, a white china bowlful of spiced faggots and peas, a hotel foyer, the grandiose Mackworth's perhaps, echoing to opinions on the state of the coal trade after the strike's end or the tense political situation in South Africa (the Boer War would break out in October 1899). An ambience piquant with the smell of warmed whisky and mulled wine mingling into the heady fumes of cigars and oil lamps lit against the winter gloom that would soon lift outside just as the glint of brass fittings and gilt scrolled mirrors inside seemed to promise. Lots of watering-holes on the way to St Helen's would fill and empty with successive thirsty travellers slapping coppers on a curving mahogany bar, scraping the light snow from their shoes on the bar rail while waiting for frothy pints of amber-coloured ale to slip down throats and slop on the scuffed sawdust floor where the dented spittoon yawned tirelessly for the attention of hawking clay-pipe smokers.

All the small noises of these packed spaces then flowed on into the main procession flattening out down King Edward's Road or along the sea-road swerving between town and the far Mumbles lighthouse, switchbacking over the humped up streets that fell over each other down from the Uplands like conscious lemmings anxious for their fate, to St Helen's. Newspapers of the day, their right to visual entertainment not denied by film and television, spelled out the full flavour of the crowds by positioning reporters in various parts:

On the one side the grandstand was packed and a large proportion of seats having been taken by ladies, their sporting favours lent enchantment to the view. On the other, standing high up above a natural terrace, which was like a sea of faces, is a large row of villas, and all the windows of these houses were filled with interested occupants who, considering the chance of rain, were envied by the less fortunate people who had failed to gain admission to the stand by the spirited competition which had bought up every inch of available room. A long range of seats inside the ropes had been reserved for old internationals ....

We were outside the ropes, standing about the cinder path where of old time Swansea had a cycling track, and like herrings in a barrel we were pressed, squeezed, jammed on that sloping vantage ground which rises above the green level on the northern side of the enclosure. This odd 15,000 or so were representative of the masses, and they talked and smoked and expectorated and swore according to their ability and inclination ... I gathered that the vast majority favoured shag for smoking and Wales to win. Rhondda colliers, Swansea copperworkers, Landore steelworkers, Llanelly tinplaters ... in abounding multitude ... argued about the respective merits of the Welsh three-quarters whether playing or not ... for man is much the same whatever chapel he does not go to.

The game itself was a triumph for a Welsh football combination that revealed club form after their coaching session in the week. Bancroft's men were praised for their willingness to vary the passing game with cross-kicks, screw-kicking to touch, punts and short bursts near the line. They added to that the unexpected thrusts of the Jameses, "Banky's" elusive runs from suicidal positions and Llewellyn's opportunism, to swamp a plucky English side which only managed a consolation try near the end. Before that, Wales had plundered 26 points. In the first half Llewellyn scored twice – first he charged down a clearance kick, gathered and darted in, then, as the Welsh pack pushed their counterparts, the Jameses stole away "on the short side" to send him in. The Welsh pack were disciplined throughout, holding or heeling when required, nursed from time to time by Bancroft "the great one who did what everybody expected he would do". And sometimes what they did not.

At the start of the second half his kick-off astonished everyone by going to touch in goal. Shortly after, receiving the ball from David James on his own line he ran causing "great deal of uneasiness", until it was cleared. Viv Huzzey's first try came when the Welsh forwards wheeled the scrum on the English 25 and Evan James, despite a split finger and dislocated shoulder, scurried away, feinting a pass left to his brother, throwing right (was Dickie Owen watching?) to Gwyn Nicholls who swerved past Royds, the English centre, and gave to Huzzey who left his opposing wing to score. Huzzey had had his second try before Llewellyn, when a rare English attack was repulsed, picked up in the open, passed to Scrines who threw to Parker who gave the trainee pharmacist his third. From a cross kick by Bancroft that Nicholls and Stout, the Richmond centre, contested, the young Llwynypia captain scored a record four tries. Bancroft goaled four of the Welsh six tries. It took thirty minutes to clear the crowd from the pitch when the final whistle went. [...]

As 1899 ended the James brothers had fled nineteenth century Wales for the last time. They were picked to play against Scotland in March but first one, then the other, had cried off through injury. Shortly after they were back with Broughton Rangers for £200 down, £2 a week and jobs as warehousemen. They took the whole family, from grandmother to children, with them, but *hiraeth* for Bonymaen was too strong for David's Welsh-speaking wife. Evan contracted tuberculosis. The Greek gods, as their Jewish mother proudly called them, came back to twentieth century Wales. David toiled in the copper works once more until he died in 1929. Evan died of tuberculosis in 1902, aged thirty-three. David, a voracious reader about the American West, had named one son Jesse and wanted to call the other Frank. His wife insisted on Llewellyn. It was a good compromise between past and future.

from *Fields of Praise* (1980)

David James Jones ('Gwenallt')
Rugby

Allt-wen was no village on the map of Wales –
Workers had no country, proletariat no borders.
We bent our knee to the fire at the stackhead –
Flame of world justice, brotherhood of man.

Yet we dreamed all week of a feast of Red Shirts
At St Helens, face to face with England –
Going mad when Bancroft kicked his Welsh goal
Or Dicky Owen scored a try for his nation.

from *Eples* (1951). Trans. Tony Conran

A.G. Bradley
Cycling to Port Eynon

Swansea, though even more finely placed by nature than Neath, is quite the most untoward-looking town in South Wales. Whether the smelting of copper is especially conducive to a dismal aspect I know not, but Swansea to the unaccustomed eye is doleful beyond words. Its well-to-do folk perched upon the mountain slopes around find infinite compensation up there, no doubt, for the hours expended in the murky hive below, which is said, moreover, to contain not a single first class street. I have threaded its highways on two or three occasions, though in hasty and uncritical fashion, I admit, but I should be inclined to think that this taunt of its neighbours was not libellous. However that may be, it is much better to be dirty and busy than ornamental and working half-time, and Swansea appeared to be working at full blast; so also was Neath, which is comparatively small and comparatively inoffensive to the fastidious eye. Indeed, industrial Glamorganshire generally, as far as one may see and hear as an outsider in such matters, seems busy and cheerful.

Now Swansea is actually in Gower, and is a leading illustration of what prodigious contrasts within a narrow compass this little island of ours can show. Port Eynon is also in Gower – very much so indeed – being almost at the extreme point of the peninsula. It is seventeen miles away, and Swansea is its nearest market town and virtually its nearest station. Now Port Eynon is at the end of the world and almost suggestive of Aberdaron at the point of Lleyn in its astonishing seclusion. But Port Eynon has a 'bus that thrice a week makes the laborious journey to and from its metropolis. I had contacted some acquaintance in remoter Wales with the nature of these indispensable but archaic survivals; so consigning my traps only to its care, I mounted a bicycle, and pursuing the now rain-soaked highway through the straggling and leafy suburbs of Swansea, and climbing up the long hill through Sketty, I found myself in three or four miles clear of every trace of urban life, and looking out from an expanse of breezy moorland over most of Gower and much of south Wales.

Gower is nearly twenty miles long by five or six miles in width, and has over fifty miles of sea coast, mainly rugged and often magnificent of aspect. Like Pembroke, it has nurtured two distinct races side by side for seven or eight hundred years. But the greater part of the peninsula is English; the smaller is Welsh, and lies on the north-eastern slope facing Carmarthenshire. The line between them, geographically and socially, is almost as sharp as that in Pembroke. It used to be said that when an English Gowerian was asked for the house of a Welsh neighbour just over the line, he generally replied: "I donna knaw; a lives somewhere in the Welsherie". Recent influences however have somewhat modified this remarkable cleavage, as in the case of Pembrokeshire.

But the Gower man outside the Welsherie is no more Welsh than a Devonian, though he is not like a Devonian. His vices and virtues are entirely his own, and his language, like that of south Pembrokeshire, is an English vernacular evolved in isolation. To use a convenient term, his stock, his character and his speech are Teutonic. The attitude of the Gower rustic when you touch on the matter of conversation with him is not devoid of humour. It is enough for him, of course, that he is a Gower man and not a Welshman, though he does not seem to repudiate the Cymric affinity with the same fervour of pride and prejudice that a Pembrokeshire man would. The community is of course a much smaller one, and he takes his racial aloofness merely as a fact, not as a happy dispensation of Providence as well. "We donna knaw exactly what we are, sir; some of the gentry says we're Flemings," is a stock reply, but there is beyond doubt some sort of satisfaction in belonging to this compact community of far back colonists, and even a little pride in that very mystery of origin which excites such interest among the gentry. A comparison between the Gower and Pembroke vernacular would have peculiar interest from the fact that they are isolated both from each other and from England. The Gower men tell you that they can detect a Pembrokian instantly. But with all their broad Teutonic speech there seemed to me an unmistakable touch of the Welsh lilt not noticeable in Pembrokeshire, and here and there a suggestively Anglo-Welsh word, such as "iss, iss" (for "yes, yes"). Till quite recently there was an old court in Swansea held twice a year, known as the court of Gower Anglicana, where the English of Gower did suit and service, and another for the Welsh, known as the court of Gower Wallica.

Gower was not included in the old lordship of Glamorgan which stretched from the Rhymney to the Tawe, but was thrown into Glamorganshire, when the new county was formed by Henry VIII. The meaning of Gower or Gwyr has defied interpretation, and exasperated generations of philologists. It was conquered independently soon after Fitz-Hamon's seizure of Glamorgan, the Norman undertaker in this business being Henry de Newburgh, Earl of Warwick, and it is said to have taken him eight years to drive the Welsh off the peninsula and make himself reasonably secure on it by a sufficient number of castles. Soon afterwards came those batches of Flemings dispatched to south Wales by Henry I. Flooded out in their own country, as tradition has it, they sought fresh territory of the English king, who, by dumping them down here, got rid of them in a graceful way, and at the same time procured a useful and permanent garrison for his own buccaneering barons.

Pembroke was the chief plantation, but the coast strip of Carmarthen, the Gower promontory, and possibly a spot or two on the Glamorgan shore, received each its supply. How these peaceful husbandmen liked it at first, when there must have been much more fighting than farming to be done, history does not say. But they proved a great success from the Anglo-Norman point of view, as well as from their own. They not only resisted the arms, but also any social intercourse with the Welsh, who probably did not press this upon them with over-much insistence, particularly as they could not understand the others' language, even had they wished to, nor, as a rule, can they now in Pembrokeshire. But the Flemings were probably outnumbered in time by English settlers. At any rate they soon became a homogeneous community, and cultivated, as I have said an English vernacular in which experts profess to find many Flemish words. [...]

The interior of Gower contains a delightful variety of scene: high ridges of heathery moorland, snug seats embosomed in fine timber, bosky glens through which bright trout streams prattle, and sea-coast peeps of every imaginable kind embellished not seldom by the presence of some imposing relic of border strife. There are ancient little churches, too, characteristic of a peculiar people and an isolated alien community; and always close at hand are vantage points whence you may look out over wide waters to the rugged capes of Pembroke, to the bounds of Cornwall, the hills of Devon and Somerset and to the lofty mountains of Brecon. Yet no one penetrates into further Gower save a few enlightened natives of the adjoining coast towns, who spend quiet holidays in the simple accommodation of its primitive sea coast hamlets.

When I pursued my solitary way towards Port Eynon, however, Gower had become but a summer memory to even these few adventurous folk. Wild and chill October winds were howling over the russet uplands, rattling the bleached leaves of the exposed wayside trees, and soughing in the yellowing woodlands of the vales. It is a breezy common above Sketty, a couple of miles or so of open fern and heather, over which the road goes trailing westward, that makes one first conscious of being actually in Gower, and of having shaken off the last trace of Swansea's remotest suburbs. Peewits and starlings, in quite remarkable numbers and of surprising friendliness, had the waste to themselves as I traversed it, and dropped down the long slope into the pretty wooded dingle of Park Mill, where together with a few other cottages, stands the more pretentious but yet modest hostelry known as the Gower Inn. It was erected in the last century by Mr Penrice of Killvrough, an old country seat above, whose woodlands contribute liberally to the arcadian charm for which the spot has some local reputation. A kindly thought for tourists or potential tourists seems to have been the motive of this former squire, for there was then no inn in Gower where any but the hardiest wayfarer might lay his head. A somewhat idyllic spot, where a bright trout stream followed closely by the road ripples through a narrow meadow fringed with woods, is here. It would provoke no particular enthusiasm on the Welsh mainland, but has somewhat the charm of the unexpected in this narrow sea-girt peninsula.

For as you emerge at what would seem to be the foot of the winding gorge, it suddenly turns to the south, and shedding its foliage runs a short course to the shore between bare hills, with the ruined castle of Pennard crowning the furthest one and overlooking the sea; an Edwardian fortress with a massive gateway, and flanking towers devoid of all ornament but the ferns with which nature decorates it. The mission and period of Pennard are obvious enough, though history is almost silent concerning it. Wastes of sandhills lie around its feet, where traces of buried buildings give great scope to the local fancy, while the view from the hill across the beautiful bay of Oxwich, with its yellow sands and its limestone cliffs, is highly inspiring. Curious bone caves, some fine rock scenery and a reputation for rare plants, give further interest to the lonely site of this really considerable fortress, whose secret seems to have died with it – a rare thing enough in Wales. [...]

[...] At Penmaen Church hanging high over the centre of Oxwich Bay, with the wooded parklands of Penrice Castle sloping seawards, the great red sandstone ridge of Cefn Bryn, which slopes diagonally nearly across the peninsula, sprang gently and invitingly from the road. The afternoon was still young; the sunshine of past weeks that had seemed gone for ever, for the moment, at least, began to reassert itself; and a tempting green track between the fern and heather wandering upwards invited one to what was obviously the highest point in Gower. The temptation to leave the rain-soaked skiddy limestone lane for another brief excursion was irresistible, so leaving my cycle on the hillside I followed the trail amid the song of rejoicing larks, and in half an hour was on the apex of the peninsula.

Though not quite a thousand feet above the sea, it was a wild and beautiful bit of moorland. But the heather had lost its bloom, the ferns were a golden brown, and the gorse retained but lingering patches of its summer glory, but the mountain turf was all the greener for the gold and russet of autumn that mantles thickly upon it, and for the late drenching storms whose drops still sparkled in the sunlight. [...]

Night was falling as I descended the long stony and perpendicular lane which dips to Port Eynon, and saw beneath me on the few occasions I ventured to look up a blur of white-washed walls and grey roofs and beyond the dark line of the sea. No anxieties as to bed and board had further embittered my journey, for I was virtually consigned to the chief government official of Port Eynon, the postmaster, in whose idyllic abode I found my effects already deposited by the faithful 'bus and good anchorage for myself. All things are relative. One may have frequently been a hundred or two miles from a railway station in distant lands, but this does not make seventeen seem any less unfamiliar on the shores of the Bristol Channel, more particularly if these long miles are represented in part by tortuous lanes, and at the moment by everywhere broken and slippery roads over which you precariously laboured. The occasional ticking of the telegraph next door, however, took away something of the romance of the situation in my particular case.

The Sabbath morn broke peacefully and auspiciously over Port Eynon, a comfortable village of more or less detached houses, whose gleaming whitewash could not hide the fact that they were mostly venerable and solid tenements. Flowers and greenery were not wanting in the generous gaps between them, and the highways wandered casually out into the waste, expending themselves in deep sand or sandy turf, which lead onward to where the waves were breaking with the lingering impulse of subsided gales, on a most delightful bay. A narrow strip of dunes backed by steep hills, themselves sprinkled for some distance with rural dwellings, curved round to the eastward. To the west a bold promontory, capped with a grassy down and girdled with savage-looking reefs rose above the village and shut out the further coastline. Across the grey and still uneasy sea the coast of Devon waved its dark familiar outline. A populous village more entirely secluded from the world I have never seen in England or Wales, for Aberdaron at the point of Lleyn, which is even more of an Ultima Thule, is but a hamlet.

from *In the March and Borderland of Wales* (1905)

Edward Thomas
Swansea Village

A great many people know that Swansea is a Welsh seaport and man-
ufacturing town, the centre of a district where it has been said that
"nine-tenths of the entire make of copper in Great Britain" is smelted;
that it has claims to be called the "Metropolis of South Wales"; that its
football team beat the South Africans; that Beau Nash was born there,
and Landor dwelt there, making love to some one named Ione or Jones,
and writing 'Gebir'; that it possesses a ruined castle and a new
'Empire'; that it lies across the visitor's road to Gower. Here and there
more can be heard of it. One of its parks, says a lady, had for some time
a clock with the hours (like Marvell's dial) marked in flowers. Another
avers that the town smells, and that the inhabitants either do not know
or do not care, some holding the opinion that one of the smells is beneficial. – It is a magnificent town, of which some, if not Landor, might
say even to-day that for scenery and climate it excels the Gulf of
Salerno or the Bay of Naples. – It is a sordid hag of a town, sitting
shameless amid the ruins of its natural magnificence. – It is as good as
Blackpool. – There is "nothing particular" in it, nothing old and picturesque, nothing new and grand or even expensive. – Many of its dark
haired and pale-skinned women are beautiful. – And so on.

But this I cannot understand: that some people should be – and
some are – indifferent to Swansea. Year after year I go there (I do not
mean to the Mumbles, but to the town, and nothing but the town), and
walk up and down it and round about, inhaling sea air and mountain
air, or the smells from copper works, cobalt works, manure works, and
fried-fish shops; year after year I have felt that only friends could bring
me again to Swansea. But the town is a dirty witch. You must hate or
love her, and I both love her and hate her, and return to her as often as
four times in a year. It is not this or that beautiful or hideous thing that
draws me. I do not go to see a woman pitching broken crockery out of
her front door into a street where children go barefooted; nor to smell
the stale fat of the skin-yard, and see shaggy cattle driven into the
slaughter-house, and a woman carrying a baby in a shawl after them;
nor to hear midnight quarrelling in the Irish quarter – a woman at first
having it her own way, shouting louder and louder and drowning the
man's bass interjections, then wildly screaming "Bastard, bastard",
until the cry is smothered in noises of scuffling and throttling, and the
victor's voice rising for a moment as he strikes, and, after that, her
sobbing and moaning, that ends in silence broken only by the child they

have awakened. I do not go because they will tell me those brand-new edifices are on the site of the old block-cottages "where the bad women lived" – as if the "bad women" were used in the foundations or had been scared out of their iniquity by the splendours of architecture. The pleasant accidents are many in Swansea. The docks are always pleasant with the smell of tar, the weaving whirl of sea-gulls, the still ships, the cold green water reflecting the gaudy figurehead of the *Kate*, the men unloading potatoes, the painter slung under the bowsprit, with a fag in his mouth, which he puts behind his ear to whistle 'Away to Rio'. For that minute the ship looks like a beautiful great captive beast, beautiful in the same manner as the neighbouring caged thrush's song of pure thickets, the sun, the wind, and the rain. I like, too, the rag-and-bone man blowing one deep note on his horn as he travels mean streets; and the cockle-women (their white, scoured cockle-tubs on their heads or under their arms) from Penclawdd, dressed in half a dozen thicknesses of flannel, striped and checked, all different and all showy – with broad hips, no waists, stout legs slowly and powerfully moving, and the clearest of complexions and brightest of lips and eyes under their fine soft brown hair. Six days of the week I like the whole Swansea crowd of factory men and girls, the shawled mothers, the seamen, the country folk, though not one element is exceptionally picturesque.

These pleasant and unpleasant things, however, have little to do with the final effect, composite but very definite, of the whole town: they colour certain days, but no more. What counts most is the careless, graceless nature of Swansea, its lordly assemblage of chimney-stacks, its position at a river mouth between mountains, and the neighbourhood of the sea. Cheapness, *clapham-junction*, squalor, or actual hideousness is everywhere in contrast with grandeur, and even sublimity, and these qualities do not alternate, but conflict, or in some way co-operate. In the central streets, broad and glassy, thronged to the point of tumult with men and beasts and every kind of vehicle; in the outward-going roads of monotonous, and dismal or unclean, cottages, threaded by electric trams and country carts, and in sunless courts where privacy and publicity are one, you have always in sight either sea or mountain.

For the greater part of the town is built on riverside and seaside ground, where the mountains open a little wider apart to make way for the River Tawe. Two steep and treeless mountains hang over it. One of them, called at different points Mount Pleasant (where the workhouse is), Gibbet Hill, and Town Hill, is more or less green, but carved by quarries, and now higher and higher up striped with horizontal lines of plainest cottages and of villas pretending to some form of prettiness, all set among wastes of poor grass, feverfew, and wormwood. The straight ascents are as steep as the street at Clovelly, the paving-stones in some being tilted out of the flush to give a foot-hold. Once the springs in this hillside fed several wells of some fame, such as the Baptist Well and St Helen's Well, which are commemorated only in the names of streets. Kilvey, the other hill, is green to seaward, but where it falls most abruptly, and the valley between it and the Town Hill is narrowest, it has been stripped by poisonous smoke and covered with a deposit of slag, except on the perpendicular juts which reveal the strata of blackish rock; a chimney pierces the summit and stands out against the sky. The lowest parts alone of this hill are littered with houses, but on a high green terrace seaward linger a white rustic cottage and a small farm-house or two, and above them, at the very ridge, an old windmill tower.

The town cannot forget these two hills, whether they rise clear in their green or their drabby black, or whether the flurries of mist reveal a momentary and fragmentary glimpse of Kilvey's hilltop chimney or windmill tower, a grisly baseless precipice and a gull passing it, a gleam of white wall. Between the hills bends the river, the yellow Tawe. The factories crowd to its right bank, opposite to Kilvey, in order to get rid of their gilded and other filth, and to receive the ships; in the mud and yellow stones rests the two-masted *Audacieuse*, of St Valery-sur-Somme, discharging phosphates, while three men in blue stand below to caulk and paint her. In spite of the colour of the water, numbers of people have fallen into it, some by accident, some after deliberation. The one foot-bridge crosses at the docks, where the character of the river is lost. Only a ferry plies from among the factories to the few undesirable houses under the steepest and barest part of Kilvey. A man, therefore, might live in Swansea without knowing of the river. But the mountains which it cleaves are omnipresent, and from many places its course can be seen far away inland through heights green with grass, grey with bare rock, or violet with distance.

The low waterside crowd of copper, steel, tin, zinc, silver, cobalt, manure, and other works is the real Swansea. The remainder, the miles of flat-faced cottages here or upon the hill, is but an inexpensive prison where the workers may feed, smoke, read the newspapers, breed, and sleep. Those works vomit the smokes which Swansea people either ignore or praise; for when the smell from the manure works pervades the town, they expect fine weather from a north or north-east wind. They take you up on the Town Hill at night to see the furnaces in the pit of the town blazing scarlet, and the parallel and crossing lines of lamps, which seem, like the stars, to be decoration. If it is always a city of dreadful day, it is for the moment and at that distance a city of wondrous night. I have seen the steel works – I think when the roof was uncovered for repairs – look like a range of burning organ-pipes, while overhead hung, or imperceptibly flowed, a white spread of smoke, hiding the hills and half of the black, starry sky, but only half-veiling the tall chimneys which silently increased it. At dawn it is worthwhile to see the furnaces paling, Kilvey very clear and dark, and the few stars white above it. Dawn climbs over Kilvey Hill into Swansea.

By day the scene is better, because the variety is greater, according to the wind and the lie of the sea mist, the river mist, and the smoke, both the accumulations and the individual tributaries of smoke; and because then can be seen the dim ridges of the greater mountains beyond the chimneys, and in the other direction a hundred moods of the sea and the coast hills. The furnaces, the vast, sooty sheds clanging and clattering, the fuming slag hills, where women crawl raking for something less than gold, and, above all, the grouped or single chimneys standing irregularly beside the river, are more worth looking at than a model town. As for the chimneys, like gigantic tree-trunks or temple pillars that have survived some gigantic desolation, these and their plumes of smoke or of flame are among the most unforgettable things that men have made. The black hills and vales of Landore, its fire-palaces and hundred smoke-stacks, compose one of the sublimest of all absolutely human landscapes. The slag heaps are venerable even in age. One of them, still growing in the midst of the town, is about a century old, and with the two blackened cottages nestling at its foot it would seem a considerable hill were it not backed and dwarfed by Kilvey. It is one of the boundaries to a characteristic Swansea waste – several uneven acres, strewn with brickbats, trodden in all directions, without grass, and on the other sides bounded by houses, a big school, and a church about as high as the hill of slag. Evidently this land once served some purpose, is now disused, and is waiting for a day when time is no longer money. Similar spaces are sometimes occupied by the town refuse, which the east wind distributes and the 'Rising Sun' washes down. Out of one broad space, black and scarred by water-courses from the mountain, a small part has been railed in for a children's playground, with swings, parallel bars, and seats; but no grass grows there. Numerous lesser wastes mark where houses have been or are to be, and at present they are useful sites for a pile of tins, glass, earthenware, rags, sweepings, tea-leaves, and fish-bones; nettle and wormwood flourish. These are in the more domestic portions of the town. Among the factories can be seen many a disastrous black wilderness, a black, empty amphitheatre traversed by the yellow river. Another kind of waste is the marshland above the town proper, invaded on one side by tips of slag, but too marshy for the most cynical builder, and still left, therefore, to rush and thistle.

Everywhere decay and ruin make their boast side by side with growth. Disused workshops are not supplanted, but are spared by some form of piety to stand and thin into skeletons, with gaping walls and roofs, to fall gradually in heaps among their successors. The sheds with rafters broken, tiles slipping, bricks dislodged, the derelict and tumbling cottages, the waste places of slag, old masonry, and dust, tufted with feverfew, the yards cumbered by rusty iron implements and rubbish, the red rivulet plunging in black gorges, speak rather of a bloodily conquered and deserted city than of a claimant to be the "Metropolis of South Wales". But round the corner a new block of buildings, including a chemist's and a sweet-shop, followed by cottages with painted wooden porches, and then a three-year-old chapel filled by a noble hymn wailing triumphantly, and next a view of twenty chimneys and of hills divided into squares of corn and grass and irregular woods, revive the claim. And yet this chapel is at the foot of a rough quarried slope sprinkled thinly and anyhow with white and whitish cottages among rushes and tufted grass, which is a scene of an almost moorland sweetness for those living in the new-old streets of eternal smoke under the mountain opposite, barren and black.

The same piety spares also the deserted dwelling. The old mountain farm-house, whose pastures entertain footballers instead of cattle, is left to gather moss and docks on its thatch, and stones (thrown at the windows) in all its rooms. The ferry-boat from the works over to Foxhole, a straggling settlement between the bare steep of Kilvey Hill and the river, lands you by a bunch of four old cottages of the colour of scorched paper, the walls of their tiny yards collapsing, and all windowless except the one which gives some reason for supposing it to be inhabited by human beings. Nearer the centre of the town other dwellings have attained a similar condition. Whole streets of houses, too old at fifty or sixty, have been condemned, but are still used because they are, at any rate, warmer than the outer air. When new cottages are built they often stand against the ruined ones instead of taking their places, just as the new church at Llansamlet stands against the partly ruinous old tower.

The houses are seldom of the material and make to be comely in their old age. The flat fronts shed their grimy plaster in flakes; the windows are like the eyes of the blind; the miniature gardens consist of fowl-houses, nasturtiums, and cats; and from the gramophone comes a frivolous London tune, or from the harmonium 'Yes, Jesus loves me', while at the back door a woman washes in the sun. Until they are well advanced in decay, they are hardly interesting, save to the occupiers and to sanitary authorities and housing committees. Almost all of them have been erected in long, straight bars or blocks during the early or late nineteenth century. They peel or split and become dirty, but their two windows and a door, or three windows and a door, have to depend for variety of expression on a barber's pole or coloured advertisements; very few have front gardens. Old age and neatness seldom adorn the same house in Swansea. As it ages it falls into worse and worse hands; the garden is given over to wormwood, and a piece of semi-rustic slum is completed. Signs of ease, opulence and pleasure, mysteriously created by men and machinery, are to be seen in the high-placed villas towards the sea, but they have no individuality except what is given here and there by a piece of cliffy garden.

The best, as well as probably the oldest, building in Swansea is the castle. It is wedged in, and actually incorporated, among shops and dwellings, though it displays a beautiful range of arcading above their roofs; a telegraph-post sticks up in the middle; but it still protects a small, inaccessible patch of long green grass on one side between it and the street wall, where a building site is advertised. Its position low down near the river, obscured by the glories of the principal street, denies it the impressiveness of the so-called Trewyddfa Castle which crowns a steep isolated hill farther inland at the verge of the town. This is a spare, craggy ruin, like a few rotten old teeth, near Landore station, but high and distinct above the pale, scrambling cottages of the slopes. Not a hundred years ago, they say, the 'castle' was built by a public man as a residence, that he might refute with ostentation the charge of penury. But he was not a Norman baron, and, lacking power or courage or imagination to raid the neighbourhood with arms, he could not endure life on his eminence very long. The forsaken mansion was let out in tenements, failed as such, and was finally offered to rain and wind as the material for an apparently feudal ruin. They have performed their task to admiration: Trewyddfa Castle is the only thing in Swansea to satisfy a taste for the mediaeval picturesque. At the foot of its hill, horses pasture among gipsy vans, slag heaps, cottages, and the remains of cottages.

Swansea is too busy to invent an Arthurian or feudal tale about this 'castle', or in any way to coin money out of it. Of the vanity of picturesqueness the town altogether lacks traces. And yet some money has been spent on making the old round windmill tower, towards the seaward and green end of Kilvey Hill, impervious to weather, boys, and the few dirty-faced cows of those pastures. Seats have been placed on two sides, because it is on the flat at the very top of the hill, and eastward, southward and northward the eye ranges without impediment. To the south are the lowest-lying parts of Swansea, the mathematical lines of the docks, a steamer hooting as she enters, many sailing vessels at rest and silent, and trains shunting with noises as of a drunken orchestra tuning up – the yellow-sanded bay curving under a wall of woods to the horned rocks and lighthouse of the Mumbles – the main sea and the aerial distant masses of Exmoor and the Mendips. A world of domed or abrupt mountains to the north is broken up by the valleys of the Neath and Tawe rivers. The waveless, effervescent blue sea to eastward is edged by dunes, and behind them by wooded or bracken-covered high hills with emerald clefts; and the white and the dirty smoke of Neath and Port Talbot rises between the sands and the hills

The seats round the windmill tower are a little worn, but I never saw anyone there, nor met anyone who had been there. Why should people go up? Not to gain a view, certainly. Swansea has as many views as smells. Every street has a view at one end or the other; some have one at both. For example, Byron Crescent, and, better still, Shelley Crescent, new streets high up on the green hill and curving with it, command so much of sea and mountain that their names are not ridiculous. Steepness forbids houses to be built on both sides of the horizontal street, and enables Shelley Crescent to look clear over the back of Byron Crescent. One end looks on Kilvey Hill, the riverside works at its foot, the lines of the multitudes of cottages, the dotted 'castle' mound, and beyond it the greater mountains. The scene from the other end includes first the docks, the slated, rectangular labyrinth of the town, hardly diversified by a few churches, a gasometer, and here and there a row of elms or poplars, or a single tree, projecting as it were out of fissures in that mass of brick and stone; and then the silver, cold, rippled sea, with slashes of foam, stretching away to the hills of Glamorgan, hazy with smoke, and to the hills of Somerset, which are as clouds. In twenty years Shelley Crescent will be old, and they will have forgotten to paint the woodwork; but the sea and the far mountains will be the same, and Kilvey can hardly avoid being still half green, half black. By that time Swansea may have a quarter of a million inhabitants; I shall not guess whether the village will have become a town. At present it is probably more a village than when the borough counted about a thousand under Elizabeth. Its activity in spreading hither and thither has kept it from thinking about anything but factories, docks, and the necessities of life. That is the dark charm of Swansea to one who has not to live in it. It is careless of itself, of its majestic position, its lovely neighbourhood, its hundred and twenty thousand men, women, and children. Compared with Cardiff, it is a slattern. Yet, being a spectator, I am glad that I have known Swansea between these hills, and not a lesser Cardiff or Liverpool. Equally shameless and unpretentious, it swarms about the Tawe, climbs over the hill with inconsiderate vitality, always allowing the magnitude and precipitousness of its hills to have full effect, while they in their turn emphasise the rustic squalor and confused simplicity of the town, combining with it to make a character which at the same moment irritates and fascinates.

from *English Review* (1914), reprinted
in *The Last Sheaf* (1928)

Paul Ferris
'a holiday gone wrong'

[During and after World War One bigamist George Shotton moves between his real wife in Penarth and his second "wife", Mamie, whom he installs in Swansea. George, a marine surveyor, is frequently absent and Mamie finds it hard to settle.]

Mrs Hearn's establishment in Trafalgar Terrace had sea views, sea winds, and often a coating of sand on the front steps that had blown across the street from the foreshore. Life with George was like a holiday gone wrong; Mamie knew what to expect of the apartment before they arrived. Masts and coal staithes in the South Dock were visible from the front room upstairs where she – or they, when George was in town – sat, ate, talked, read; where home was. The one-sided terrace ran west to east between a cricket ground and Swansea Gaol. Sometimes a bell tolled from the prison; Mamie didn't know why.

The houses were respectable but unsecluded. Steam trains passed almost under the windows, following the bay's curve until the line (the L. and N. W. Railway, which George used for journeys to the north) turned inland and disappeared up a wooded valley. Another line carried the electric Mumbles train, which looked like a tram, to the far end of the bay, where a pleasure pier and a lighthouse ended miles of urban sands, and a lonely coast of cliffs and coves began. Mamie went that way for bracing walks on the sands.

More often she wandered into town, where Mrs Hearn had shown her the places to go for life's necessities, apparently cheap food and weatherproof clothes. A youngish woman, with dyed hair, Flo Hearn had an invalid husband, two boys and the house to look after. She was proud of Swansea's facilities, particularly of the covered market with its dismaying mounds of cabbages, bowls of cockles and white enamel trays splattered with what looked like blackish-green cowpats, a local so-called delicacy made of seaweed and misleadingly known as laver bread.

For Mamie real shopping consisted of inspecting skirts and hats at Davis the Bon or Lewis Lewis and, best of all, visiting the thirty-odd departments of Ben's, Swansea's version of Binns. The town also had six cinemas and two theatres, so every week she could see up to a dozen shows, depending how many cinemas changed their programmes on a Thursday. A bag of sweets and stories in the dark suited her. But she was terrified it might go on for ever.

As a way of life it was so laughably unlike anything she could have imagined for herself that at first the absurdity that this was her, Mamie Stuart, buying vegetables and baking powder, seemed to confirm its temporary nature. She had thought the same in Bristol; six months later it began to feel permanent. There were even watery winter days, rain pouring from clouds that came down to street level as she hurried in to the Carlton or the Castle for her daily helping of romantic adventures, when she felt so low in spirits that dissent was out of the question. Stare at Lillian Gish in a five-part Love Triangle Drama, a Pathé Gazette and some Mutt & Jeff; go home to tea; think kind thoughts about George and the undying love he always mentioned at least once every visit. Love wasn't to be laughed at.

A few shillings a week, spent carefully, made domestic life easier to bear. The skivvy who brought the coal up from the cellar could be bribed to stay and dust. Flo would make an extra dish of faggots and peas for sixpence, and Mamie could pretend it was hers, convincing George that she had improved since Bristol. Sometimes he worked in Swansea and the small ports nearby for days on end, so he spent more time at home. "Much nicer for you," said Flo, and so it was, except when they quarrelled, or the lovemaking went badly or failed to happen at all.

Marriage left you with less room for manoeuvre. When she was just a woman who liked men, Mamie could offer them, and more importantly herself, endless helpings of whatever seemed opportune: not only dirty acts but mysterious depths and the harmony of naked souls in love as depicted in her library books. She could pick and choose. Whereas marriage was a fixed condition that you didn't invent; it invented you. She had joined the Florence Hearns and Edith Silvers. She even wrote to Edith, poking fun at George and his funny ways, asking how women put up with it all, and got a letter telling her to pull herself together.

Mrs Hearn often invited her down to their sitting room in the basement, where she liked to hear about Mamie's exciting life. As a rule she had no time for theatrical persons, the kind who stayed in certain

Trafalgar Terrace boarding houses and misbehaved. Mamie, having been redeemed by marriage, was exempt. [...]

It was nearly spring, the first sunny day for weeks. George had departed for London after breakfast, leaving her slightly more miserable than before. This couldn't go on, could it? She dressed up and swept into town, aching to feel like Mamie Stuart used to feel. At Ben's she spent one pound seven shillings and sixpence on English Violet Perfume and English Violet Soap. This impressive splurge paved the way to opening an account in George's name. The assistant manager barely looked at the receipted bill she produced, for an emerald velour hat that George bought her in January; he concentrated on the hat itself, which Mamie was wearing, and on the other smart things (purchased up north) that covered her: blue serge costume, blue kid gloves, dark-blue kid shoes. All-powerful in his striped trousers, he authorised a monthly account of up to ten pounds.

"I would prefer fifteen," said Mamie.

"Fifteen it is, madam."

Knowing that whenever she felt like it she could stock up with spring lingerie and shoes and a hat or two improved her morale. But the same dusty streets led away from Ben's; she saw herself in a shop window and wondered if she was wasted on George. When a man smelling of beer moved into the seat next to her at the Ritz, a cinema down a lane off High Street where she had gone to see Wallace Reid in *The World Apart*, and she felt fingers on her leg, she made a terrible scene, instead of responding with a quick slap in the normal way.

She enjoyed seeing the miscreant flung out. She enjoyed being mollified by the proprietor in his cubbyhole and offered a month of free seats. He also owned the Elysium, so she could have seats there too. "Edwin Morgan, madam, at your service," he said. "The patron is always right." His crisp cuffs and slender hands reminded her of the man she fell for when she was nineteen, who ran Cornishe's in Leeds, or was it the Avenue? Reputation was everything at a picture house, said the just slightly oily Edwin. Madam was welcome to bring someone with her, friend or husband; the way he said 'husband' made it sound like a question. He saw her to the foyer, touching her arm. Would she make herself known to him whenever she returned? They would fetch him at once if he wasn't there.

Men like Morgan were two a penny, and she would have to be desperate to take them seriously. Still, there was a degree of satisfaction in knowing that they were there, admiring her, going out of their way to be nice to her on the off chance of scoring a hit.

The man from the garage might or might not have been in that category. He came round to Trafalgar Terrace in a Ford motorcar one afternoon in early April, asking for Mr Shotton, and, finding him not at home, suggested that Mrs Shotton herself might like a spin.

At last, an event to lift her out of herself. The scar and a sporty jacket gave Captain Andrews a worldly look. They raced the Mumbles train, overtook a coal lorry and various motorcars, and arrived at the Mumbles Pier in – he consulted his watch – eight minutes fifteen seconds. He hoped she would tell Mr Shotton about her nifty acceleration and the very low vibration factor.

"Don't build up your hopes," she said. "If it was me, I might be persuaded. Do you sell many motorcars?"

Leaning back in the driver's seat, he spoke of postwar economic conditions and the boom that would undoubtedly come. He looked at her sideways. "Not many."

Watery sunlight glinted on the bonnet, on the bay. They might have been a couple out for the afternoon, the handsome ex-officer who had been in charge of a motor-transport section in France (he told her about his war; he got the scar when a tyre burst and his vehicle overturned) with the enigmatic young woman who might or might not be his fiancée.

from *Infidelity* (1999)

E. Howard Harris
On Approaching Landore

I heard a wag within the Irish Mail
Say, "This is what they call down here Landore.
Old Billie Burke, when three sheets in the wind,
Sleeping from Paddington, dreamed that he had sinned
And wakened up in —, well
Some place I need not tell."
I looked without; the blackened hillside
Heaved with ant-hills of rough slag;
The furnace glared; the smoking stacks beside
Were there; but — I forgot the wag.
For I could see beyond; an arch of golden sand,
A lighthouse on its pedestal of rock,
And the blue sea push tongues of water in the land
And meet the cliff with thunder of its shock;

The chimney-stacks had faded from my view,
Or perhaps to speak more true,
Passed through the alembic of my heart and brain,
And were rebuilt again.
Such alchemy is in the heart of man;
Through smoky air,
That now they seem more fair
Than domes and minarets of Ispahan.

from *The Singing Seas* (1926)

Dylan Thomas
Reminiscences of Childhood

I was born in a large Welsh industrial town at the beginning of the Great War: an ugly, lovely town (or so it was, and is, to me), crawling, sprawling, slummed, unplanned, jerry-villa'd, and smug-suburbed by the side of a long and splendid-curving shore where truant boys and sandfield boys and old anonymous men, in the tatters and hangovers of a hundred charity suits, beachcombed, idled, and paddled, watched the dock-bound boats, threw stones into the sea for the barking, outcast dogs, and, on Saturday summer afternoons, listened to the militant music of salvation and hell-fire preached from a soap-box.

This sea-town was my world; outside, a *strange* Wales, coal-pitted, mountained, river-run, full, so far as I knew, of choirs and sheep and story-book tall hats, moved about its business which was none of mine; beyond that unknown Wales lay England, which was London, and a country called 'The Front' from which many of our neighbours never came back. At the beginning, the only 'front' I knew was the little lobby before our front door; I could not understand how so many people never returned from there; but later I grew to know more, though still without understanding, and carried a wooden rifle in Cwmdonkin Park and shot down the invisible, unknown enemy like a flock of wild birds. And the park itself was a world within the world of the sea-town; quite near where I lived, so near that on summer evenings I could listen, in my bed, to the voices of other children playing ball on the sloping, paper-littered bank; the Park was full of terrors and treasures. The face of one old man who sat, summer and winter, on the same bench looking over the swanned reservoir, I can see more clearly, I think, than the city-street faces I saw an *hour* ago: and years later I wrote a poem about, and for, this never, by me, to-be-forgotten 'Hunchback in the Park'. [...]

And that Park grew up with me; that small, interior world widened as I learned its names and its boundaries; as I discovered new refuges and ambushes in its miniature woods and jungles, hidden homes and lairs for the multitudes of the young, for cowboys and Indians and, most sinister of all, for the far-off race of the Mormons, a people who every night rode on nightmares through my bedroom. In that small, iron-railed universe of rockery, gravel-path, playbank, bowling-green, bandstand, reservoir, chrysanthemum garden, where an ancient keeper known as Smokey was the tyrannous and whiskered snake in the Grass one must Keep Off, I endured, with pleasure, the first agonies of unrequited love, the first slow boiling in the belly of a bad poem, the strutting and raven-locked self-dramatisation of what, at the time, seemed *incurable* adolescence. I wrote then, in a poem never to be published:

> See, on gravel paths under the harpstrung trees,
> Feeling the summer wind, hearing the swans,
> Leaning from windows over a length of lawns,
> On tumbling hills admiring the sea,
> I am alone, alone complain to the stars.
> Who are his friends? The wind is his friend,
> The glow-worm lights his darkness, and
> The snail tells of coming rain.

But before that, several years even before those lines, that cry from a *very* happy heart waiting, like an egg, to be broken, I had written:

> Where could I ever listen for the sound of seas asleep,
> Or the cold and graceful song of a swan that dies and
> wakes,
>
> Where could I ever hear the cypress speak in its sleep,
> And cling to a manhood of flowers, and sing the
> unapproachable lakes?

I am afraid the answer was, the Park. (I had 'the swan' on the brain in those days; luckily, there were very few rhymes for 'parrot'.) The answer was, the Park; a bit of bush and flowerbed and lawn in a snug, smug, trim, middling-prosperous suburb of my utterly confining outer world, that splendidly ugly sea-town where, with my friends, I used to dawdle on half-holidays along the bent and Devon-facing seashore, hoping for corpses or gold watches or the skull of a sheep or a message in a bottle to be washed up in the wreck; or where we used to wander, whistling and being rude to strangers, through the packed streets, stale as station sandwiches, around the impressive gas-works and the slaughter-house, past the blackened monuments of civic pride and the museum, which should have been in a museum; where we scratched at a kind of cricket on the bald and cindery surface of the Recreation-ground, or winked at unapproachably old girls of fifteen or sixteen on the Promenade opposite; where we took a tram that shook like an iron jelly down from our neat homes to the gaunt pier, there to clamber *under* the pier, hanging perilously on its skeleton-legs; or to run along to the end where patient men with the seaward eyes of the dockside unemployed, capped and mufflered, dangling from their mouths pipes that had long gone out, angled over the edge for unpleasant-tasting fish. Never was there such a town as ours, I thought, as we fought on the sandhills with the boys that our mothers called "common", or dared each other up the scaffolding of half-built houses, soon to be called Laburnums or the Beeches, near the residential districts where the solider business families "dined" at half past seven and never drew the curtains. Never was there such a town (I thought) for the smell of fish and chips on Saturday nights; for the Saturday afternoon cinema matinees where we shouted and hissed our threepences away; for the crowds in the streets, with leeks in their pockets, on International Nights, for the singing that gushed from the smoky doorways of the pubs in the quarters we never should have visited; for the Park, the Park, the inexhaustibly ridiculous and mysterious, the bushy Red-Indian-hiding Park, where the hunchback sat alone, images of perfection in his head, and "the groves were blue with sailors."

The recollections of childhood have no order; of all those every-coloured and shifting scented shoals that move below the surface of the moment of recollection, one, two, indiscriminately, suddenly, dart up out of their revolving waters into the present air: immortal flying-fish.

So I remember that never was there such a dame-school as ours: so firm and kind and smelling of galoshes, with the sweet and fumbled music of the piano-lessons drifting down from upstairs to the lonely schoolroom where only the sometimes tearful wicked sat over undone sums or to repent a little crime, the pulling of a girl's hair during geography, the sly shin-kick under the table during prayers. Behind the school was a narrow lane where the oldest and boldest threw pebbles at windows, scuffled and boasted, lied about their relations –

"My father's got a chauffeur."

"What's he want a chauffeur for, he hasn't got a car."

"My father's the richest man in Swansea."

"My father's the richest man in Wales."

"My father's the richest man in the world." –

and smoked the butt-ends of cigarettes, turned green, went home, and had little appetite for tea.

The lane was the place to tell your secrets; if you did not have any, you invented them; I had few. Occasionally, now, I dream that I am turning, after school, into the lane of confidences where I say to the children of my class: "At last I have a secret."

"What is it? What is it?"

"I can fly!"

And when they do not believe me, I flap my arms like a large, stout bird and slowly leave the ground, only a few inches at first, then gaining air until I fly, like Dracula in a schoolboy cap, level with the windows of the school, peering in until the mistress at the piano screams, and the metronome falls with a clout to the ground, stops, and there is no more Time; and I fly over the trees and chimneys of my town, over the dockyards, skimming the masts and funnels; over Inkerman Street and Sebastopol Street and the street of the man-capped women hurrying to the Jug and Bottle with a fish-frail full of empties; over the trees of the eternal Park, where a brass band shakes the leaves and sends them showering down on to the nurses and the children, the cripples and the out-of-work. This is only a dream. The ugly, lovely, at least to me, town is alive, exciting and real though war has made a hideous hole in it. I do not need to remember a dream. The reality is there. The fine, live people, the spirit of Wales itself.

from *The Broadcasts* (1991) [broadcast in 1943]

The Hunchback in the Park

The hunchback in the park
A solitary mister
Propped between trees and water
From the opening of the garden lock
That lets the trees and water enter
Until the Sunday sombre bell at dark

Eating bread from a newspaper
Drinking water from the chained cup

That the children filled with gravel
In the fountain basin where I sailed my ship
Slept at night in a dog kennel
But nobody chained him up.

Like the park birds he came early
Like the water he sat down
And Mister they called Hey mister
The truant boys from the town
Running when he had heard them clearly
On out of sound

Past lake and rockery
Laughing when he shook his paper
Hunchbacked in mockery
Through the loud zoo of the willow groves
Dodging the park keeper
With his stick that picked up leaves.

And the old dog sleeper
Alone between nurses and swans
While the boys among willows
Made the tigers jump out of their eyes
To roar on the rockery stones
And the groves were blue with sailors

Made all day until bell time
A woman figure without fault
Straight as a young elm
Straight and tall from his crooked bones
That she might stand in the night
After the locks and chains

All night in the unmade park
After the railings and shrubberies
The birds the grass the trees the lake
And the wild boys innocent as strawberries
Had followed the hunchback
To his kennel in the dark.

from *Collected Poems 1934-1953* (1988)

Andrew Lycett
Swansea Grammar School in the 1920s

Just before eight o'clock every morning, a mad scramble occurred on the hill outside the imposing Gothic Revival edifice of Swansea Grammar School. For several minutes beforehand, caretaker William Marley had tolled a bell summoning pupils from all quarters of the town. Then two or three minutes before the hour, he stopped, slowly walked across the courtyard, and then abruptly brought down a bar across the main front door. Anyone still outside was late and was duly punished.

On his first morning at his new school in September 1925 Dylan almost certainly made the journey there with his father. Florrie had dressed him in his uniform of bright red blazer, with matching cap, and had added a scarf to protect the sickly boy against Swansea's changeable elements. Then he and D.J. took the back route – a fifteen-minute stroll along Terrace Road to the school on Mount Pleasant.

Founded in 1682 by the Bishop of Waterford and Lismore, Hugh Gore, and set in a commanding position overlooking Swansea Bay, the Grammar School was, like its senior English master, D.J. Thomas, a curious mixture. A visitor might imagine he or she had strayed into a typical British public school, with its quaint traditions, daily religious observance and academic bias – a scholarship at Oxford or Cambridge University being the goal for the more ambitious pupils. Nevertheless, headmaster Trevor Owen, a stocky North Walian with a top degree in Mathematics from Cambridge, had little of the usual public school enthusiasm for games. Beatings did occur and masters were known to cuff pupils around the head. But generally the atmosphere was easygoing and discipline relaxed. Certain teachers had to endure endless ragging, among them W.S. 'Soapy' Davies, the senior classics master who was D.J.'s regular Wednesday lunch-time drinking companion at the nearby Mountain Dew. Classroom wags would torture Jimmy Gott, who taught art during Dylan's first year, by asking him distractedly, 'Sleep with your wife, sir?', and when asked for clarification, would say 'Lend me a knife, sir?'

The school had moved up the hill from the town in the 1850s. A carved inscription above the main door read 'Hear instruction, be wise and and refuse it not', a sentiment subtly echoed in the school motto, 'Virtue and Good Literature'. Arms of the founders and early trustees adorned the stained glass windows in the main assembly hall where the mitre was the most obvious decorative motif, though another surprising feature was the preponderance of pen nibs. A favourite pastime was to steal a fellow pupil's pen, add a dart-like paper tail and launch it at the ceiling where dozens of these lethal missiles were imbedded.

During the First World War the school had sprung dutifully to the defence of the Empire. A cadet corps was set up and drilled by the physical training master, Sergeant O.A. Bird, a former NCO known to Dylan and his friends as 'Oiseau'. But the conflict took a heavy toll: of around 900 old boys who volunteered, seventy-six were known to have died, including all but one member of the 1917 upper sixth form. Nearly a decade later the losses were still mourned. With so many former pupils among the casualties, D.J. felt some shame at having avoided the blood-bath. Commemorating the dead became a personal crusade. Daniel Jones (Dylan's best friend at the school) recalled how, beneath his outward calm, the senior English master seethed with a barely controllable rage. Once, when a pupil dared to giggle while a war poem by Wilfred Owen was being read, D.J. lost his temper and administered a savage beating. D.J. had had 'a hard time schoolteaching' during the war, remarked Jones.

D.J.'s unease was not helped by a new breed of younger master, usually without a university degree, but with a maturity that came from wartime service at the front. Their casual manner was in marked contrast to older teachers in their stiff collars. One of the school's most distinguished old boys, Llewelyn Gwynne, Bishop of Egypt and the Sudan, and war-time Deputy Chaplain General to the British Army in France, came back to address the pupils. The general atmosphere of a nation still struggling to come to terms with the battlefield carnage could not fail to have made an impression on young Dylan. When the school commissioned a bronze memorial, unveiled by local grandee Lord Swansea in June 1924, Florrie noted that her nine-year-old son was 'very impressed'.

By then the school had long outgrown its Victorian shell. Seventy years earlier it had taken boarders, but now its dormitories were commandeered for use as chemistry laboratories, while the main classes were conducted in a filthy asbestos-ridden corrugated shed at the back of the main building.

A traditional feature of the establishment was the ritual chastisement meted out to new boys by their peers. During their first week, recent arrivals would be taken to the lower of the school's two playgrounds, beside the fives courts and cricket nets, and unceremoniously thrown into the brambles and bushes beneath. With a resilience that belied his delicate physique, Dylan survived this barbaric initiation and began making his mark on the school. For his first couple of years, he played the game as a member of Mansel House, called after an early patron of the school. In the fast-stream class 3A, he had a reputation for being bright but lazy. When, despairing of Dylan's repeated failures to complete any homework, his young Latin master, J. Morgan Williams, boxed him around the ears, he was surprised to hear a staff colleague advise against such punishment, as D.J. would disapprove. Dylan usually played on this perception, trying to get away with doing as little as possible, because he knew that most masters stood in awe of his stiff father.

Initially at least, Dylan's Latin improved under this regime and he may not have been as bad a student as his proud boast of being thirty-third in trigonometry would suggest. One of his physics exercise books survives, and it shows a conscientious second-year pupil who, despite a tendency to scribble random verses and sign his full name – Dylan Marlais Thomas – wrote up his experiments neatly and regularly received good marks. One doodle showed his interest in the physical properties of light. 'Light', he wrote. 'Light is invisible/Light travels in straight lines.' It could almost have been a draft of his early poem 'Light breaks where no sun shines.' [...]

His plummy voice proved an asset when he picked up the acting career he had started at Miss Hole's. If asked for an enduring image of Dylan, his contemporaries would almost certainly have pointed to one of his roles in the school plays. It might have been him as a fourteen year-old impressing as Edwin Stanton in John Drinkwater's *Abraham Lincoln*, or the following year in the title role in the same author's *Oliver Cromwell*, when his character's distinctive wart lacked adhesive and kept slipping to other parts of his face. Most likely he would have been recalled as Roberts, the strike leader, in John Galsworthy's *Strife*, in the spring 1931 production. The school magazine praised his performance, though with reservations, for he 'seemed to lack the coarseness and toughness of fibre necessary for the interpretation of Roberts; his vowels were occasionally too genteel; and he was innocent of gesture, an essential part of the demagogue's equipment.'

Dylan was clearly too much of a respectable Uplands child to be entirely convincing. As the magazine had joked in an earlier feature on 'Things We Cannot Credit', 'That D.M.T. should mispronounce a word'. And there was indeed an irony in his well-endowed Grammar School mounting a play about class conflict during a period of growing industrial unrest. Part of the school's income came from an estate in the upper Ogmore valley in Glamorgan where a coal-mine had been sunk in the 1860s. South Wales had suffered crippling unemployment for the best part of a decade, though Swansea, with its new oil refinery at Skewen and its seams of 'modern' anthracite, had been spared the worst effects. In the late 1920s, however, the slump came to Dylan's 'ugly, lovely' home town. Dole queues lengthened, conditions in St Thomas became more difficult, and boys in the Grammar School's distinctive red cap were targets of abuse if they strayed outside their narrow suburban confines. Pupils had always been politically conservative and socially exclusive, an inevitable consequence of their type of education. But now these traits became more pronounced. One young master was surprised to find that noone in the sixth form supported him in his opposition to capital punishment. When he remarked on this in the staff commonroom, he found that everyone there was a hanger and flogger as well.

Dylan could not escape the effects of this social conditioning: as he would later tell his girlfriend Pamela Hansford Johnson, 'You don't know how True-Blue I really am, and what a collection of old school ties my vest conceals.' A couple of months afterward, he was capable of making a complete volte-face: 'Don't you go about jeering at my Old School Tie. I hate Old School Ties.' Finding an appropriate attitude to his socially exclusive alma mater was always a problem, one made no easier by the fact that the school was so clearly identified in his mind with his father. So a solution was to bury and later find himself in poetry.

from *Dylan Thomas: A New Life* (2003)

Harri Webb
That Summer

The first thing I remember is the General Strike,
My father in his shirtsleeves leaning on the front gate
Smoking his pipe in the sunshine,
Miss Davies the shop calling across to him,
Are you out, Mr Webb? I hear now
Her bright amused voice, see Catherine Street
Empty and clean, hear the nine days' silence
As the last ripple of a lost revolution
Ebbed into history and the long defeat
Began to mass its shadows. The ambulances
Were absent from the road beside the hospital,
Garn Goch Number Three, Great Mountain, Gilbertsons,
Elba, the names I learnt to read by, names
Of collieries and tinworks, names of battlefields

Where a class and a nation surrendered
The summer they killed Wales.

We spent the time on the sands, played all day.
We had the whole place to ourselves,
Or so it has always seemed, from the West Pier
To Vivian Stream. When you are five years old
There are things you understand more easily
Than ever afterwards, that the sea is huge
And goes on for ever from Swansea, the moon
And the hospital dock inhabit the same sky,
Neighbours. But there are other things, and these
You only understand later, much later.
Inland, in those ambulance villages, the other side
Of Town Hill, from stations further up the line
From Mumbles Road, already it was beginning,
The losers' trek, the haemorrhage of our future.
But for a child there is only the present.
Dad, I said, there'd be lovely if the strike
Was all the time, then you and me could come
Down the sands every day and play. He laughed.
It wouldn't do, son, he said, it wouldn't do,
There's got to be work, see, there's got to be work.
Chasing a ball I didn't stop to argue, forgot
I'd ever asked the question till later, long after
The summer my country died.

from *A Crown for Branwen* (1974)

Peter Hellings
A Local Habitation

In this seatown forty-five years ago
I lived
            on names
                        like Constitution Hill,
Salubrious Passage, Goat Street, and Black Pill;

but most I lived on those I did not know:

Loughor and Llangyfelach and Gorseinon,
Cwmrhydyceirw, Clydach, Fforest fach,
Brynhyfryd, Danygraig and Mynydd Bach,
singing out from Port Talbot to Port-Eynon.

These were the names of places I grew up with,
but never saw:
                        they seemed so far away
I'd never get home from Brynmill to Waunarlwydd
unless I left home for more than a day.

What I liked best was being
                           in this place
where local names inhabited blank space.

From *A Swansea Sketchbook* (1983)

Barbara Hardy
Sweets

I walked again the way we went to school
from 22 Cradock Street up Carlton Terrace
where every day I counted cracks in walls
played Daddy Daddy Can I Cross the Water
and the Big Ship Sailed on the Ally Ally O
to Heathfield up the stone steps by the Green
where I picked bitter wormwood and blanched barley
near the corner house where Valerie Williams lived
whose parents talked fast Welsh in front of the children
past the quarry where we dared Alpine climbs
and Peggy Petters told me the facts of life
while I gaped and gasped noone would do it
near steep Primrose Hill whose iron rails remain
a bit bent now where we hung like wobbly bats
telling tall tales about the gory stain
and my tightroping brother cracked his new front tooth
just across from the Spanish chestnut tree
felled long ago but the grassy slope we searched
for skeleton leaves and tender nuts still green
by Cromwell Street where Glenys James told me

boys liked big breasts and her old grandfather
recited Poe's *Raven* in deep solemn tones
as we listened rapt and nearly died laughing
then Norfolk Street where the school's still standing
Terrace Road School with its weathervane veering
gold glitter on a tower above the playgrounds
high flights of steep sharp steps we jumped
where bold as a heroine from the Abbey school
I punched a rude boy teasing Valerie
as we played orphans and cruel guardians
and I sulked when Miss Clemonts sent me out for talking
saying I couldn't be a fairy in her Christmas play
where we had singing games with Loopy Loo
ran out to icecream carts and raspberry vinegar
or an old hunched man swopping rags for goldfish
near the twin sweetshops on opposite streetcorners
Mrs Davies for the boys and for us Mrs Lily
yellow sherbetsuckers and cocobutternuts
pied peardrops flinty mints and lucky packets
windows filled with everlasting sweets.

from *Severn Bridge: New and Selected Poems* (2001)

Saunders Lewis
[from] Monica

"Good-morning to you now."

From their window the two sisters watched their neighbour crossing the road back to her own house. She walked unhurriedly. She knew that they were watching her, but did not once turn round.

"She's like someone on her way to be hanged," said Lily. "Look, the cats have come to meet her at the gate. Why's she standing there so long?"

Monica had flung open the door and was waiting for the cats to go in first. The morning sun was shining from the south-east and her shadow was cast before her into the porch. Suddenly she turned to face the sun and raised her hand to wave to the sisters. She seemed to be bidding the sun good-bye. Then she stepped into her own shadow and, closing the door firmly, shut out the light. A shiver ran through Alice.

Monica closed the door and went upstairs to her bedroom intending to change. She opened the window. Her cigarette-case was near the mirror on the dressing-table. She took out a cigarette, lit it and sat down on the feather bed to smoke. It was ten o'clock. In half an hour the milk-boy would be calling. Then the grocer's cart would come round and the fishmonger's after that. Thus she would get the provisions necessary to make herself a meal at mid-day. She ought to go into the village to buy meat by the time Bob came in for dinner at six. It was high time she swept the parlour. She would have plenty of work to fill her morning and then she could wash and change and call on Mrs North for an afternoon in town. She could change her novel at the library, go to a café for tea and cakes, look at the latest fashions in the shop-windows, have her hair done perhaps and a shampoo. She could be home about five and still have an hour in which to prepare dinner, and in the evening she and her husband might go to the cinema together or for a walk by the seaside. That had been her daily routine ever since coming to live in this new suburb five miles from Swansea.

And then it would be night, for which the daily round was but a preparation, when she and Bob would climb the stairs together and come into this room. She would sit here on the edge of the bed while he closed the heavy orange curtains, and then he would turn to her with his languid, importunate eyes and imploring hands.

Monica made a grimace of distaste. She nipped her cigarette between finger and thumb and, going to the window, leaned out to observe the street below. There was the milk-boy. Monica called to him from the window:

"Two pints. The jug's by the back door."

Now a road in a middle-class suburb is something unique. Its character is formed and its social life completely run by women. From nine in the morning till six at night, their minions – the shopkeepers' delivery-boys, the postman with his bag, the curate and minister on their rounds, the uniformed employees of the gas and electricity companies – are the only men to be seen about the place. It is the women who determine all personal contacts between the houses; they who, by bestowing or withholding their 'good-mornings' and 'good-afternoons', decide each family's social standing. The men may hobnob with one another as they please on the train or bus on their way to and from their places of business, but when they go out with their wives of a Sunday afternoon or do the gardening under their watchful eyes on Saturdays, if one family should bump into another whom they consider inferior, great is the husbands' discomfort as they endeavour not to see each other. On those occasions they are stunned to observe the

Olympian blindness of their wives and the perfect bows of their lips, their surprise turning to astonishment when one wife says just after the other has passed out of earshot:

"Did you see her new coat? Four pounds ten at the Bon Marche last week."

Monica lit a second cigarette and gazed out at Church Road about her. This was the hour when the wives went into the village to do their daily shopping. The first to set out this morning was Mrs Clarence, a widow who lived in a house at the top end of the road, a plump, jolly and affected woman of about fifty. A heavy responsibility had fallen to her since her only daughter had married the son of the Archdeacon of Llangenith. On this account, Mrs Clarence as she walked along was looking at the windows of every house she passed, in a most judicious manner, and she stared straight at Monica without seeing her. She kept a watchful eye on the lives of all her neighbours but she greeted none save Mrs North and the two Miss Evanses. She had been at school with Mrs North, and the two sisters came of an old Newton family who had lived there before the rural village had become a populous suburb. Yet to Mrs Clarence's ears, the way the two old maids spoke, though she could not deny they were gentlewomen, was too rustic and unrefined. She had been shocked one morning when she caught Lily Evans, shovel in hand, standing in the middle of the road:

"Whatever are you doing, Miss Evans?"

"Collecting this manure for the garden."

"Oh, Miss Evans, *manure*. That's not a very nice word."

"What should I say, *dung*?" asked Lily innocently.

"My dear Miss Evans! If you must mention it, say *droppings*. And it would be far better not to notice that such a thing is ever to be found in our road. But that's the worst of coming to live so near the country."

On first arriving in Church Road, some four months previously, Mrs Clarence had prevailed upon the Archdeacon himself to attend her 'at home' and he had taken tea with her. The clergyman was a genial old fellow, with a body the shape of a barrel on the legs of a duck. After tea, Mrs Clarence escorted him as far as the end of the road, and as she passed some of her neighbours had said in a voice loud enough for them to hear:

"Archdeacon, I feel it's easier to put up with this street now that you have graced it."

"Very likely," said the barrel, and off he went on his splayed feet. Mrs Clarence's cup overflowed. The Archdeacon had done all the right things that afternoon. Later, she told the wives who came to drink her tea:

"The only thing I dreaded was that he mightn't come in his gaiters, but he did. You know, there's nothing as effective as clerical gaiters for putting neighbours in their place."

Monica did not mind being ignored by Mrs Clarence. The widow's bliss, as well as her pride, put her outside Monica's world. But when she saw Mrs Amy Hughes following her to the shops three minutes later, Monica hid for a moment behind her curtains. She recalled the first time she had set eyes on Mrs Hughes, in one of the village shops a week after she had moved into Church Road. They had walked home together and Monica learnt that her neighbour, too, was a new-comer to the district.

"You're not from around here?" asked Mrs Hughes.

"No. From Cardiff."

"I'm from Bangor."

"Did you move here directly?"

"No, from Birmingham. My husband was transferred to a better position in the bank here. I expect he'll have another promotion soon. Have you decided yet which day your 'at home' is to be?"

"What's that?"

"Don't you know? The afternoon you'll be at home to receive friends."

"I don't know anyone around here," said Monica.

"You must join the golf club. It's a most select and classy place. I've just become a member. Of course, my husband's being a cashier at the bank makes it important that I cultivate a good social circle. The last Wednesday of the month is my day. If you come over and leave some cards, I shall introduce you to some well-placed people who will be of some help to you."

Monica learnt, moreover, that Mrs Hughes was a graduate of the University of Wales, and being naïve she took that to be a mark of culture. Mrs Hughes had also been a school teacher. She was not pretty; she dressed grandly but without taste. For a fortnight the two were bosom friends. Monica began to entertain an ambition that was quite unusual for her, namely a desire for social success and going up in the world. But one morning, when the two women met in the street, Mrs Amy Hughes walked straight past her without so much as a word or smile. Monica thought it was inadvertent and called out to her. The woman did not turn round. Monica was troubled. A few days later they again came face to face and Monica stopped:

"Whatever's the matter, Mrs Hughes?"

"I beg your pardon?"

"Why do you pass me by without saying hello?"

"Oh, I'm sorry if I offend you, Mrs MacEwan, but I'm surprised that you don't understand how out of the question it is for us to be friends. I had no idea your husband was in trade. Good-morning to you."

Monica was not lacking in dignity. She walked on without uttering a word. She had a vague but persistent idea that her own spiritual malaise was of a more aristocratic nature, after all, than the base craving of her neighbour. At least she had never paid very much attention to the whispering of others.

Can any heart know the bitterness of another? At that very moment, as she passed beneath Monica's gaze, despair was weighing heavily on the feeble shoulders of Amy Hughes. Her 'at home' had come and gone. She had spent that morning in the kitchen making pretty little pasties, and putting them flat and floury in the oven and then taking them out again all light and golden, like the bubbles of a waterfall. She was a dab hand at making pastry. Then she had tidied her lounge, dressed, and waited for her guests to arrive. At least two or three wives of her husbands' colleagues should reciprocate, for she had gone to visit them. But nobody had turned up. She and her husband had had the bitter pleasure of having to eat her handiwork. Why was she such a failure and such a pariah? So unfortunate in all her opinions and scheming? There was that Mrs MacEwan; on seeing her for the first time, and noticing how elegantly she dressed, Amy Hughes had thought she would steal a march on her neighbours by making her acquaintance. Then she had heard from her husband that MacEwan was only a clock-mender in a shop with a wage of less than four pounds a week. Why aren't I more attractive? Amy Hughes complained inwardly, Why can't I dress like that Mrs Valmai Briand? There she is now coming out of her house. Why don't I have a melodious name like hers instead of Amy Hughes? I've always been held back by being shy and not forward enough. She's the one I should have greeted, not that clock-maker's wife. Mrs Briand was once a mere shop-girl, and yet now her circle of acquaintances is to be found, not among the people of Church Road, but among those living in the large houses all around us, each in its own grounds. We've been neighbours for months and we ought to say hello to each other. And when she came to do just that, – a Daimler was waiting at Mrs Valmai Briand's gate and a stout woman was sitting in it with a small fortune in squirrel's pelts draped around her shoulders, – Amy Hughes said in a loud voice, looking confidently into a face that had opened wealth's doors:

"Good-morning, Mrs Briand."

But the cupid lips did not move, and the proud eyes under eyebrows that were like new moons swept in one contemptuous glance over the frumpish figure of Amy Hughes, until it brought a blush to her forehead and neck, whereupon Mrs Valmai Briand had got into the limousine to join her fat friend.

Nor could Amy Hughes have known that it had been that very morning the bank's manager had told her husband:

"Hughes, you'd better return Mrs Valmai Briand's cheque to this tailor. Briand doesn't have an account with us and she has no funds, as far as we know, with which to honour her cheque."

Mrs North now came up the street like a schooner under full sail. There was nothing of the snob in Mrs North. Once a month, late in the evening, she filled her house with friends, got reeling drunk, and at about midnight came out into the road to see off her guests, shouting her farewells after them along the silent street, until she woke every baby and dog in the vicinity and caused cursing and the gnashing of teeth in many a heavily laden bed. Mrs North's keenest pleasure was in gossiping. Her imagination delighted in creating drama and excitement all about her. She mingled with everyone in Newton, rich and poor alike, in order to listen to her neighbours' stories, which she worked up shockingly in her own mind and then spread abroad wherever she happened to go. When Mrs Clarence reproached her for her undignified ways, she would instantly retort:

"And if I didn't chin-wag with the fishmonger's wife, what would you have to tell Mr Davies the curate this afternoon that's of any interest?"

Even now as she was making her way home, a brand-new scandal was seething in her breast. She looked about her, sniffing for someone who would listen to her. Seeing Monica at the window, she hailed her and rushed through the garden up to the house. Monica came to the door:

"Have you heard about Mrs Rosser?"

"No."

"Thank heaven for that."

Mrs Rosser, a young woman with a three-month-old baby, lived at the far end of Church Road. After the child's birth she had taken on a girl from the village as a daily help. On this particular morning Mrs Rosser had stayed in bed with her baby in the cot beside her. Her husband had said good-bye and left, so she thought, for his business in town. Half an hour had gone by. The fire in the bedroom was burning low and so she had rung the bell for the maid. She rang twice without getting any response. She flung on a dressing-gown and ran downstairs in her slippers to fetch some coal. The door of the back parlour was ajar and there on the sofa her husband and the maid were lying together. In her distraction Mrs Rosser had run out into the garden, where she encountered the milk-boy. "Come here," she shouted hysterically, pulling him into the parlour to show him the pair on the sofa. The lad had had a most glorious morning peddling the story from house to house.

"Frightful, isn't it?" said Mrs North, her eyes dancing. "What will my friend Mrs Clarence say? She'll have to invite the Archbishop of Wales, no less, to tea, to get over the shock. But just think of that poor woman with her little baby," – and crocodile tears came to Mrs North's eyes, – "What would you do, Mrs MacEwan, if you were her?"

Monica laughed, the shrill, mechanical laugh she had adopted since her marriage.

"Will you be coming into town with me this afternoon?" her neighbour asked.

"No, I can't today, thanks all the same."

"All right, good-morning. I must fly to tell my daughter all about it. It's best she hears it from me than from anyone else. You'll soon have to be thinking about the difficulties of being a mother yourself, Mrs MacEwan."

As Mrs North went off, a small boy came up the garden path with a bundle of newspapers under his arm. Monica took her paper, closed the door and went into the lounge. She sat down at the table on which lay a half-full box of chocolates. Opening the paper, she began perusing it, reading and eating at the same time. She chewed the chocolates rather than sucked them, her jaws working vigorously. She went on turning the pages, reading a passage here, another there, the report of a child's murder, an actress's Paris divorce, an advertisement for toothpaste, another for a soap for washing silk. She did not look at the political news, nor at the report of a fire and casualties at a coal-mine in Monmouthshire, but she read the twentieth installment of the novel, despite not having followed it up to then. It was an adventure story set among the tombs of Luxor and the pyramids of Egypt. One after the other the chocolates disappeared from the half-full box.

from *Monica* (1930). Trans. Meic Stephens

Dylan Thomas
I have longed to move away

I have longed to move away
From the hissing of the spent lie
And the old terrors' continual cry

Growing more terrible as the day
Goes over the hill into the deep sea;
I have longed to move away
From the repetition of salutes,
For there are ghosts in the air
And ghostly echoes on paper,
And the thunder of calls and notes.

I have longed to move away but am afraid;
Some life, yet unspent, might explode
Out of the old lie burning on the ground,
And, crackling into the air, leave me half-blind.
Neither by night's ancient fear,
The parting of hat from hair,
Pursed lips at the receiver,
Shall I fall to death's feather.
By these I would not care to die,
Half convention and half lie.

from *Collected Poems 1934-1953* (1988)

Mervyn Matthews
Coal Trimming

My Father was a docker, more precisely a 'coal trimmer', which meant
that he loaded coal into ships. His work cast a gritty shadow on our
whole manner of living. He came home black, like a miner, and his
working clothes had to be washed daily. Nobody in Lamb Street had
a hot-water system, let alone a bath, so my Father's arrival was always
preceded by the boiling of iron kettles on the kitchen fire. He washed
in a zinc bath in the wooden lean-to behind the house. Trimmers did
irregular shifts, depending on the ship movements, so sometimes I did
not see him for days on end. I was always being told to be quiet
because he was asleep upstairs.

The coal-trimmers considered themselves to be a sort of elite
among manual labourers, which fitted my Father's assumed superiority. Before the war coal exports were very important in Swansea, and
the trimmers had an agreement with ship owners whereby they
received not a wage, but a percentage of the cost of coal loaded. In this
way they reckoned to do considerably better than men on fixed pay,

and indeed, until the war stopped exports, they enjoyed a relatively good income.

My Father's love of refinement meant that he dressed with care, never used bad language, and strange though it might seem, was very sensitive about his hands, which were at once gnarled and delicate. He wrote quite neatly, and was for many years Secretary and a valued member of the Coal Trimmers' Committee. The deliberations of this body took place on a Sunday morning, when my Father would leave the house attired in a blue pin-striped suit and slim black shoes, with perhaps a smart overcoat and trilby. The committee, need I add, met in close proximity to the beer pumps of the Labour Club, one of the very few places where alcohol was available on that day.

My Father's ideal of gentility was maintained against truly hellish conditions at work. I well remember the only occasion he took me on board ship to show me what it was like. What a thrill I had going up the rickety ladder, and clambering onto the iron deck. In no time at all we were approached by a tall Indian sailor in a dirty coal-smeared turban: such headgear was never seen in the streets of Swansea, and I was quite overcome. The man underneath gave me a murky smile.

"How many children?" he asked. My Father was never one to tell the truth when he could manage something more spectacular. "Ten," he replied, showing him ten fingers. The Indian was obviously impressed.

After that we went 'below' to see the trimmers at work. Trucks filled with coal were shunted out onto a sort of gantree above the quay-side, and tipped into an enormous iron shute leading down into the ship's hold, or bunker, as the case might be. The coal, sometimes in huge lumps, came thundering down into a confined space below decks. It had to be spread evenly, or 'trimmed', so that the ship did not list at sea: the trimmers did this with the help of shovels and large boards, mostly as it poured in. One man, chosen by lot, had to stand on deck and regulate the tipping, with shouts and a whistle. It could be dark below, and the men sometimes worked by the light of long, tallow candles, bending down as the level of the coal rose and headroom was reduced. The air was thick with coal dust which swirled and glinted near the flames.

Given these conditions, coal-trimmers could expect only illness and lung disease as they got older. The fact that my Father had such an awful, if well-paid, job was always a matter of sorrow on his side of the family: and although my Grandfather had been a founder member of the Coal Trimmers' Association, both he and my Grandmother, or Gamma, as I called her, had wanted my Father, always known in the family by his full name of 'William Alfred', to do better in life. Their house in Osterley Street, St Thomas, was almost middle-class. I often wondered why my Father had chosen coal-trimming: it was not thrust upon him, and a trimmer's 'cap' was not easy to get. He had in fact started life as a telegram boy, and switched. I think the pay, access to the club, and the irregular hours attracted him. Earlier, I was told, he had had Saturday afternoons free for the football match. He later regretted his choice, but lacked the initiative to change. Even when I was a child he urged me to get an office job in which I wouldn't have to 'work hard', as he put it.

Trimmers had to provide their own tools, and I was always interested in the tough but simple implements my Father brought home for repair – large, shining shovels with long handles, lacking the cross-piece found on ordinary garden spades. My Father also made hangers for the tallow candles. For this he used strips of metal, bent to fit the wax stalks, with sliding collars and loops which allowed them to be suspended from a convenient bulkhead. Oil skins were another essential thing, and one of my Father's regular duties was to tar these peculiar garments for use when he was on deck. Like all trimmers, he had a couple of large tarpaulin-covered chests in which he kept his belongings at the dockside. Together, that is, with any useful objects he could pick up.

Indeed, pilfering was regarded by the coal-trimmers as part and parcel of their job. We never heard of anyone who was caught least of all my Father. Despite a rigorously honest upbringing, he never hesitated to boast about his acquisitions. "I got it off the dock, son," he would say, with his slightly twisted smile. "I stole it." The thieving always made my Mother and me very uneasy, for it was quite outside our family ethic as well. There were many small marine fittings, curiously-shaped hooks, knobs and brackets. Pints of the drabbest paint you could imagine – brown, buff and a lugubrious mauve – found their way into the toolshed down the garden, and then onto our woodwork. The use of a mysterious substance called 'driers' meant that it took days, rather than weeks, to go hard.

One day my Father staggered into the house carrying part of a carcass of beef with the first whiff of decay about it. He loved salting meat, so that it would keep longer: this particular piece, however, only led to another row with my Mother, who said it was uneatable. On another occasion a number of brass Catholic madonnas, with dangerously spiked haloes, made a miraculous appearance in the parlour. God knows where my Father got them from, but they had no beneficial influence on our household. Other such items which came our way from the docks included occasional flat-fish and cutlets, per favour of Mr Bennen, who worked down the fish market. I don't think my Mother ever refused those.

from *Mervyn's Lot* (2002)

Dylan Thomas
Once it was the colour of saying

Once it was the colour of saying
Soaked my table the uglier side of a hill
With a capsized field where a school sat still
And a black and white patch of girls grew playing;
The gentle seaslides of saying I must undo
That all the charmingly drowned arise to cockcrow and kill.
When I whistled with mitching boys through a reservoir park
Where at night we stoned the cold and cuckoo
Lovers in the dirt of their leafy beds,
The shade of their trees was a word of many shades
And a lamp of lightning for the poor in the dark;
Now my saying shall be my undoing,
And every stone I wind off like a reel.

from *Collected Poems 1934-1953* (1988)

Barbara Hardy
Happy as a Sandboy

I never thought of sandboys as boys. They were creatures made out of sun and sand and salt. Once I turned round on Swansea sands and saw my elder daughter Julia running along the beach as fast as she could, laughing as she ran. That was it. She was happy as a sandboy. And so were we, though we didn't know we were lucky children, with Swansea Bay and the Mumbles and Gower as our playground. [...]

The first wild place you could go to without grown-ups, first with big children, then your peers, then on your own, was Swansea sands. To go down the sands was to go anywhere between the old West Pier, by the docks, and Blackpill. The sands were lovely to look at, dark brown from the tide or yellow in the sun, but littered and polluted with trippers' rubbish, mud dredged up from the Channel, and sewage.

The bay curved from the derelict West Pier to the three points of Mumbles Head, and the Mumbles train's twin carriages moved all day between the two points. The first boats you knew by sight were the dredgers, the tugboat and the pleasure-steamers that crossed to Ilfracombe or round the Gower coast for evening cruises. I remember going once with my mother and brother, leaning over the side, seeing a fish, and being proud of not being sick. It was calm as a millpond, my mother said, but I knew I wouldn't have been sick even if the waves had been mountainous, as they were in Mother's stories about Father's storms. I boasted of being a good sailor, savouring the phrase. Though the sea wrecked my parents' marriage, my mother would say, "The sea's in your blood." This was confirmed when I recited Masefield's 'Sea-Fever', misquoting, like everyone I've ever known who has quoted from the poem, "I must go down to the sea again," improving on the archaic and affected, "I must down to the seas." Having a father who was a sailor was romantic, though I wished he was a captain not a chief steward. And after a while, when I got used to missing him, I wanted to be like my friends and have a father at home. I didn't want to be different. I wished my mother was happy.

The big sewage pipes ran at intervals into the sea, emptying their contents at high water, concluding in brown but sea-smelling pools when the tide was out. We were told not to paddle in those pools, but the pipes were lovely for playing. You could run along the sand and spring up on to their high sides, to balance, jump and fool around, then jump off the end. The beach was threaded with little streams, clean and running, nameless except for Vivian Stream and the river that ran down Clyne Valley to become Blackpill. We played round the old pier, but paddled and tried to swim in the more salubrious regions near the Slip and Brynmill. Swansea Bay was really no good for bathing. At high water you could get deep enough quite quickly, and there were no dangerous gullies or pools or undertow or currents, but the water was never clear. All kinds of bits and pieces floated round you. And at low tide you walked for miles to get even thigh-deep, plodding patiently, lifting your legs high in and out of the squish, feeling soft, nameless ooze between your toes or hurting the soles of your feet on the ripple of hard banks. Sometimes you gave up and went back, relieved if a friend suggested it first. Though we lived by the sea and played in it, we weren't taught to swim. My uncles could swim, but only Renee out of the aunts. I doubt if my grandparents ever went in except to paddle, and my mother always regretted that she'd never learnt. I used to go to the old Swansea Baths, by Victoria Park, until they were closed some time in the war because of a polio epidemic.

Once, I cut my lip on the rough bottom, trying to dive at the shallow end, and that put me off for years. You didn't learn to swim at school, but with the help of a few lessons from Ron and Walter, and a rubber ring, I learnt to float, do an erratic dog-paddle, and eventually a side-stroke which I still resort to when tired or lazy.

The beach had many pleasures. There were old lumps of peat which were the remains of ancient forests. Wood became peat and peat became coal. You could pop bladder-wort and skip with long strands of some other seaweed. You could look for shells. The best ones, always rare and now gone for good, were the exquisite ancient oyster-shells worn into transparent mother-of-pearl slivers. Mother-of-pearl was on my list of beautiful words, which I added to from time to time. It was a word that meant more than pearl, a poetry half understood. And the shells were silvery, gold, copper, rainbow, in frail saucers and half-moons. We were told how real pearls were made and searched amongst the big, thick, newer oyster-shells, still pretty ancient, because it's more than a century since the rich oyster-beds flourished which gave their name to Oystermouth, the village at the west point of Swansea Bay. You found shells of mussels and cockles and whelks too, and some-times after the weekend you could pick up ha'pennies and pennies left in the sand by the careless, happy trippers who came down from the Rhondda in charabancs. [...]

We knew the whole curve of the bay. Every summer my mother bought season tickets, one and two halves, for the Mumbles train. It ran along the bay, separating the beach from the promenade. We'd walk down from Cradock Street to the terminus, where there was a shelter to wait if there wasn't a train in. The train was bright red, with two coaches and a wonderful hoot. It looked a bit like a tram, though there were no overhead lines. When I introduced my husband to Swansea he teased my family by calling our famous train the Mumbles Tram, arousing local patriotism I thought I had outgrown. Destroyed by short-sighted planners, it was a unique means of transport. For us it was the vehicle of summer journeys to the first Gower seaside, Bracelet Bay.

The journey round the bay was a series of pleasures, punctuated by the familiar stops. First there was the grim fastness of Swansea Gaol, with high, stony walls. Mean streets were succeeded by a terrace of smart boarding-houses, still there with old ads for bed and breakfast and new ones offering television and *en-suite* luxury rooms. They still have the old white-painted verandas and names like 'Seahaven' and 'Bayview'. Then you came to the Slip, with one of the several arches which led across the railway line from road to sea, and the Vetch or Vetchfield, where my uncles watched the Swans win or lose on

Saturday afternoons. When they first talked about them, I didn't know the Swans were human animals. I saw my first and last football match there, taken by my grandfather to see Swansea boys playing. There was the smallest and most boring of the Swansea parks, Victoria Park, whose attractions were the Patti Pavilion and a floral clock, brilliant before the war but ugly when it was restored. Next you came to the Rec, a recreation ground enlivened by circus tents or the fun-fairs, or a waste of dry and battered grass where boys and men in shirt-sleeves idly kicked balls about. Then came Brynmill Lane, leading to two parks. At the entrance to Singleton Park is a fake-mediaeval lodge built over the archway, one of my enchanted dwellings, admired for its supposedly ancient pointed arches, windows and turrets, and for its small compactness. Just right for my romantic community of children without adults, constructed out of imagination and eccentric architecture. My castles in Spain were mostly built out of Swansea pseudo-Gothic and mock-Tudor. After the Park you came to the university buildings, tiny compared with their later spread, opposite the small golf-course, which seemed vast and wild. Then past Ashley Road stop, undistinguished except for a couple of dolls-house villas, to Blackpill. Here Gower and the country began, at the old Roman bridge, where the river ran down from Clyne Valley. This was the halfway point, the turn in the bay where you looked straight ahead to the Mumbles with the lighthouse and the three pointed rocks. The lighthouse might be a misty shape, or invisible in sea-fog, or a clear and shapely telos. It flashed its warning by night, and marked the destination of every August day. After Blackpill you came to West Cross, an expensive suburb before the housing estate lowered values and caused a class exodus, Norton Road, then Oystermouth, with its ancient castle and rows of swaying coloured boats and buoys, and last of all Mumbles Pier. The train stopped, we got out, the driver changed places, and the second coach became the first. There might be blasting there for the new sewage works, the first explosions we ever heard. We might go on the pier, which had slot-machines where you could get a penny fortune or pull a lever, threepence a go, and stamp a silvery slip of metal with your name in print for the first time, or see the famous Mumbles lifeboat, saver of lives, braver of storms. We'd walk up the short, deep, tunnelled road round to the cliffs, where there were harebells and thrift in the soft, sweet, cropped grass. A short scramble took us to the rocks and caves and beach, a wide strip of shingle, then golden sands.

My mother would find a sheltered spot on the rocks, or a small sandy inlet, and we would undress, pull on our cover-all bathing-suits, and make for the sea or the rock-pools. Memory sets a small white

cotton hat on Bill's head, and gives him a shrimping-net and pail, and
a fisherman's smile. I go off to find a pool big enough to lie in, with
rocks to sun myself on, red anemones to poke and shrink, and long
tails of seaweed for a mermaid. You could look out at the ocean, see if
it would stay fine or rain, and pretend you could swim as you held on
to a rock with one arm or found a stony corner to prop your head. The
pools were dark and deep, with crabs and pink, crimped sea-plants,
but they held you safe and warm and floating in a secret embrace.

from *Swansea Girl* (1994)

John Prichard
Swansea Bay

Here would seem a mastery of time
And sufferance of that academic death.
Here delivered by grace of water, conspiracy
Of wind and moon are foreigners commuted
For a tide's abidance to this instant slate,
Stranded on the littoral; shells without tenant,
A ruffled, rare-lidded gull in shroud of oil
And a dog snarling with rib and tooth
In a lethal embrace of needy stones.

The static, shipless sea of false waves
Poised and propped beyond the claybeds, the blind
Lighthouse, the map sun set in a barren
Sky, a painted flat, and these starched gravegrooms
Scaring like laid by the wayside coffins and all
The hushed, unweathered beach, still and spent,
Irreducible as its sandgrains, compose
A breath-holding scene, a daylight exhumation,
Life's pattern caught and built in a moment's pose.

Extremity is nearest to eternity.
This pedestalled world behind a dike of time
And this petrified emotion snapped
In the flat, heraldic seascape now tell
Life in tableau, show time in statuary.

from *Modern Welsh Poetry* (1944)

Leslie Norris
Percy Colclough and the Religious Girls

This is not my story at all. If not to Percy Colclough, then it belongs to my friend Tom Bevan, who told it to me in the taproom of an inn five miles out of Chichester on the A-286, the road to Midhurst, in Sussex. The name of the inn is the Horse and Groom, and it is about a hundred and fifty miles and thirty years away from the scene of the story Tom Bevan told me.

Tom had left school in 1935, when he was fourteen years old, and gone to work in the mines. Anyone could tell he'd once been a miner. He has the high, heavy shoulders that years of hacking and shovelling give to a man, particularly to one working in the South Wales pits, where there was never enough room to swing a pick properly. He also carries on his face a few of the thin, indelible-blue scars all miners wear.

He told me this story in his emphatic voice, his fanatical pale eyes fixed over my shoulder on the resurrection of his memories. I had never known Percy Colclough, but as soon as Tom Bevan began to speak I could see him plainly. He had started work on the same day, at the same age, and in the same Aberdare pit as Tom Bevan.

For four years they had worked near each other, Tom Bevan with his father and Percy Colclough with an older brother. Tom paraded before me the two young men, hard, spare, muscular. I saw them clearly; I knew the way their cheekbones shone after the ferocity of their evening shaves, I could see the extravagant care with which they brushed their hair, docile with hair cream.

Work was brutal and hours were long in the mines in the late thirties. Together, Percy and Tom would walk over the mountain to the pithead, and they'd stumble home together after eight hours of back-breaking toil, too tired to speak, too tired almost to go to bed.

Their lives were extraordinarily narrow. From Monday morning until Friday night, they worked and ate and fell heavily to sleep, and all their pleasure would be packed into the brief weekend respite of Saturday and Sunday. Even this was an unadventurous leisure, almost ritualistic in its regularity: football, dancing, a visit to the cinema, drinking in the evening with one's friends. They never went farther from home than the dance hall at Pontypridd, eight miles down the valley. There they would gaze at young men from valleys four or five miles distant as if they came from the other end of the world.

Once a year, on a Saturday in August, they would go to Barry Island, or Porthcawl, or another South Wales coast town, in company with other miners, to a meeting of their trades union, the Miners' International Federation. I have a sepia image, as clear as if I myself had taken a photograph, of Tom and Percy, caught in midstep as they walk along the promenade, their white collars open, their jackets over their arms, the wide trousers then fashionable blown around their striding shins by a wind off the sea. That would have been a great journey for them – like a journey to Siberia, almost.

So it was enterprising of Tom when, on a Saturday morning in the cold spring of 1939, he walked breezily along to the railway station, its one platform empty in the pale-yellow sun, and bought a return ticket to Cardiff. Cardiff, twenty-four miles away, was the big city; in the evening, its lights warmed the sky with orange promises of the exotic as far north as Tom's village.

Tom went down on the nine-fifteen, walked like a famous dandy around the two main streets, looked at the expensive shops and the girls newly blooming in the sun, had lunch in Woolworth's, went to a football match, and was home by seven-thirty. This was living. He told nobody of his escape from the valley, not even Percy Colclough. And the next Saturday he went to Swansea.

This was a longer journey and lacked the intoxicating, headlong directness of Tom's first venture. There was, for example, a change of trains at Neath, and he had to wait for ten minutes in a cold rain that drifted inexorably over the nearby hills and settled, as if forever, on the whole of Wales. Then his carriage was full of comfortable families going shopping. On his trip to Cardiff, Tom had had a compartment to himself, so that he could take two steps from window to window and miss nothing of the scenery on either side. He had sung loudly, in his resonant baritone, the popular songs of the day – 'Begin the Beguine', 'Blue Moon', 'Stardust'. But now he was forced to sit, silent in his steaming raincoat, between two plump women, pinned in by their elbows. He lost, gradually and hopelessly, the bold spirit of exploration with which he had begun the day.

He was depressed, and a little awed, by the iron magnitude of Swansea Station. As gray and wet as the rain outside, it glowered down at Tom, its metal noises ringing ominously through his head as he gave half of his ticket to the man at the gate.

Tom stepped cautiously out into the world. A huge square, as big as a village, stretched in front of him, its raucous traffic checked by an eloquent policeman on a dais. He was buffeted by people; the wind ripped at his slapping coat. It was all too much for Tom. He sidled along the pavement, his head down, searching for haven.

What he found was a small Italian café, squashed incongruously between the splendid buildings of more prosperous concerns. It was warmly shabby, its windows carried an array of advertisements for concerts and boxing matches, maroon paint peeled in strips from its door. With a sigh of relief, Tom stepped into its odorous darkness. A long counter stood along the far wall, the gleaming coffee machine, hissing to itself, at one end. Plates of sausage rolls, curling sandwiches, and doughnuts lay limply under glass covers. Behind the counter, a muttering, fat old man was just visible. You could order tea or coffee or Bovril or Horlick's. A little pot of crusted mustard stood on each of the four marble-topped tables. It was exactly like Carpanini's, in Aberdare. Tom was at home. He sat down in an upright and comfortless chair.

"I'll have a coffee," he said firmly, "if you don't mind."

"One coffee," said the fat old man. "Yes, sir."

"And a doughnut," said Tom.

"And a doughnut", said the old man. "Yes, sir."

The only customer in the safe dark of the café, Tom dozed away the remaining morning, his eyes half closed, like a cat. At one o'clock he took off his raincoat, hung it on a hook on the wall, and pondered over the menu the old man handed him. He liked its restraint and conservatism.

Pie and chips
Sausage and chips
Egg and bacon
Egg and chips
Sausage, egg, and chips
All with bread and butter and a cup of tea.

He read with approval.

"Sausage, egg, and chips," he said. "I like a good meal in the middle of the day."

"Yes, sir," said the old man. "Sausage, egg, and chips."

He shuffled off to do the cooking.

Tom ate slowly, with conscious enjoyment. From time to time he glanced out the window, watching the rain stream down the glass through the advertisement for Typhoo Tea, seeing the hurrying wet figures of the passers-by. He was very happy. He wished only that he had a daily paper, and when the old man, without a word, brought him a grimy copy of the Express, he was pleased but not surprised. Propping it against the sugar bowl, he read placidly, sipping his tea like a young man with time to spare.

When the two girls came in, Tom lifted his cup to them in gentle courtesy and wished them a good afternoon. They were pink from hurrying, they shook out their wet coats with exclamations of relief and surprise, they smiled at Tom Bevan. One of them was tall, fair, and elegant. She moved like a colt.

"What a day," one of them said. "The usual, please, Algy."

"Egg and chips," said the old man. "Yes, Miss."

The girls sat two tables away from Tom Bevan, examining the contents of their parcels, chattering away as briskly as starlings. Tom looked at them with pleasure. He pushed away his paper and spoke to them.

"How do you girls like living in Swansea?" he said.

They stopped talking and considered.

"I've never lived anywhere else," said the tall, fair girl. "It's all right, though, living in Swansea. Very nice, really."

"I don't live in Swansea," the shorter, darker girl said. "I live in Dunvant, just outside. It's a village."

"We went to school together, didn't we, Elsie?" said the fair girl.

"And now we work together in an insurance office," said Elsie.

The old man came in, two plates held in front of him.

"Ooh! Thank you, Algy," said the girls together. "It looks lovely."

What nice girls, thought Tom Bevan, what pleasant manners. "I had sausage, egg, and chips," he said. "I believe in a good meal in the middle of the day."

"We've never had that," said Elsie, "although sometimes we have pie and chips. Mostly in the evening we have pie and chips, after the cinema. Don't we, Margaret?"

"That's right," Margaret replied. "In the evening." She looked up at Tom Bevan. "Where do you live?" she asked.

Tom Bevan told them. He told them about his journey to Cardiff; he told them of its glittering shops and its streets; he told them of the Taff River, black as oil, running through the heart of the town; he described the football match he'd seen. Then he told them of his work in the mine, and they listened carefully, interrupting him now and then with flattering little gasps of amazement.

"It's a world of its own, down there," he said. "I've seen things down there that would make you laugh, yes, and make you weep, too."

"You must have," said Margaret with admiration. "We don't know how you colliers stick it as you do. Now, our work isn't exciting at all."

"Not exciting," agreed Elsie, "but we have some fun, you know, in the office."

The girls looked at each other, smiling, their eyes shining.

They took Tom Bevan into the small universe of their office, described the manager, the clerks, the other typists, told him of the little practical jokes that enriched the passing days.

"That Mr James can be a pig sometimes," said Elsie, "but he can't help it. He has asthma."

"There's nothing worse," confirmed Tom Bevan, "than a bad chest."

He held the palm of his hand for a moment on his own shirtfront.

"Do you know," he began, "that two winters ago, I had bronchitis so badly I couldn't breathe? I had to sleep all night sitting upright in an armchair, the blankets wrapped around me."

The girls, full of sympathy, nodded softly to him.

The afternoon sped by. Tom, preserving what he hoped would prove an interesting reserve, did not join the girls at their table, but he bought chocolate biscuits that they all three shared. He couldn't remember ever having met such attractive, sensible girls. He looked with satisfaction at their sophisticated clothes, their delicate shoes. There was no doubt that girls in the big towns knew how to behave.

When the girls got up to leave, Tom, springing to his feet to help them with their coats, felt keen disappointment. He handed them their parcels and moved to open the door for them.

"Good-bye," said Elsie. "It's been nice meeting you. I enjoyed our chat."

"Thank you," said Tom. "So did I."

"We might see you again," Margaret said. "We always have our lunch here on Saturdays."

"I'm often here myself," said Tom, with pardonable exaggeration. "I might see you next Saturday."

The girls stepped into the street, ducked their heads against the wind, and disappeared.

A glint of sun broke through the cluttered windows of the café. The rain had stopped. Tom took down his coat and shrugged himself into it. The world was warm and pleasurable. He said good-bye to the muttering old man, immobile behind the counter. "Nice little place you have here, Algy," said Tom. "Very nice little place."

The old man did not reply.

Outside, the streets had regained their normal proportions, the traffic was amiable and controlled. Tom strolled about for half an hour, returned to the station, caught a train, and departed for home. His carriage was empty, the late-afternoon light was golden, and Tom sang all the way to Aberdare.

On Sunday morning, Tom went to church, meeting, as he usually did, the tall and elegant figure of Percy Colclough. Percy was a deeply serious young man, and attended church three times every Sunday.

He was astonished to learn that Tom had been to Swansea, but, keeping the Sabbath for solemn matters, asked no questions.

The next morning, however, on the way to the pithead, he spoke out boldly.

"What's it like in Swansea, Tom?" he asked.

"Lovely," said Tom. "Fine. They've got a huge station and a very nice café there."

Percy Colclough laughed.

"It was raining," said Tom defensively, "and then I met these two charming girls."

Percy Colclough stopped laughing. "Two charming girls?" he said.

"Margaret and Elsie," confirmed Tom. "I'm meeting them again next Saturday. You can come along if you like."

Percy whistled pensively. "I might," he said. "I just might, at that."

All week long Percy found opportunities for nudging Tom with an elbow, for winking slowly at him.

"Saturday," he'd say. "Still all right for Saturday, Tom?"

"I'll see you at the station about half past nine," Tom would answer.

Tom was at the station early on Saturday. He had hurried through the holiday streets, bright with strengthening spring, but he knew that Percy Colclough would be there before him. He bought his ticket, moved through the barrier, and walked on to the platform. Tall, slim, his dark suit pressed and cleaned, Percy Colclough stood alone at the far end of the platform. He turned his head but gave no other sign of recognition. His black hat sat prim and straight on his head.

Tom hurried up to him, noting with approval the details of Percy's appearance – the glossy white shirt, the discreet small flower in his lapel, the shoes polished like mirrors. Under Percy's arm was a Bible.

"Good morning, Percy," said Tom, "and a lovely morning for our little escapade."

"Good morning, Tom," said Percy. "I think we may enjoy ourselves today."

Together the two young men stared down the track in the direction from which the train would come.

A heavy silence deepened until Tom could stand it no longer.

"For God's sake, Percy," he said hoarsely. "Why the Bible? Why the Bible, Percy?"

Percy Colclough stepped nearer. He looked with extreme care up and down the deserted platform. He lowered his voice, as if in fear that the heathen wind of April would lift his salacious words and scatter them broadcast over listening Aberdare.

"I was thinking," he said, like a convict, out of the side of his mouth. "Well, tomorrow being Sunday ... and if these girls were any good ... you know ... we might stop over until tomorrow."

When Tom Bevan told me that, in the Horse and Groom, I couldn't stop laughing.

"And did you," I asked, "did you stop over?"

"No," said Tom Bevan. "Of course we didn't. Those were two very nice respectable girls. Went to church every Sunday, the same as we did."

Tom Bevan is a schoolteacher now. He lives in Hampshire, only a dozen miles from me. I rang him up to tell him I'd written this story, and he laughed.

"It's all true," he said. "Every word of it. And I'll tell you something else. Although he was so religious himself, when Percy Colclough found out that those two girls were also religious he was white with anger. He was angry for weeks, not speaking to me for over a month. And I never heard him say a good word about Swansea after that."

from *Collected Stories* (1996)

John Ormond
Poem in February

Walking besides the lank sea-shore in February
with the faint birdmarks, triangular,
and the grave curve and cry of the whirlpool bay,
I set a line the wave cannot destroy,
wave turning upon the dunes, beyond the rock
first searched and sought out by the renewing tide
that leaves no hidden sanctuary.

The line is valid as a winter dream; upon no rack of logic,
under the point of nails, proving some non-existence
of a spirit by a manrib cracking before pain;
it is no wreck of ghostship on the shore,
gone in the daylight, only there on moon;

so when the reedwinds come to seek me out
my hair is seagrass, fingers sand,
and over all the watermarks they pass;
there is no enemy; here is friend.

The slender sun combing the grey hair's cloud
drops the insistent shadow on the distant castle;
broken like bone. Yet on the beach the skull's no alien,
and the black woods around above witness no burial
of the dead seas. They are not alone

for under them all and the leafmoulds, and the waters
through the late winter boughs, and under the stones,
the skull and I are handlocked like a flood,
a flood in February when first the primrose breaks.

Three Cliffs Bay
from *Modern Welsh Poetry* (1944)

Waldo Williams
The Peacemakers

Rose-red sky above the snow
    Where bombed Swansea is alight,
Full of my father and mother I go,
    I walk home in the night.
They are blest beyond hearing,
Peacemakers, children of God.

Neither, within their home, abuse
    Nor slander could be found.
Mam would look for an excuse
    For the biggest scoundrels round.
They are blest beyond hearing,
Peacemakers, children of God.

It was the angel of poor homes
    Gave my father two rich pearls:
Brotherhood the mission of man,
    God's largesse the invisible world.
They are blest beyond hearing,
Peacemakers, children of God.

Nation good or nation bad
    (So they taught) is fantasy.
In Christ's light is freedom had
    For any man that would be free.
Blest, the day dawns that will hear them,
Peacemakers, children of God.

What is their estate tonight,
    Tonight, with the world ablaze?
Truth is with my father yet,
    Mother with forgiveness stays.
The age will be blest that hears them,
Peacemakers, children of God.

from *Dail Pren* (1956). Trans. Tony Conran

Denis F. Ratcliffe
Mayhill in the Blitz

That winter, late in January, the bombing started. Not very frightening at first, the raids developed into three consecutive nights of mind-numbing noise and destruction which wiped out the heart of the town with fearful accuracy. Very few bombs strayed on to residential areas, but even those few wrought great alarm and panic out of all proportion to the damage done. It was an awesome sight, and D. roamed the local streets the mornings after, to see houses bombed flat, to hear neighbours discussing deaths and injuries.

The first of the three nights' alarms came at midnight. Not many people in the neighbourhood took much active notice at first. Then the sound of anti-aircraft gunfire convinced them that there was serious business afoot, and D. and his sisters were roused, rushed downstairs still in pyjamas, clutching a blanket.

Dazed with sleep, they ran down the sloping cinder path to the shelter and clambered over the sharp lip into the damp bowels of the freezing black cavity that gave them safety. There they crouched on the sharp steel slats of the two-tiered bunks, shivering with cold and fear.

The night was a clear moonlight frozen black and white map. A dusting of powdery snow drew outlines of roads and buildings sharply, though this meant little to the bomber crews sitting aloft, who relied on a radio beam system to pinpoint their target and bomb-release point.

Such technical impartiality did little to comfort the thousands of souls crouching in dread all over the town, each of them expecting a personal and painful assault from the unseen enemy.

As the bombers drew closer their engines developed a sympathetic resonance, giving the world below a strong three-four waltz time beat, as though from an orchestra of giant muted double basses. The anti-aircraft guns, few enough for the conflict, faded away as the aircraft began to fly overhead and out of elevation range of the clumsy, large-calibre, slow-firing barrels which were reluctant to turn around and shoot bursts over the town.

There followed a strange period of waiting, the whole world slowly yielding to the hypnotising throb of hundreds of engines, like a reluctant patient surrendering to a powerful masseur. They began to relax.

Then the whistling bombs began to fall. Each whistle ended in a thumping roar and in the shelters they twitched and clenched their teeth, and their fingers and toes curled tight. At the height of the raid the bombs were falling so thick and fast that the explosions merged into one huge noise, extinguishing even the warning whistle of approaching death.

As the main stream of bombers did their work and turned for home, stragglers began to arrive, and dropped their bombs anywhere. These were the most fearsome. Not only did the stragglers drag out the raid by hours, but they inflicted real punishment on the packed housing estates surrounding the industrial centres.

After three and a half hours the all-clear sounded. For some reason, the siren of the Cwmfelin steel works always got off first, even though it didn't have a proper siren that wailed up and down the scale as all the other works did. The Cwmfelin siren sounded like a tired fog horn, with a single note broken into three-second burps for a warning, and continuous for the all-clear.

D. heard his mother burst into tears. It was over. They were safe, and as far as he knew, their house was still there.

His father had been outside in the open, on locally-organised air raid rescue duties. He poked his head into the shelter and said reassuringly, "OK. It's all over now. Let's get to bed." As D. stirred his father said in surprise, "What's D. doing here, on his own? On the top bunk?"

His mother sniffled away her tears. "He's only a boy. He can look after himself. I was looking after the girls on the bottom bunk."

"It's safer down below," said his father. "He should be on the bottom bunk." He sounded disapproving.

There was no further discussion, and they trooped out of the shelter, frozen, stiff and sweating with nervous exhaustion. As they tumbled wearily into bed D. wondered why his mother had said "only a boy." If she had said "He's a boy, and can look after himself," he would have been proud. But "only a boy"? He wasn't up to it, and fell asleep.

They stayed at home the next day, listening to visiting adults discussing the bombing. Names were mentioned, in hushed tones. People, places, whole families had "gone". Wrecked buildings were described second and third-hand. D.'s father had wanted to go to work but he was persuaded to stay at home like other men in the street, to offer help if needed. He dished out Christmas supplies of whisky, and more neighbours came to talk and to give each other reassurance. Soon the gathering had spilled on to the tiny lawn outside the back door, and someone picked up the bottle of whisky and passed it around. Those without a glass took a swig from the bottle, and someone else called for more liquor. His father obliged, his mother protested, and someone broke into song. [...]

That night they came again. This time there was no hesitation or doubts about taking shelter. Drawing on the previous night's experience, they found time to dress fully, and his mother took a prayerbook with her. This time they were joined by the Michaels, their next door neighbours, whose shelter was only two sheets long, without bunks and too small to lie at full stretch as all the best Ministry of Information advice told them they should do. The Michaels were the only Welsh-speakers in the street, and thus considered "odd". Mr Michael ate his peas with his knife, a marvellous achievement that D. tried to copy with conspicuous failure.

They all prayed in Welsh and sang hymns from the local Baptist chapel as the cascade of death exploded all around. More bombs went astray this time, including one that fell into the Michaels' back garden, a scant ten yards from the shelter where they all crouched. There were incendiary bombs too, small blunt-nosed phosphorous ordnance that was rumoured to be able to burn holes through thick steel sheets. Sometime during the raid their father was reported to be blinded, but this was an exaggeration – the glare from an exploding firebomb had temporarily disoriented him, and he was seen in the nick of time as he staggered towards the lip of the crater dug out by the HE bomb that had fallen just a few minutes before in the Michaels' garden.

D.'s mother lay at the bottom of the shelter, wailing and bemoaning her fate with a blinded husband, wisely making no move to leave the relative safety of the shelter to give aid to her spouse.

It was generally agreed that the raid was worse than the previous night. As well as fire bombs, the anti-aircraft guns had continued to fire, even when the debris of bursting shells was bound to fall away over the houses, and this had provided an alarming hail of metal fragments, peppering roofs and roads. Slates were dislodged, and the scraping rattle as they slid down roofs, followed by a short silence then a crash as they struck a concrete pathway or a glass-roofed lean-to, added to the strain. Sometimes the slates were stopped by guttering until it could hold no longer, and collapsed with a frightening clatter. It seemed the whole world was disintegrating around them. And then they heard the siren bomb for the first time. This was truly frightening. One or two German planes flew higher than the rest and dropped small bombs with air-activated sirens attached. These seemed to drop for ever, the sirens getting louder and louder and always in the direction of the listener. The tone of the siren was a lot lower and more musical than the whistling scream of the heavier bombs, and easily distinguishable. To the children, their mother's agonised shout of: "There's another one!" meant only the emergence of a siren bomb. Paradoxically, before the night was over, they were almost ignoring the real heavyweights and their whistling announcement of death and destruction, and concentrating on being the first to claim a hearing of the smaller, less deadly sirens, though these were quite as capable of demolishing a house and killing everyone in it.

They emerged weary and exhausted from the shelter. The bright, crisp moonlight and frosted snow was a bizarre background to the sound of fire engines and shouts of men in the streets calling for tools, bandages and blankets for the trapped and injured of houses hit in the raid. As they walked up the garden path one side of the house reflected dancing shadows against the yellow glare of a house on fire just down the street. Curiosity numbed by tiredness and cold, they trudged upstairs and fell asleep.

D. didn't know who the Patons were, but they had been hit. One half of a semi-detached house had been destroyed and father, mother and baby killed outright. They had sheltered under the stairs because their steel shelter was too small and cold for the baby. The remaining half was exposed like a doll's house, floor by floor, with all the furniture and belongings on view. D. watched with others as the man of the house tried to recover a pram, parked incongrously at the edge of a sagging floor of the main bedroom. Neighbours shouted advice. "Use a pole." "Throw a rope over the handlebar and pull it." "Lower it down" ... and so on. "The brake is on," snapped the man. "I have to get to it to release it."

Later that day the pram appeared in D.'s house, complete with baby. Reggie Squires was the man's name, and he, his wife and baby stayed with them for a week while the authorities found somewhere for them to live. D.'s elder sister Jean was sent off to her grandmother for the time being to make room.

The bomb that killed the Patons was one of a stick of three. The second one fell just twenty yards away and cut the water main and sewer. Why these should run side by side in a relatively modern housing development was anybody's guess. For weeks the families in the street performed their toilet functions in an old bucket behind the air raid shelters, and clean water came from a bowser truck that called once a day until the pipe was repaired. It was D.'s job to take two buckets, the maximum allowed, fill them and carry them home. On the third day, his mother found a frog in one bucket.

A row with the Army bowser driver followed on the lines of: "How do 'they' expect us to use water with live frogs in it?" and "'They' ought to do something about it" and "We pay our taxes ..." etc, etc. Uncontrollable sniggers from a group of boys close by resolved the confrontation. The Army driver first twigged the joke, and began to smile at D.'s mother, fuelling her rage. D. also saw it, but did not smile. The bowser driver climbed into his cab, promises of reporting to his seniors ringing in his ears, and drove off.

D. inspected the crater of the bomb that had exploded in the neighbouring garden. He was impressed by the size of the hole, though he was assured by his father that it was a very small bomb. The neighbours' shelter didn't appear to be seriously affected, though anyone in it could have been killed by blast, he was told.

Again, today, leaning from his bedroom window, D. could see the brown-black haze of fires in the docks and town centre area. There was nothing else to show what a terrible night they had spent.

Reggie Squires brought a box of plums in, and gave them to D.'s mother. She took them with ill grace, asking petulantly what she could do with them. They were sour and unbeatable. Mrs Squires suggested she should make jam. Reluctantly, because gas supplies were cut off, D.'s mother agreed, borrowed a large aluminium pot, added a little water, and set the plums to stew on the stove, pouring in precious packets of sugar.

In the evening, the gas supplies were restored, and the plums were set up on the gas ring atop the stove, where they bubbled away interestingly. There was no electricity that day, or in the sharp winter night, as they crowded into the kitchen for warmth. One candle was not enough even to play cards, so the adults talked and the children fiddled and got on everyone's nerves until they were packed off to bed early. People had been warned not to light fires in their homes, because this increased the risk of fire if the house was hit by a bomb.

It was cold in bed, and the air was full of nervous expectation. From below D. could hear the muffled voices discussing the war. Was it true, D.'s mother was asking, that the Germans ate the babies of their enemies? No one was sure about this. They certainly were heathens – they had dressed up as nuns and parachuted down behind Dutch lines, where they shot people and then hid their guns under their skirts. They even had bombs disguised as rosary beads tied around their waists. D.'s mother said this was terrible blasphemy, and the Pope should do something about it.

"What religion are they, Frank?" she asked. Perhaps they were Hindu or something. The Pope would be seriously handicapped if they were.

After a pause where D. could detect some embarrassment, his father said that they were the same as in this country. "A bit of a mixture. Catholics and Protestants."

"And a lot of neither," said Reggie Squires.

"Those bomber pilots can't be Catholics," said his mother, her voice rising in disbelief. "They can't be. It's a mortal sin to kill people."

"It's not very nice to frighten them, either," said Mrs Squires.

"Cliff is a Catholic," said his father. "He flies a plane that carries bombs."

"And a lot of guns," said Reggie Squires.

"But that's different," said D.'s mother.

There was a long pause. Cliff was the husband of D.'s favourite aunt.

"They won't come again, will they, Frank?" His mother's voice was fearful. "They say there's nothing left in town."

"No," said his father. "They don't have enough planes. Hundreds were shot down yesterday. They found wrecks all over the place. Even if they get up another raid, they'll try somewhere else. Somewhere nearer, and safer to bomb. We're a long way from their airfields."

Comforted, D. fell asleep. He slept in his parents' bed, head to toe with his sister. His elder sister wasn't here tonight, and there was more room. His parents slept in his bed, and the Squires slept in his sisters' bed. Complicated and unsettling, but the disturbed nights were taking their toll, and sleep came easily.

They came again that night. There was less warning, and the Cwmfelin hooter was groaning its call as the bombs were falling. On their way to the shelter, D.'s mother, who was in front, asked his father, "Do you think they can see us, Frank?"

"No. Of course not," said his father. He sounded slightly impatient.

"But they tried to drop a bomb on us last night, though, didn't they? They must have seen us running. There's so much light."

As they reached the shelter entrance D.'s mother stopped, waiting his father's answer. His younger sister wriggled past and dropped down to the bunk. His father turned away, his shepherding duties done, and ran out to the road with Reggie Squires, ready for rescue work.

Inside the shelter, D.'s mother crouched whimpering on the bunk with his sister. D. lay on a top bunk, face down on the steel slats, above the Michaels with their baby, and Mrs Squires with hers. He had never felt so lonely.

The night was worse than the previous two combined. The Germans dropped a new kind of bomb, as well as the incendiaries and siren bombs. This was a 'land mine', complete with parachutes it was said, though the advantages of this kind were not clear. Anyway, they made a much bigger bang, and there was no whistle.

They were in the shelter for two and a half hours, praying, singing hymns, calling comforting messages to one another. "That's the main wave gone" or "They're turning for home now." They were always false comforts. The bombs continued to whistle and scream, the guns went on firing, slates crashed to the ground, whistles blew, bells rang, men shouted, women and children whimpered, dogs barked and the ground shook.

Then the engines faded, and the sirens struck a clear continuous note and they wept with relief. Numb with cold and fright they clambered out of the shelter, thankful that their house was intact. Inside the kitchen, the plums were still bubbling in the pan over the gas ring. D.'s mother wailed as she examined the pan's contents. The jam had boiled away all this time unattended and had turned to the consistency of rubber. What a waste of sugar, she complained to the world. The incongruous novelty of the gently purring gas flame, undisturbed by the exploding madness of the world outside, escaped her.

Sleep came less easily that night. It was colder than before. R.A.F. planes roamed the air, raising a lurching fear of enemy aircraft returning to make a sneak raid, and there was a growing nervousness that it was only a matter of time before they all came to the same end as the Patons. There didn't seem to be a time limit for the punishment they were taking. It might be better to be sentenced to certain death rather than undergo the never-ending threat of a nasty end.

On a short tour the following morning D. found that Reggie Squires' remaining half of the Patons' house had disappeared. By a chance in a million a straggling bomber had released three bombs, exactly as on the second raid the night before last, and they had struck the ground within a few feet of their previous pattern. The water and sewer mains had been cut again. There were other houses too, which had been wrecked. In some of the longer five or six-home blocks there were gaps, neatly cut out sometimes by fire, often by smaller bombs. One of D.'s cousins, he was told, had been killed with all his family. D. remembered his cousin, who had been in his class at school. He had a very pretty older sister.

When he returned home D. found his mother in the kitchen, gibbering insanely over a cup of whisky held by a woman neighbour. She couldn't stand any more of it, she blubbered. Not any more. "What do they want?" she cried. D. watched impassively. Why was she crying? There was no danger now, at this moment.

"I haven't done anything wrong," she continued to wail. "I go to Mass every week. I've never missed. It isn't fair."

Her knees began to wobble, and she permitted herself to be guided to a nearby chair, where she collapsed over the table, arms outstretched as though to Allah, and sobbed theatrically. The neighbour patted her back sympathetically, but was clearly embarrassed. Nobody in the street had caved in like this. D. became ashamed, and went out of the house to have another look at the bomb crater next door.

He returned to the house to inspect the hole in the ceiling. The base-plate of an anti-aircraft shell had struck the slates near the edge of the roof, barrelled its way through, bounced off the floor boards, hit the ceiling again and come to rest on the bed. Exactly where D.'s head might have been. He looked at the ugly piece of metal, placed by his father on the mantelpiece. Black, with jagged edges on one side where it had disintegrated when it had exploded miles above. His mother had been very annoyed. "Somebody could have been hurt," she said. "You'd think they would aim better than that, wouldn't you? They'll be killing their own, at this rate."

Later that day two Army engineers called, checking on the utilities supply. The water still fountained from the evil-smelling, mud-filled crater where a dozen men worked feverishly for hours. D.'s mother invited the two men in, and now, completely recovered from her breakdown, flirted with them and made them a cup of tea. This was a golden opportunity to pick up news from the soldiers – what delays on the water and gas supplies, where the bombs had fallen, how many dead, the size of the fires, and so on. She would hold centre stage at a street chat later on. [...]

The Germans went somewhere else that night, but there was a false alarm, and they spent half an hour of biting cold in the shelter, hardly believing their luck as the Cwmfelin hooter moaned the all-clear. There were no bombs, throbbing engines, crashing slates or clenched hands. There were no prayers or hymn singing either, and God seemed a little further away than the night before.

In early March the King and Queen paid the town a visit. Nobody could say why they had come, but the town was flattered and people turned out in their thousands to wave and cheer as the Royals toured the streets in a huge open-topped car. The Queen caught D.'s eye as he stood gazing, mystified at the entourage, and she raised a hand and smiled. Then she passed in regal progress and the crowds moved off. He wondered who she was.

As the hard winter of 1941 drew on, alarms and threats of further raids faded, and by D.'s eighth birthday at the end of March, the only enemy activity had dwindled to single-aircraft raids aimed at vital targets. This collapse of activity seemed to inspire the government to order the evacuation of all schoolchildren to places of safety in the country, and a general order was issued.

from *Second Chances* (1996)

Vernon Watkins
[from] The Broken Sea

My lamp that was lit every night has burnt a hole in the shade.
A seawave plunges. Listen. Below me crashes the bay.
The rushing greedy water smothers the talk of the spade.
Now, on the sixth of November, I remember the tenth of
	May.

I was going to fly to your christening to give you a cup.
Here, like Andersen's tailor, I weave the invisible thread.
The burnt-out clock of St Mary's has come to a stop,
And the hand still points to the figure that beckons the
	house-stoned dead.

Child Shades of my ignorant darkness, I mourn that moment
	alive
Near the glow-lamped Eumenides' house, overlooking
	the ships in flight,
Where Pearl White focussed our childhood, near the foot of
	Cwmdonkin Drive,
To a figment of crime stampeding in the posters' wind-blown
	blight.

I regret the broken Past, its prompt and punctilious cares,
All the villainies of the fire-and-brimstone-visited town.
I miss the painter of limbo at the top of the fragrant stairs,
The extravagant hero of night, his iconoclastic frown.

114

Through the criminal thumb-prints of soot, in the swaddling-
    bands of a shroud,
I pace the familiar street, and the wall repeats my pace,
Alone in the blown-up city, lost in a bird-voiced crowd
Murdered where shattering breakers at your pillow's head
    leave lace.

For death has burst upon you, yet your light-flooded eyes
    do not tremble
Where pictures for waking life stand in the spray's wild bead.
You are guarded, shrined in the torrent, fast-locked in the
    cave of the Sibyl,
In that terrifying delay of the waters' magical speed.

Asleep tonight in Paris, not knowing I walk your world,
You are deaf to the schoolyard's voices, where, escaped, the
    children meet,
The world of a child's one town, renascent, in rage unfurled
Between Cwmdonkin railing and black-faced Inkerman Street.

Waves, hooded, raging, thunder, hiding contagious guilt,
Tossing, high on the shale, the hard and scribbled stones.
An anchor's dirge is buried under the waters' quilt.
Dazzling sunbeams have hidden the hook and the barnacled
    bones.

O indifferent grains of sand, O mother-of-pearl of the shell,
I hear the inconstant water, the blind, the wandering one.
The groan of Sophocles, and the groan of the leper's bell
Burst on annihilation: through your window breaks the sun.

I hear the breath of the storm. The engulfed, Gargantuan tide
Heaped in hills by the moles, hurls to the mountain's head
The streets of sunrise. O windows burning on Townhill side,
O light of annunciation, unearthing the unknown dead!

from *The Lamp and the Veil* (1945)

John Ormond
[from] City in Fire and Snow

By the city, the mask of the city in snow,
By the city in fire, the city split in two,
Between the elements,
Between the snow and the fire I went,
Between her midnight and my own;
Where the town was taken and destroyed
And where the town still stood
In corridors of two ways of light
In streets where the red world met the white
I walked away from her death in the middle grove
Between my fear and my love.

Here buildings flowered red upon the air
And here a street, inaccurate and pale,
Lit but unconquered by the flame;
And here the fire burst tall
And there the snow furred on a wall;
Between two seasons of the soul,
One in its roaring end, the other asleep and slow,
I walked and watched the terror leap
But fail to destroy the further snow.

And as I turned to the only way to the sea
I passed where fire had had its way
And saw such faceless figures stalk,
The lost in blood, the torn, the terrible walkers
Seeking impossible safety blindly
Lost in the heart of the fire's fringe;
And from them stepped unscathed and strange,
One man living among the living dead;
And there he followed me,
There where I fell, he leapt, moved easily.

I waited for him. Here was one, I thought,
Who knew this part of what had been the city
Well, and would lead me
By some passageway underground.
But when I stopped and signed
To call him to come on

There as a roof and a wall tumbled red
Petals of fire like a rose,
Motionless he stayed under it, and did not move
Until I moved again, and then he followed on:

Through the arcaded gardens of inferno,
The narrow avenues, the mazes
Peopled by dead,
Their arms outstretched to embrace the fire,
The dead struck kneeling in homage
At the cry, the words of the giver of peace,
The dead as in stone but moaning in their age,
The children dead where the windows fell
To the familiar street
As if they had gladly watched the snow
Then suddenly were wise,
The white dust of the world upon their eyes.

And once I saw his shape
Stoop where a child lay beautiful and dead,
A golden-headed girl. He touched her head,
Lifted her up and laid her where
Fire left an alcove.
Then he came on
But would not walk with me
Though I beckoned again
And he coming ever nearer
Pointed on still
Until I saw his meaning
— Safety in separation from each other
Under the buildings' fire-drunk leaning
And falling, the steel veins bending
And falling under the unending wind of fire
Scattering the sky's broad arch of blazing snow.

And when at the edge of the town
He came towards the sea
Again the vortex snow spun endlessly
Over the shore, puffed up and winnowed down,
White poplar leaves blown red
Away from the angry breath
But still in the dome of fire.

The shuttling threads of snow worked in the air
To a hanging pattern of blood.
I waited for him, but he had disappeared.

Glad then to be alone
I started on the arc of the bay
For at the end there lay
The inland road to the hills,
Until I saw him come
Walking the lit waves
Near the shore
With his limbs in flame,
Leading three children,
Naked each one for the whip of spray.

As they came near I ran
And saw him leave them sink to drown
Washed by the tide and the bloody foam.
He waded to the sands
Ahead of me, and with fiery hands held out
Waited to greet me.

This man I saw with the bright body,
Had darkness in the holes that were his eyes.

from *Requiem and Celebration* (1969)

Harri Webb
In Gower

The last bus home, blue-lit, draughty
rattling along country lanes and the road over the common
the end of leave, somewhere the war is waiting.
I have been seeing my people and pass now the lonely houses
where they were born and the churchyard
where they lie close together
the wood my grandfather planted ready now for felling
and the fields the men made fruitful
who are my blood.
Alone in the last bus with my quivering reflection
in the dark window deepened by the night

I see my own eyes drowned in darkness
and in the contours of the face
drifts of shadow
where the country night has gathered
making me strange.
Who are the strangers who look through my eyes?
My fathers' fathers the unknown the forgotten
and their night has risen with all its tides of shadow
the tired generations drowning my gaze
in the depths of my blood.
So the shivering mask now caught in the nervous pane
looms intangibly between the dead and the wind
returning no answer to the staring eyes.

from *New Welsh Review* (1995)

Graham Allen
Out of the Dark

Old fellow, old one,
    sing me a song out of the dark,
    a scullery one, and I'll beat time still
on the tin-bath.
How clear you looked free of the work's dirt
and gay with evening, your time for taking the air
– you'd think breathing it was a work of art,
my mother said.

Sometimes before dressing, suds long at the elbow,
you had me punch away at your bicep:
always this strength; always the body,
you tested everything on it,
all life's fifty-year long shift.
Suddenly, you must lie down with its strange
stillness.

Older, I thought all you left of yourself
at home was a black ring round that bath,
water down the drain, and me, cold leavings,
to remind my mother bitterly of you.

But do you remember sometimes on nights
out of the street's noise never got used to,
you slept in my back-room, slipped carefully
into the rumpled shape of warmth I left you there,
each morning that ghostly crossing, you worn-out,
me head-full of Donne, Shakespeare and Keats?
– *Hyperion* to you was a beery windfall.

Now I get you into bed and out of it,
ashamed.
My body was never my meal-ticket
in the burrow of street and foundry under
the rattling viaduct, the canal's dark bridges.
Do you think if I could give you this strength
I wouldn't?
With finger-tip touch I steady your shoulders
pretending you sit alone on the brand-new
commode.

Old fellow, old one,
    sing me a song out of the dark,
    twenty years later,
    (must it be twenty years late?)
    let the morning find
    that shared shape in the bed,
    – no more cold crossings for us –
    but the same flesh and warmth and need,
    a father, a son.

from *Out of the Dark* (1974)

Vernon Watkins
Rhossili

Pushed out from the rocks, pushed far by old thought, long into
               night, under starlight,
At last, tired from my coastal labouring, I come to you, sleepless
               Rhossili.
I have cut through the mirror-bright sea in the long, slender boat
               with two paddles,
And ground in the sand. Dawn breaks. I stare, amazed, at the
               marvel.

Coiled sand, gold mountains, grass-tufted dunes, unending,rising,
descending,
And the cat-spotted, wind-crafty tide, spitting serpent-white tongues
drawn slack,
Soon reaching the barnacled wreck, quivering, recoiling, bending
Stung eyes to the rasping whisper of gongs, of songs that will not
run back.

Rhossili! Spindle of the moon! Turning-place of winds, end of Earth,
and of Gower!
Last one, shivering like a shell, cold with thought that is fiery and
new!
A tent-pole. The cries of seabirds. And over our fingers the power
Of perplexing starlight, entangling our threads in the field soaked
with dew.

Worm's Head! The rock of Tiresias' eyes! From the world's very
verge
I listen to the locked bell-ringers, the impetuous thunder and crash
Of the flying, flagellant waves, torn into two by the surge
From the strata of winkle-stuck rocks, and caverns where claw-
mussels flash.

Terrified, the nesting-birds mount as I climb. Mantles of fugitive
blue
Drain blood, and the bull of the sea falls pierced in the spindrift
dance.
Up from the mirror of the waters to the summit a seabird flew.
I creep to the verge of the pard-breathing tide. Cries turn round the
rock's turning lance.

Flat on my face I lie, near the needle around which the wide world
spins.
Three eggs are balanced there, mottled in cushion-soft, quicksilver
grass, on the final rock.
Far out in the deep blue water the razorbills fish, and their skins
Dazzle, where they flutter blown wings drenched white, nor scatter,
nor break their flock.

I watch them like bright-winged ants, on the deep, unresting swell
Where they rise and fall, fly clear of the crest, or hover with sea-
                              touching wings.
High overhead wheel the herring-gulls, each with a plummet; they
                              drop, and a bell
Rocks in each bird, swung away by a thread, spun out from these
                              rock-rooted things.

Sheer down they rush at my head, crazy with fear for the loss
Of their locked, unawakened young, hidden in those brown shells
On a perilous ledge. They scream; and their wings divide and cross
In a shuddering shadow of piston-like bones, in a rain of farewells.

From the navel of rock, birth's pinnacle, the hovering wings hurled
                              wide,
Flying out and ever returning to this unseen point of fear,
Watch witchcraft, the snakelike movement of the enchanted tide.
I reach to the razorbills' verge. My fingers clutch the rock spear.

Light screams: Look down at the mad, mazed frenzy of the
                              destroying moon!
Gasp at the cockle-sucked heaven! Tide-blown the castaways lie
Peeled to the parched and weary grains where the beaked ships spin
                              and are gone.
Blood-light on the wings of the sea! O the bull and the dragonfly!

The Sibyl keeps watch for Tiresias. In the dumb yet singing rock
The brother of light is dead, or sleeping, transfixed like a shell in a
                              cleft,
In a thunder of floundering timbers, where pine-logs and rum-
                              barrels knock.
Sun-dazzled the book-leaves have opened; but only his vision is left.

Look! The sea-threads! Thought begins there! In a million rainbows!
                              The zenith
Stares at the long flat beach, no bend, no break in the dance
Of sandgrains and seawaves, drenched in gold spray, where the
                              downs fly on to Llangennith:
Dolphins, plunging from death into birth, you are held by the Sibyl's
                              trance!

from *The Lady with the Unicorn* (1948)

Ode to Swansea

Bright town, tossed by waves of time to a hill,
Leaning Ark of the world, dense-windowed, perched
High on the slope of morning,
Taking fire from the kindling East:

Look where merchants, traders, and builders move
Through your streets, while above your chandlers' walls
Herring gulls wheel, and pigeons,
Mocking man and the wheelwright's art.

Prouder cities rise through the haze of time,
Yet, unenvious, all men have found is here.
Here is the loitering marvel
Feeding artists with all they know.

There, where sunlight catches a passing sail,
Stretch your shell-brittle sands where children play,
Shielded from hammering dockyards
Launching strange, equatorial ships.

Would they know you, could the returning ships
Find the pictured bay of the port they left
Changed by a murmuration,
Stained by ores in a nighthawk's wing?

Yes. Through changes your myth seems anchored here.
Staked in mud, the forsaken oyster beds
Loom; and the Mumbles lighthouse
Turns through gales like a seabird's egg.

Lundy sets the course of the painted ships.
Fishers dropping nets off the Gower coast
Watch them, where shag and cormorant
Perch like shades on the limestone rocks.

You I know, yet who from a different land
Truly finds the town of a native child
Nurtured under a rainbow,
Pitched at last on Mount Pleasant hill?

Stone-runged streets ascending to that crow's nest
Swinging East and West over Swansea Bay
Guard in their walls Cwmdonkin's
Gates of light for a bell to close.

Praise, but do not disturb, heaven's dreaming man
Not awakened yet from his sleep of wine.
Pray, while the starry midnight
Broods on Singleton's elms and swans.

from *Affinities* (1962)

Bishopston Stream

River last seen in Spring, you race in the light of Autumn.
Now, as you run through hazels, their leaves are already falling.
Out of the wood I come, astonished again to find you
Younger and swifter.

There were two voices then, moving about in foliage.
One called the other voice, then a great bird made silence.
This was their meeting-place, here where the heron paddling
Stepped on the square stone.

Crossing an open space, haunted in June by mayflies,
Into the gloom of trees you wind through Bishopston Valley,
Darting, kingfisher-blue, carrying a streak of silver
Fished from oblivion.

Over your tunnelled song, pulled in the year's declining,
Lies an uprooted elm, struck by a gale or lightning.
Trout in the shadows hide; black is the hurrying water,
Thronged once with Spring stars.

May not the two I saw be in this hour united
Who are gone different ways? Water, that young Rebecca,
Naomi, Ruth, once heard, voices above a pitcher,
Late let me stoop here.

Yet if I listen closely, singing of separation,
Singing of night you go, through a continual darkness,

River of exile's voice, harps that were hung heard plainly
Now, in the clear dusk.

Even by day you run through a continual darkness.
Could we interpret time, we should be like the angels.
Always against your sound there is a second river
Speaks, by its silence.

from *Affinities* (1962)

Dannie Abse
Sea-shell for Vernon Watkins

A stage moon and you, too, unreal, unearthed.
Then two shadows athletic down the cliffs
of Pennard near the nightshift of the sea.
You spoke of Yeats and Dylan, your sonorous
pin-ups. I thought, *relentless romantic!*
Darkness stayed in a cave and I lifted
a sea-shell from your shadow when you big-talked
how the dead resume the silence of God.

The bank calls in its debts and all are earthed.
Only one shadow at Pennard today
and listening to another sea-shell I found,
startled, its phantom sea utterly silent
– the shell's cochlea scooped out. Yet appropriate
that small void, that interruption of sound,
for what should be heard in a shell at Pennard
but the stopped breath of a poet who once sang loud?

Others gone also, like you dispensable,
famed names once writ in gold on spines of books
now rarely opened, the young asking, 'Who?'
The beaches of the world should be strewn with such
dumb shells while the immortal sea syllables
in self-love its own name, 'Sea, Sea, Sea, Sea.'
I turn to leave Pennard. This shell is useless.
If I could cry I would but not for you.

from *Way Out In the Centre* (1981)

125

G.S. Fraser
Memories of Swansea

Like the Bay of Naples, Landor said. I remember
Beer at the Mumbles, a little railway, gone now:
And to your right along the coast the dragonish
Sea-gobbling rocks, and Vernon Watkins' neighbour's
Greenhouse on the cliff that a sea-wind had come into
And broken like a too large hand in a too small glove.
That also had a twisted dragonish look.
We ate tomatoes plucked green from the tomato
Plants in the greenhouse, with that fruity dust
And pungent prickly smell of the freshly plucked.
Vernon said that the whole Gower Peninsula
Was a Saesneg enclave (Watkins is a little Wat).
A windy day. On the cliff, my children, small then,
Were swung off their feet between our hands.
A steep path down to the sea. My wife undressed
Under a rock shelter, in the slapping wind,
With Gwen, who said: 'If after you are forty
You give up this sort of thing, you *do* give up!'
The boiling boisterous slaphappy sea!
Vernon at ease on a surfboard. I sometimes
Floated over the rise of the big waves,
More often they bounced me gasping back. My son
Climbed a high rock and he could not get down.
I could not get up. Vernon swam up the surface,
As if rock were water, all casual muscle and nerve:
How right he should go in the sweat of a set of tennis!
We had tea later. Looked out of the window at
The play of light on clouds and birds and rocks,
The endless iteration, endlessly different –
A sort of metaphor for God in Nature –
Shape, colour, spray, all changing and unchanging,
He had become a bank clerk in Swansea to stare at
All his life, making slow poems of praise:
But I thought also, a long bus journey
For Gwen to go and do her shopping in Swansea
And rocks are not as talkative as neighbours.

I can still see his litheness, active on rock and surf:
And his beautiful horn-like asymmetrical face.
Much later at Leicester, at our Arts Festival,

His saying with Empson in the audience,
How Dylan's little smack or swoop at Empson,
That tiny parody intended to go into
John Davenport's spoof teccy (dear drunk, dead now!)
Was on the whole a joke rather than a tribute.
Blessed are those who bless a moment of memory.
Bless Kingsley Amis, also, since he lent me his
Terrace house with a greenhouse that had green
Just edible grapes, near Cwmdonkin Park.
Harold Frankel organised our Arts Festival,
Adored Vernon. This year I revisited Swansea
To visit Harold in the Morriston Hospital,
A fat man down to nine stone, a mature student
Of fifty eight, with a tube in his oesophagus;
Bouncing in bed, scattering press cuttings,
A dying man, still crazy about poetry,
The nurses kind to his untidy ways.
Bless the peculiar openness, the utter
Surprising openness to the receptive stranger
Of fiery, tetchy, hospitable Wales ...
Harold died in another month or two
In Oxfordshire, in a private adult
Educational College, Braziers, run by
Marianne Faithfull's father. Kingsley became
A public image, now I never see him:
But strangely, Braziers, Horace-Walpole Gothick,
Sheep nibbling right up to the ha-ha,
Is where Ian Fleming was born. In the library,
His nursery once, I thought of Kingsley and Harold
And of Swansea, and Vernon Watkins. A funny world.

I slam on all this loose associational gossip:
I ought to have done some research on Dylan Thomas:
I had a look at the terrace house of his childhood:
I found no hunchback in Cwmdonkin Park.

Memory, Landor said, is the Mother of the Muses
But not a Muse herself. These memories move me.
Gossip becomes a tired man's poetry.
Swansea and Naples. Mabon will understand.

Note: *Mabon*, a Welsh literary magazine in which Fraser's poem was first published.

from *Poems of G.S. Fraser* (1981)

T. Harri Jones
Swansea

Landor in Italy longed for an old bay
That even holidayers cannot spoil,
Smutch, litter, peekaboo it as they may,
Or violently rest there from their toil.

I would not walk now in that memoried town
In case I met the all too affable
Ghost of the wave's son, and with him drown
Happily saying life is terrible.

Drown in mixtures thinner than Mallarmé
Dreamed for Poe, but blacker in their way.
St Helen's, Sketty, and Cwmdonkin Park –
O Iesu, what's there left for me to say?

Only that that old bay and that old park
Are there, as Dylan still is there for me.
No bloody air-raids ever rubbled away
The birdridden and sea-assaulted country

That belled our Dylan out over the bay.
Voice of the sea, and murmur of the land,
Bayvoice, seavoice, birdvoice, o silent voice,
Where you belong is all I understand.

from The *Beast at the Door* (1963)

John Arlott
Cricket at Swansea

(Glamorgan in the Field)

From the top of the hill-top pavilion,
The sea is a cheat to the eye,
Where it secretly seeps into coastline
Or fades in the yellow-grey sky;
But the crease-marks are sharp on the green

As the axe's first taste of the tree,
And keen is the Welshmen's assault
As the freshening fret from the sea.
The ball is a withering weapon,
Fraught with a strong-fingered spin
And the fieldsmen, with fingers prehensile,
Are the arms of attack moving in.
In the field of a new Cymric mission,
With outcricket cruel as a cat
They pounce on the perilous snick
As it breaks from the spin-harried bat.
On this turf, the remembered of rugby –
'The Invincibles' – came by their name,
And now, in the calm of the clubhouse,
Frown down from their old-fashioned frame.
Their might has outlived their moustaches,
For photos fade faster than fame;
And this cricket rekindles the temper
Of their high-trampling, scrummaging game:
As intense as an Eisteddfod anthem
It burns down the day like a flame.

from *The Cricketer's Companion* (1960)

John Ormond
Homage to a Folk-singer

Phil Tanner, born 1862

This evening is colder, but sit here by the hedge
The first leaves fallen on fire at your feet.
That thrush knows that cold will come. The stones
On the downs will not warm in the sun
Again this summer. This season, autumn, this silence,
Singer, is yours, for an old tune out of the sea.

Turn your face to the channel. Gaze past the headland
Where in the rock silence breeds secret wishes,
Death seeds itself in stone and, set to mark birds down
And their notes, would lock the charmed sea out.

In air and sea bells strike and death runs back
To sleep in the river-bed, the cliff-face:
So silence keeps its place, fixed with a dead shot.

Late? It's too soon for sleep. Past times are up
With us to-night and shake their bells at our bones,
Bury in waves of ringing the step that could sound
On the stair, this, any winter, drown striking clocks
As under the sure frost the sure spring dreams.

Those bells are yours that wave the sea's waves up
To sing of shipwrecks in the bay
And gold that shines like the moon
That lights lovers, love in the green lane.

Do not sleep yet. The tune turns with the wind
For the white sprays of silks and flowers,
Decks dancing weddings, wassails and whistles, brings
Time from the century's grave and furrow, unstops
Old music; and silence, rock, frost, fire, must wait.

★   ★   ★

Rocks are arrayed, are worked with green
Of weeds that have no words, being of rock.
The sea in our sight is green nearly always;
For it is green at the spine
Of each wave, and fragile blues soon break
With weather. So true sea waters speak
From green for those who sailed or drowned
Down the deep main, whose eyes sea closed,
Salt found, sand settled round
To wind long strands and stories in their brain.

The silent grey of the rocks would prove
That shade outlasts all loves, all lands,
All pure colours of the prism.
But children will clap their hands
For the spring because of the green
That gladdens them at the window-pane
When old men have told them wisely,
'Yes, one more frost is due.'
The children do not understand:

'What is the frost but silver?' they demand.
Green is the colour they best know
By dreams of prophecy,
Their careful sleep's experience
And emerald innocence.

They can afford to sleep, being young,
To feed on stuff later years lie about
Saying, 'Green fails'. Black frost is on that tongue.
Age must hold out, keep waking when the eye
Would close its lid perfidiously,
Disprove the stony lie,
And tell of all green sounds that ever rang
When April sprang and girls were garlanding.
I hear them as you sing.

★   ★   ★

Now it is nearly dark. Before we go
Sing as the moon comes up
Of wassailing's white cup
And Henry Martin's story
Of robbing the salt sea, too long ago.

And sing of Fair Phoebe
In a silken gown
With her dark-eyed curly sailor
Whose glance for her was crown.
And for her cruel beauty
Sing, too, of Barbara Allen
Dead in Scarlet Town.

As the moon rises
Sing of the Green Bushes,
The Banks of Primeroses,
Of lovers arm in arm who are gone
To cold, yet who laugh immune
From cold in the long days of a tune.

Sing of every bride for whom
'Green trees the shaded doors did hide'.
Bells would have clanged their iron thin
To keep their quiet bodies from the tomb,

From the deep grave, the hands of stone.
But they still ring for true love,
And those figures shall remain:

And look, in moonlight now
They walk with us.
Dancers, lovers, sailors kiss their brides.
O, they are gone now!
But listen, hear them cry
Where the long waves ride:
There, suddenly, hear them!
They sing with their hearts' green bells, merrily.

from *Requiem and Celebration* (1969)

J.C. Evans
Crofty Flats

The slipping ponies driving home
pulling the jack-knifed carts heavy
with sandy clefted shells, birds
screaming above the selvedged sea,
the bowed men slowly following.

Evening waits the springing tide,
attends the children's pleasure
curving further the tumid shadows.
Turf edges the crazed runnels
moving me with its graceful style.

Bonded he and she, with love
cementing personalities,
bounding like old gladdened fools;
she trimming her dainty steps
leaping on resilient grass

he himself lobs a stone
rough, no tide lops it smooth
over the stalking cyclic years,
at the curious grubby bitch
immoderately loping.

Sensing tongues of crawling sea
ghosting the secure paths
coming surreptitiously
wet and askance, peremptory
raising the fearsome tang of night,

I call through the oyster catchers' cries
and am not heard. The periapt
of the dull moon begins to show
scintillating the lumpy waves
scheming over the salted fields.

from *The Survivor* (1990)

Bryn Griffiths
Scarred Landscape

This is the scarred land where the soil
is scorched almost beyond recall.
This is the valley of the Tawe where a river
the colour of rust gropes through black banks
of slag towards a sea fouled, as always, by man.

Strangers ruined this landscape. Their greed
made the first metal industry here flourish;
packed the harbour, quay to quay,
with Horn-weathered windjammers; brought
a million tons of copper to flow –
a blinding river of liquid wealth –
from glowing furnace after furnace.

But the strangers never settled here,
near the smoking desert of their making;
they preferred the gracious living
and the softer landscapes of England.
They came just to rape a timeless beauty;
to warp and buckle men with breaking toil;
to make money and leave to loot elsewhere ...

They are long gone, just shadows in history,
but their marks remain, scarring the land,
to remind us of the past again and again.

from *Scars* (1969)

Bryn Griffiths
Days of Sail

Here our river, a calm chemic green,
sweeps green and silent to a sea
where the avian scavengers squall and wheel
above the drifting debris of our decay;
where tanker and tramp
slice the liquid squalor into poison white;
where man has turned around
the sea's slow rhythm till it seems
our time is dying,
drowning in the waste of these blind decades ...
Here the clipper ships once lay,
packing the river quay to quay
like a vast raft of birds at rest
upon the Tawe's tidal flood;
here they once weighed anchor into time's night,
birds of stormy passage ready for flight,
beating white-winged down river
outward bound for the Horn,
Valparaiso horizons never known to us ...
But they live today only in memory –
the tall tales of time's castaways,
the old capehorners come ashore to die,
marooned for life in their desert suburbs.
And when the water ebbs now, calm and green,
the timbers of the dead ships
grope like rotting fingers upwards, up,
up and up through the river's scum
and black slime to the uncaring skies
as the memories of beauty, the days of sail,
fade forever with the falling tide.

from *The Dark Convoys* (1974)

Kingsley Amis
Aberdarcy: the Main Square

By the new Boots, a tool-chest with flagpoles
Glued on, and flanges, and a dirty great
Baronial doorway, and things like port-holes,
Evans met Mrs Rhys on their first date.

Beau Nash House, that sells Clothes for Gentlemen,
Jacobethan, every beam nailed on tight –
Real wood, though, mind you – was in full view when,
Lunching at the Three Lamps, she said all right.

And he dropped her beside the grimy hunk
Of castle, that with luck might one day fall
On to the *Evening Post*, the time they slunk
Back from that lousy week-end in Porthcawl.

The journal of some bunch of architects
Named this the worst town centre they could find;
But how disparage what so well reflects
Permanent tendencies of heart and mind?

All love demands a witness: something 'there'
Which it yet makes part of itself. These two
Might find Carlton House Terrace, St Mark's Square,
A bit on the grand side. What about you?

from *A Look Around the Estate* (1967)

'looking to the heart of a man'

"Sit down, please, Mr Lewis," Gruffydd-Williams said, smiling faintly.
I was surprised, and tried not to feel pleased, to find him evidently
taking the chair. (I found out afterwards that the regular Chairman
was away ill.) Gradually, like a herd of big game scenting man, the
members of the Committee began turning their heads in my direction.
As each gaze reached my face it became keen and searching, and soon
they were all engaged in that activity which Welshmen love and in
which, more than most things, they like to think they excel: summing

the fellow up. It seems, though I didn't think of this at the time, that my countrymen have long been noted for this idiosyncrasy. I can remember finding, in a pile of coverless books lying about the library, a rotten old play about Welsh humours in which the following occurs:

> *Ap Hughe*: Py Cot, coufin, you think to finde me as Green as a *leek*. Think you not I fhall *fmell out your Knauerie* in ij VVaggs of yr Tong, py Iubider? Know you not a *VVelfhman* can euer look een to the Hart of a man and know her, by what Deception soeer her hope to fcape knowing. Now *Cots plutter and nailes*, get you gone or as I am a Knights fon I will peat you to death.
> *Exeunt, Ap Hughe beating Maggott*

When a dozen Welshmen are looking to the heart of a man, or even thinking they're doing so, the man can't help feeling a little hemmed in. My impression was that nobody loved me.

I was sitting at the mid-point of the longer side of a rectangular table, with Gruffydd-Williams opposite me. Throughout the interview I was to be conscious of disquieting mutterings and fidgetings at the two lateral extremities of my vision, and was to wonder all the time just what conundrum or death's-head they might be rigging up for me on the flanks. I tried to show I didn't mind it much when the Committee asked each other my name, went on looking to the heart of me, and turned through their sheaves of papers to find the stuff about me. The stuff about me had been provided solely by me, in association with the younger of the Library's two typewriters (né c. 1913). A mere twenty copies of the application had been required, so it definitely hadn't been worth while to go to a printer. All the same, it did strike me occasionally – for example, just after putting 'Assitsant' instead of 'Assistant', rubbing it out on original and all four carbons, and then putting 'Asistnat' – that you could do a lot worse than go to a printer, and even that it wasn't really worth putting in for the job at all. While I pursued this vein of reminiscence I tried to give a bodily and facial impersonation of the thoroughly good, sound, honest, reliable, trustworthy, competent, responsible, steady, sober, level-headed chap, with just that touch of imagination which makes all the difference. I moved my lips forward a couple of millimetres to indicate this last property, but kept my brow trustworthy and my eyes competent.

The interview began. Prompted occasionally by the clerk, Gruffydd-Williams took me through my application, making sure that I wasn't an impostor, or at least wouldn't own up to being one at this stage. An alderman sitting on the other side of Gruffydd-Williams then asked me whether I thought I could do the job, and I said I thought I could. Next he wondered aloud whether I wasn't too young for such a responsible position, and I said I didn't think I was, at the same time trying to show that I found his wonderment both subtle and instructive. He asked me finally why I wanted the job. I'd have liked to match his impertinence by asking him if he was all right with God, but I said only that I wanted the extra money, felt an urge to rise in my profession and would like to have a crack at the problems of organisation which the post involved. This was a pre-selected answer, designed to avoid the pitfalls of mere avarice (too crude), mere ambition (too crude), and mere vanity (too unworldly).

This part clearly went down all right, but it was only a limbering up on both sides, an overture saluted chiefly by yawns but which all the same plays over some of the main themes, a phase corresponding to the mutual circumambulation of two dogs, like the components of a binary sun-system, before they fly at each other. A man in his early thirties with a savage red face now cleared his throat and looked at Gruffydd-Williams from a couple of places along. He was Salter, an interfering Liverpudlian who lectured on constitutional history at the local University College, and who, by patiently going on losing his temper in the Library, had got himself co-opted on to this Committee. "Mr Salter," Gruffydd-Williams said. This was it.

"Oh, Mr Lewis," Salter said in his thick, retching voice. "You did History at the College under Professor Furriskey, didn't you? Would you tell the Committee what class you obtained in the degree examination in your final honours year?"

To be fair to him, Salter's prolixity was intended, I could tell, to give the other people on the Committee a chance to follow him along the difficult path of academic technicality. "Yes, sir," I said. "I got a Two A."

"A Two One, yes," Salter said, giving emphasis by variety.

Before he could go on, one of the several Trade Union members present, a big sallow man from the T. & G.W.U., slewed his head towards the middle of the table and said: "What's this Two One A business, please? I'm afraid I didn't just grasp that."

Salter bowed his own head before turning it, so that his eyes and voice were coming upwards into the interrupter.

"Class Two, Division One, Mr Jones," he said, unexpectedly deferential. "A good Honours degree."

"Aw, Honours, is it?"

"That's correct, yes. And ... Mr Lewis, you have your A.L.A., I believe?"

"Yes, sir."

"Don't bother with all this Two One A.A.A. business, Mr Salter," Jones said. It's not the letters after his name that interests us. If he got his School Cert and went through the College all right, it's enough for me, see?"

Salter looked at me with undiminished hatred, but in a way that suggested I wasn't its only object. His face was a little redder, and when he spoke again it was as if his already over-large tongue had been stung by a wasp. "I'd like to tell the Committee," he said spitefully, "that I've found Mr Lewis extremely helpful in seeking out the kind of obscure and little-known books that only a scholar like myself would want. I will say that he seems to have an excellent knowledge of what the Library contains in that way."

Wishing that Salter hadn't used the rather double-edged term 'scholar' I bowed my head as if my health had been proposed.

"Now, Mr Lewis," Salter went on; "do you consider that that kind of knowledge is an important qualification for the post you've applied for?"

"Well, sir, that's not a simple question," I said, meaning it. To minimise the importance of 'that kind of knowledge' would antagonise Salter and possibly others; to stress it would establish me as an intellectual. "I think I'd say that the first duty of a Sub-Librarian – as of a librarian of any grade – is to the ordinary borrower," ("Hear hear" Jones said robustly) "but anyone with any self-respect would of course regard catering for the expert as an integral part of his duties." Yes, that's right, I thought as I said this: showing the expert where to find the *Encyclopaedia Britannia* or the *Cambridge History of English Literature*. But I was pleased with what I'd said.

Salter wasn't; his mouth tightened and his face seemed to grow narrower. "That's all very well, Mr Lewis, but it doesn't tell us much, does it? Don't you think a Sub-Librarian should have some particular field of study in which he himself is something of an expert, if only so that he can understand the problems of the expert?"

"Yes, I suppose that would help him."

Salter's mouth became asymmetrical; he was smiling. "In that case, Mr. Lewis, what's your special field?"

I paused for a moment; I couldn't say 'constitutional history', because Salter would at once shoot me down on his own subject, and that would look bad even to those who didn't like Salter or constitutional history. On the other hand, it was about the only subject I knew at all well in library terms, except science fiction and the modern American novel, and they wouldn't do. Almost at random, I said: "The drama," thinking of the time I'd helped a man from Brynbwrla Community Centre to confirm the absence from catalogue and shelves of *The Duchess of Malfi*.

Ω"Do you mean to tell me, Mr Lewis," Salter said with luxurious elaboration, "that you regard that as a specialist field?"

"I do."

"Why? How?"

At this awkward point, the pressure was relieved by another interruption from Jones, who'd been showing more and more plainly by wriggling and fiddling about that he thought this had gone on quite long enough. "The drama is a most important field indeed," he declared. "I agree with the applicant, Mr Salter."

"I didn't say it wasn't important, Mr Jones, I was just querying whether the degree of specialisation involved in ..."

"Perhaps you aren't aware, Mr Salter, that there are no fewer than sixty-three amateur drama groups in this town and its neighbouring environs?"

"No, but I wasn't trying to ..."

"And you tell our friend here that drama isn't important? I'd like in that case to know what you do see fit to consider important, Mr Salter. In this area, as in many others in Great Britain as a whole, though I thank God we've less to contend with here than in some other places I happen to know of, well anyway, we've all got to bear in mind the problem of juvenile delinquency which has arisen as a result of wartime conditions. We have to keep our young people off the streets, and provide them with some leisure activity. Myself, I look upon the recent growth of these amateur dramatic groups as a most hopeful sign. I don't know what other people think ..."

Several other people thought to say "Hear hear," notably a middle-aged clergyman with a dry withered face like one of last year's nuts. This man now said: "What Wales needs today is an upsurge of the native Welsh culture, and the Welsh drama, I agree with my friend Mr Jones, with whom I've disagreed so often in the past, and so it gives me particular pleasure to agree with him now, I say the Welsh drama is a fundamental form of Welsh cultural expression, though Mr Salter, who's only recently come to live among us, may not think so. The Welsh drama ..."

I was sure for a few moments that this, delivered in the accents of a film Welshman and accompanied by continuous gesture, would beat Salter into the ground, but he came back strongly with: "That's not my point at all, Mr Chairman. I wasn't running down anybody ..."

"I don't think you realise either, Mr Salter," Jones cut in, "that many plays by local authors have aroused considerable ..."

The clergyman had taken longer than Jones to work out what Salter had just said, but having done so he saw no reason for delaying his response to it. "It is the point, it is the point. Here we are, seeking to provide the cultural needs of a growing Welsh industrial area, with all these new factories ..."

Jones took him up: "... like the mounted toy soldier factory near Fforestfawr, they're making dentures boxes just on the other site of Llantwrch, and then there's the bicycle saddles starting up next month at Cwmpant ..."

During this, I glanced at Gruffydd-Williams, wondering when he was going to interfere. He sat there, his eyebrows raised, his eye on the scribble he was making with a pencil, looking very intelligent and clearly not caring. Why didn't he care? What was the point of him if he didn't care? Was he too important to care?

"But the drama as a specialist field, Mr Chairman," Salter said desperately.

Gruffydd-Williams gave him an encouraging smile, as if to say he'd be glad to hear Salter on this subject at any time, particularly now.

"I know Mr Salter won't think we've done much so far," the clergyman was going on, "but we haven't had everything made easy for us in Wales. You must give us time, Mr Salter. Really, you must be reasonable."

There was an assenting rustle and mutter. When it had quite died away, Gruffydd-Williams said quietly, but moving his mouth a lot: "Have you any more questions to ask the applicant, Mr Salter? Anything to add?"

Salter let his body sag and flopped it to and fro for a moment, like a cretin; then he said, in a tone of fairly impressive weariness and contempt: "Let it pass, Mr Chairman. Thank you all the same."

An interlude followed, during which one of the block-headed doctors who abound in Aberdarcy (this one was crazy about collecting antique inkwells so as to be able to boast of his extravagance, and had recently joined the Labour Party in a vain attempt to get on to the Council) asked me a question about redecorating the Library and how important I thought it was. Reflecting that his head was if anything smaller than Bill Evans's and more blockish, and how both heads would roll when the Day came and Ken Davies was appointed Minister of Culture, I said I thought redecoration was pretty important. The interlude was upset by the others for the lighting of pipes and cigarettes, nose-blowing, and a brisk rattle of conversation. At the end of it Jones spoke up.

"Perhaps I might ask a few questions, Mr Chairman?" He said it like a teacher at a meeting of a pupils' society.

"Mr Jones."

"Now, young man, I shan't keep you long if you answer up and stick to the point. Now, speaking as ... um," he pawed with a frown, "as

Secretary of the Fabian Society, as you know, Mr Lewis, we've for years enjoyed the privilege of using the Reference room at the Library for our meetings – Mr Rowlands and Mr Webster have always been very co-operative in that particular. But, er, thinking on what I might describe as a wider front, through the experience I've had the good fortune to acquire as Literature Secretary of the Aberdarcy Labour Party, I know for a fact that many people would welcome opportunities for smaller, more informal discussions than the kind I've just mentioned. I'd like to know your views on this point, Mr Lewis. I feel myself that we must try to make the Library less of a ... what shall I say? an institution of the intellect, purely of the intellect, and more in touch with the needs of the people. After all," he looked seriously round at his colleagues, "we are public servants. Now, what would you say to that?"

"I'm quite in agreement there, sir. Our first duty is to the public, after all."

"Quite so." He stared at me with his blunt bus-inspector's face, a face empty of all curiosity, all uneasiness, all spite, all humour. Why had he taken the trouble to speak at all, or even come to the meeting, get on to the Committee in the first place, work his way up in the Union and the Party? He began to speak again; he hadn't finished yet. What hadn't he finished? "You feel we'd do well to widen our field in the way I suggest?"

"I think there's a great danger in proceeding on too narrow a front, sir. No facility ever suffered through being made available to a more extensive cross-section of the community."

"That's very well put indeed. As Class Secretary of the W.E.A., now – as you know, our class on modern political thought is one of the oldest-established classes in the area – well, occasional meetings thrown open to the public would broaden the basis of appeal, and I feel strongly that the Library should play its part in this. Do you agree?"

I said I did. What Jones was really saying was that he intended to go on organising people, organising more and more people, causing complications with the caretaker about locking up, leaving lights on, losing the keys, re-arranging the furniture and not putting it back, holding meetings so as to clash with bookings made by bodies like the Coed-y-Môr Old Age Pensioners' Eisteddfod Organising Committee (Vocal Section). Well, in a way I didn't mind him doing it all.

Jones, after informing me that his official capacity at this meeting was as the representative of the Secretary of the Trades and Labour Council, went on talking, but somehow I had to stop listening. Gruffydd-Williams was looking at me with a faint smile, much as at my entry into the room. Was he laughing to himself at what that librarian fellow of his wife's was undergoing? It was nice of him to back me, if he was backing me. For a moment I wished I'd got to know him in some other way, nothing to do with Elizabeth or jobs. In spite of his commanding air he seemed a very nice chap. I wondered what went on behind that bored but appraising expression, what he really thought of Whetstone and Theo James and Evans and the dentist and the dentist's mistress, not forgetting his own wife. It would be difficult to find out. I now heard Jones ask me what I thought the service provided could be improved.

"Well, sir," I said capably, "I feel we have nothing to be ashamed of in our progress up till now in this matter ..." It was good to see a man who hadn't said anything so far nodding his head vigorously at my tribute to our progress up to now in whatever matter it was. "... But as far as the future goes we should give all possible improvements our earnest attention – and I mean that not as a mere piece of vague approval, but as something quite real and urgent."

"Thank you," Jones said. "Now you can imagine that this also affects me in my capacity as the Workers' Educational Trade Union Committee representative. Do you think it desirable that the type of literature I've mentioned should be freely available in the Library?"

This, so late, when Jones seemed to have announced the full muster of his titles, nearly floored me. Was he talking about books containing mention of the sexual act, or did he mean things like those frightful pamphlets on the history of the tin-plate industry and so on with which I was steadily filling up Jenkins's room? "I do, sir," I said loudly, staring fervidly at him.

It was the right answer, but before I could congratulate myself a woman who didn't look like a woman was saying in a rapid monotone and without taking breath: "I think, Mr Chairman, that the type of literature supplied in our libraries, without seeking to provide propaganda, should nevertheless help the working class to shoulder their responsibilities in striving for progress and a more equitable distribution of the means of production and exchange – what are the applicant's views?" The restiveness at the flanks of the table grew very marked during this short speech.

I opened my mouth to utter some superlatives of agreement when I saw one of the aldermen glaring at me. I knew this old shag by repute: he was the most prominent of Aberdarcy's outfitters, sat as an Independent (i.e. Tory) Councillor, was President of the local British Legion Branch and completely controlled the Golf Club. Since the imposition of that control, he was known to boast, no Jew, Catholic or non-Britisher had had the impertinence even to put up for membership. I said in a lukewarm tone: "I would maintain at any rate that the Library stands behind every individual in his or her search for the fuller life and in equipping everyone to play his or her part in the community." It would take a Central or South American President (of a Republic, I mean, not a British Legion branch) to object to that.

A pause followed, in which I speculated how much more there could be of this, considered that this Committee had slipped up badly in not co-opting Mrs Davies, and felt I wouldn't say no to a cup of tea. The nut-faced clergyman was next. As before, he waved his arms about all the time while he talked, which he proceeded to do at length. The first few minutes of his address were devoted to thanking the Committee for letting him know and letting him come and letting him speak, and in saying, with profuse illustrative detail, how good he was. This old shag I also knew. Like many another minister, he'd brought a busload of his congregation to pack the public meeting about Sunday cinemas three or four years previously. Again, like many others, he'd found the hall already bursting with squads from other chapels who'd turned up even earlier to make sure nobody who wanted Sunday cinemas could get in to vote. So he'd set up his pitch outside the hall and led an inflammatory and very loud rendition of 'Caersalem' (the noted Congregationalist hymn). It was still one of his chief claims to importance that when, ten years or so ago, a task force of Welsh Nationalists had torn down and burnt the 'English' flag at Treherbert aerodrome, he'd only just not been among them. Each time I met him I was re-convinced, for the first couple of minutes, that he was trying to be funny. But I've often been wrong about that sort of thing.

He now began to include me, by degrees, within the bounds of his discourse, and before many minutes had passed had gone on to seem to be asking me what proportion of books in the Library should, in my opinion, be in Welsh. I said I thought these should be supplied as asked for. Holding out his arms to me as if he wanted me to run round the table and jump on to his lap, he said with emotion: "I wonder if you know that two people out of every five in this part of Wales are Welsh-speaking?"

"Monoglots?" I asked offensively.

"Welsh-speaking, I said," he said.

I shrugged my shoulders. "I very seldom get asked for books in Welsh. People want to read stuff about Everest and the Kon-Tiki expedition and escapes from prison-camps and so on. They might still want to if the stuff was translated into Welsh and the English copies burnt. It's difficult to be sure." There was a slight but fairly general laugh at this. The clergyman spread his arms out sideways like a conductor allotting to his orchestra their share of applause. "It is our solemn duty to encourage and popularise our local authors," he said, glaring.

"Which authors are you referring to, sir?"

"I'm referring to such poets as Owain, Siôn and Wiliam, and ... to take a different kind of instance, to my own colleague, the Reverend Traherne Williams, his history of the Rhondda Baptists ..."

"I'm afraid I'm not familiar with ..."

"Our greatest poets? Him with six bardic chairs?"

"I've never been asked for ..."

"A scandal, that's what it is. A scandal and a tragedy."

"We have other duties, sir, which I would regard as more ..."

Nobody who hadn't been interrupting people for years could have interrupted as the woman now did, saying: "I think we agreed, Mr Chairman, that what we have primarily to consider is the equipping of every person to play his or her part in the community. That and giving our full support to each and everyone in his struggle to attain a fuller life."

There was silence. Gruffydd-Williams drew in his breath. "Well, if there are no more questions ..."

A little man in a check suit near the end of the table said: "Just one, Mr Chairman." Every head switched angrily to him, but he held on bravely. "Won't take a minute."

"Mr Wynn."

"You perhaps are familiar with the cultural habits of normal families in this area, Mr Lewis?"

Liking 'normal' a lot, I said I was.

"Could you say, in the light of your experience, whether, in your opinion, the rents of council houses should be economic?"

"Yes, they should," I said instantly. "No question about it."

The little man began nodding, slowly at first, then stepping it up. His lip pursed tighter and tighter as he wrung every drop of significance from my answer. His eyes gradually shut. After a time, he said: "Yes," then, galvanically rousing himself, added: "Thank you, Mr Chairman."

Gruffydd-Williams conferred with the clerk and at last said I could go. As I went out, it seemed to me that I was just on the brink of realising why he'd taken so little notice of what had been going on, but the thought eluded me and I couldn't bring it back. Someone was saying "No" loudly as I shut the door.

from *That Uncertain Feeling* (1955)

Martin Amis
Memories of a Swansea Childhood

It Im Again, Dai

I was idling away at the kind of thing that eight-year-old boys find very fascinating. A plump pebble was wedged between the bars of a drain in the gutter, and I with a sandalled foot was trying to kick it through, to stomp it down, to hear that satisfying plop as it joined the water-ways of the city's innards.

– Oi! You by there! What ewe doing with that drain?

– Nothing! I'm just...I'm just...

He was about fifteen, swarthy, curly-haired, his good looks under-mined by his fraudulently bright green eyes. It was dark, it was wet – but in Swansea, in winter, an inky drizzle was the very air you breathed. 'When the lights come on at four / At the end of another year,' wrote Larkin, well north of us in Hull; but he needed his asso-nance and his monosyllable, and couldn't say 'half past two'. Still, memory informs me that the time was illicitly late. I shouldn't have been tarrying with this pebble, this drain, this green-eyed boy.

We stood on the busy and well-lit foothill of Glanmore Road. Now we started off together, up into the steepening gloom. In a practised but roundabout way the youth asked me if, following his leniency with the pebble and the drain, I might consider doing him a favour. 'What?' I asked. He said he would give me a chocolate toffee, a Rollo – 'or pos-sibly two' – if I would oblige him. 'What is it?' 'Oh, it won't take a minute. Just show me . . . ewe willie.'

I came to a halt and received the pressure of tears on my chest. Strange: we know that children cry from fear, but this felt more like grief. I crossed the road. He watched me as I climbed the hill. I said nothing to my mother when I got home. A couple of weeks later I reencountered the boy with green eyes. I was a block from home, on a side street I crossed every schoolday (it had a good dirt lane, a short-cut, up the other end of it). Again it was dark, late, wet.

– Oi. What ewe doing down here on my road?

He had a companion with him, a stocky little boy, considerably and reassuringly younger and shorter than me. This terrible toddler, I would soon learn, was called David and answered to the usual Welsh diminutive.

– What ewe doing down here on my road?

– Your road?

It him, Dai.

With explosive alacrity, like a fast bowler at the moment of release, Dai hurled his closed fist into my forehead. I didn't know that boys that size could hit that hard. But I did know two things. One, that the attack was revenge for the favour earlier denied. Two, that little Dai, at least to begin with, had enjoyed Rollos by the tubeful. But Christ knows what they turned into, this pair. And Christ knows what *their* children turned into.

– Who said ewe could walk past my house?

– I didn't know it wasn't allowed.

–...It im again, Dai.

And so on for about ten minutes, the same question, and the same command. When I got home I told my mother how I had come by my swollen face. I gave her the bare facts, and not the subtext. Immediately she leashed up the three big dogs: Nancy, certainly, and Flossie? and Bessie? With anxious adoration I watched her go down the hill, like Charlton Heston or Steve Reeves wielding the reins of the chariot. The dogs, no less indignant than their mistress, were almost upright on their leads.

She returned half an hour later, still furious and still unavenged.

Dunker Castle

I first made front-page news when my age was in single figures. The banner headline of South Wales's premier evening paper (it was the *Evening Post*, I think) ran as follows: THE SAGA OF THE AMIS BOYS. It turns out that I am a much more anxious parent than my mother ever was. I once spent half an afternoon – Spain, a picnic, I was a childless twenty-eight – standing with my arms outspread under one tree or another in case Jaime, then four or five, fell out of it. My mother looked up from her sandwich, and flicked a hand backwards through the air.

– I let him do *everything*. I let *you* do everything.

She did. She let us do everything. We spent all-day and all-night car journeys on the roof rack of the Morris 1000, the three of us, in all weathers, slithering in and out while my mother frowned into the windscreen ... I don't think we did this when our father was in the car, and he was perhaps in general rather more cautious. As for the decisions leading up to the saga of the Amis boys, well, he wouldn't need or want to be consulted about a matter to do with the open air. He was in his study. He was always in his study.

The Amis boys, and primarily Philip, put it to their mother that they should canoe alone from Swansea Bay to Pembroke Bay, a distance of several miles west along the (notoriously and, in that direction, increasingly unpredictable) Welsh coast. And my mother said yes. In secret I had always thought this an ambitious plan. I was not exactly emboldened when I saw the height of the sea at our starting point (Swansea Bay was usually more docile than the others we would pass), and saw also the extreme difficulty we were having in getting the boat past the surf. Repeatedly and brutally the waves rebuffed us until, already half drowned, we were in our slots and paddling, Philip up front, towards the bay's western limb. All went well for several minutes. Then our paddles fell silent as we assimilated an oceanic effect that remains unique in my experience. A violently confused kiloton of water was driving *laterally* along the bay towards us ... I have seen seas disgracefully tousled and disorganised, in the epilogue of hurricanes, sick-green and crapulent after their atrocious splurge, and meaninglessly milling, flapping, cringeing. The cross-tide we now faced, while formidably muscular, had the same deracinated air as it sidled loutishly towards us. We could have turned back (this was my firm preference); but I knew that Philip would not turn back. On the whole the younger brother has an easier time of it, watching his elder not turning back – going on, into unlit territory, and not turning back. Philip was, as always, positioned ahead of me. But this time I was in the same boat. Staring straight ahead he shouted,

– Goodbye, Mart.

And we paddled at battle speed, at attack speed, at ramming speed into the advancing foam. 'Saga' suggests something endless and arduous (and uncomplainingly Nordic); but those few seconds, as we slapped and bounced our way through, were really the extent of our adventure. That was in any case quite enough for me. Reaping much fraternal disgust, I asked to be dropped off at the next beach along. I called home from the snackbar at Caswell Bay; then I stood on the steps leading up the cliff and watched Philip as he tried, again and again and again, to manhandle the tall canoe over the taller breakers; and each time, with his boat all over him, he came thrashing back into the shallows. His body was untiring; I couldn't see his face but I knew it would have an implacable look on it by now.

At Pembroke Bay my mother and I spent the afternoon vainly scanning the mountainous seascape. And at this point the alarm was raised...But let's face it. The *Evening Post's* front-pager, adumbrating an ordeal of maritime endurance that would have stunned a Patrick O'Brian, was a near-total sell. Because my brother never did get the canoe past the breakers. And all the time the coastguards were unscrambling and the helicopters were clattering down the coast, Philip was drinking Tizer and trying the phone in the snackbar on Caswell Bay.

I felt more embarrassed than flattered by the headline. My position was especially fraudulent, Philip having at least tried to go on getting killed.

So the press got everything wrong. But this was the first and last time that it cast me (wrongly) as a hero.

[Punishment]

This was Swansea, and I had been sent upstairs to be beaten, or at any rate hit, by my father in his tiny study at the end of the long corridor. The long corridor, the tiny, tawny study facing the steeply sloped back garden: that means we were still at 24 The Grove, and hadn't yet moved up the hill to Glanmore Road, making me unbelievably and embarrass-ingly young to have committed such crimes – six and three-quarters at the outside. More and more recklessly I had been stealing money and cigarettes from my mother's handbag and coat pocket. I knew a reck-oning was coming. Earlier that day, almost legless with apprehension and self-disgust, I had secreted a handful of stolen change under a bench in a bus shelter – and gone home, where my mother told me to present myself at my father's study, to be hit...*-I remember the increasing gloom of the corridor. I knocked (we always knocked). He stood with his back to me at the window. He turned – with the signifi-cant face. What happened next is darkly shadowed and escapes all memory. My mind knows nothing about it. Afterwards he said: 'What do you want to do now?' I said: 'I want to go to bed' It was a summer evening. Plenty of fervently hurrying footsteps in the street, and people calling out to one another with a buoyancy and hopefulness unimagin-able in the nighttime ... As for the cancelled memory of the beating: the void is so perfect and entire that I sometimes suspect it never hap-pened. But I would have remembered its not happening. And my mother told me he wept that night, as he always did when he hit us.

He turned from the study window. His face was in quarterprofile (and shouldn't this have been *my* face?): childish, softly frowning, entering a plea for mitigation, for leniency, asking for things to be seen in a kinder light.

Although, in the novels, with their permanent blitzkrieg against bores and boredom, pointmissers, poseurs, much violence is sum-moned, hammers, pokers, bayonets, knuckledusters, flaming stakes,

148

swarming anthills, starving crocodiles (Dad. Yes? If three anthills and two crocodiles...), firearms, mortars, flamethrowers (this list is by no means complete), together with common assault ('Ronnie had been standing for about half a minute...considering whether to run up and hit Mansfield a lot would convey to him something of what he felt about him'), Kingsley was in some sense a profoundly unviolent man. He didn't leave my mother and he didn't leave Jane. They left him. Divorce 'is an incredibly violent thing to happen to you'. Above all he feared escalation.

from *Experience* (2000)

Peter Thomas
The Lascars

When I was a boy they came in blackness
from black ships together, gripping an unseen circle
protected from the pack of the crowd.
Lascars, my father would say,
they'll empty the pubs tonight,
– and we'd see them in Wind Street by tailors' windows
huddled together, left alone.

One Monday, the *Evening Post* said blood had been found
on the pavement across the road from Sidney Heath's,
so *Lascars* my father said, and I stopped writing homework,
feeling the deft slit of the knife.

Then I was looking at coats in the window,
a man at the edge of means, indifferent to the town,
aching to be away. Quietly
they ringed me, staring into the same tailor's window,
dark in their quietness, unsure of the strange town,
nudging each other like schoolboys, they giggled
and fingered the frayed collars of loose shirts.

And *Lascars* I thought, as my dead father tugged,
but they smiled at me shyly, turning
to walk down Wind Street
to their ship.

from *Anglo-Welsh Poetry 1480-1980* (1984)

149

Sally Roberts Jones
Rhossili

Tomorrow the tide will come at the proper time,
The sun burn hot on the rocks,
The clean sheep move
Idly across the pathway we do not walk.

Tomorrow – but now, today, the proper time
Curves into distance along the bay,
The gulls
Turn on the wind, slow as a stopping clock.

Wave after wave the pattern appears; we walk
Alone in a peopled land, no longer alone,
In a moment as long as our lives,
As short as a breath.

from *Poems '69* (1969)

Moira Dearnley
College Ball

I had always fallen 'in love' with men I knew scarcely anything about, and Charles Sinclair was no exception. But in the past, my lack of knowledge was compensated for by the fact that external beauty was likely, in the platonic sense, to be a pointer to inner grace. But Charles Sinclair was not beautiful – at least, the casual observer would not think him so. The fact was unpalatable. I pulled back the bedroom curtains and knelt at the low sash-window. Resting my elbows on the sill, I looked down Bryn Mawr, beyond the dark moving tree-tops to the long terraced rows of slate roofs, and down to the town-centre, brilliantly lit but now almost empty of traffic. There were the familiar landmarks, the mediaeval tower of St Botolph's, illuminated by floodlights (little Bethesda was overwhelmed by darkness), the neo-classical Town Hall, the gothic railway station, the black space denoting the rugby pitch, the hospital punctuated by rows of dim yellow windows, and out there the black mud flats of the estuary. I was always looking down, judging other people's lack of spiritual perspective by my own preoccupation with the way of negation as a path to religious truth, starving myself of food, and leisure, and love ... Was I not, in fact, myself giving in to the shamelessly secular? My mind, far from being composed for prayer and meditation, was running back over the years, to Michael's beautiful face, to Tom's beautiful body ... I shivered at the memory of my virginal terror of male beauty. And why, I thought, over the hammering of my heart, did the very thought of Charles Sinclair now make me prickle, shiver all over in the same sort of way? Why did I not recoil with distaste as I had recoiled from Frank and Raymond and Dave ...? I turned from the window and went to bed without saying my prayers formally, though I asked God to forgive me, wildly, twenty times over. What He needed to forgive me I did not put into words.

The next morning I bought some Spicers' Calligraphy writing paper and envelopes (I normally used Basildon Bond) and wasted three sheets of expensive paper before finally contriving a note of acceptance:

Union
21st January

Dear Charles,
Thank you for your invitation to College Ball.
I should very much like to accept, and look forward to
hearing from you.
Sincerely,
Gwendoline

I hoped that this sounded friendly without being over-eager. [...]

I managed to get a 'bus home from college, but the snow was beginning to fall heavily, and by evening the buses had stopped running from the town centre up and down Bryn Mawr. So I had to walk. I wore wellingtons lined with a pair of my father's old socks and on the slippery rubber soles I slithered gaily down the one-in-seven gradient, protecting my mantilla hair-style with an umbrella and carrying my shoes and handbag in a vanity-case. I managed the descent without accident, and in the town, three hundred feet below, the snow hadn't had a chance to settle in the main streets, so that I was able to approach the hotel at a more dignified pace. But before I turned the corner into King George Street, I sheltered in a shop doorway and quickly changed my wellingtons for court-shoes. I squashed the boots into a polythene bag, stuffed the bag into my vanity-case, and hoped that the catch would hold. That done, I was able to turn the corner and mount the steps to the main entrance of the hotel feeling my usual high-heeled, high-coiffured, dignified self. At the same moment, Charles Sinclair, wearing a dinner-jacket, was crossing the foyer towards the door. I spun through the revolving doors as he sauntered up, head back, hands in pockets. It was one of the head-spinning big moments of my life.

"You made it!", he said, kissing me on the cheek.

"I did, Mr Sinclair, even though I've had to walk all the way."

"Hard luck," he said, taking my elbow, and leading me across the royal blue carpet towards the staircase.

I was quite dazzled by the expensive interior, the soft carpet, the pink lighting, the curved reception desk, the sleek receptionist. I noticed with delight the display cabinet of Nantgarw china, white fragility and delicate fruits and flowers, and the exhibition of pictures along the staircase wall, mountains in dark purples and magenta. I noticed with even greater delight that Sinclair had obviously washed his hair and instead of the ginger plaster against his scalp, it was thick and floppy and almost golden – red gold as in the *Mabinogion*, I thought romantically.

"We're drinking in the Ddraig Goch lounge, he said, making it rhyme with The Hague and making no attempt at the 'dd'. Some of my friends are there already. Come and meet them." [...]

Since it was now past nine o'clock, it was generally agreed that we ought to be getting to the Ball, and there was a scramble for coats and belongings variously deposited on chairs, under chairs, and under the table. In the middle of the scuffle, Kevin Finch, who had not uttered another word since reciting from 'The Blessed Damozel', suddenly cleared his throat and stiffened his body. Then, throwing back his mane of hair, he looked at the perforated ceiling and began another recital. This time it was Belloc. Although I shared the acute embarrassment of the rest of the customers in the Ddraig Goch Lounge Bar, I could see that our party registered only vast delight. "It was a *chilly*-day for Willy/When the mercury went down ...." There was loud applause and cries of "good old Kevin", but he ceased as abruptly as he had begun, pulled the hood of his duffel-coat over his head, and shuffled like a cowled monk out of the room. The rest of us followed him – with every eye disapprovingly upon us.

Keith Dent drove an ancient Citroën with an endless bonnet. He brought it round from the hotel car-park and seven people were eventually packed inside it. In the back seat, Jenny sat on Phineas Larkin's lap and I on Charles's, with Kevin Finch squashed between us. Jack Rowe rode in front with Keith. The car smelt of petrol and musty old leather. I was wearing my best coat, the emerald one with a big fur collar, and I had my arms tightly around Charles's neck. He held me round the waist and we said nothing as the rest of the party giggled and sang 'Cwm Rhondda' and snatches from *The Pirates of Penzance*.

The neon lights in the town centre sent flashes of green and amber light across our faces and then the windows began to steam up.

"Sorry, ladies and gentlemen, but we'll have to have a window open." Keith lowered the window and a draught of icy air blew through the car. We drove cautiously out of town, through Pont-newydd, and up the valley towards college. The main road was free of snow but Jack Rowe kept reminding Keith that he was likely to meet icy patches. Jack sounded very nervous. I was feeling blissful but awfully sleepy. I fought the urge to put my head down on Charles's shoulder. There must have been gin in the orange.

"Happy?" whispered Charles.

"Mmm."

When at last we drove into the car-park behind Union and every-one clambered out making a lot of fuss because it was so freezing cold, Charles said to me,

"Jack and I are nipping back to Hall. Coming?"

"Why?" I asked suspiciously and probably coyly.

"To get our dancing shoes and that's *all.*"

He sounded annoyed again.

"All right. But will I be allowed in at this hour?"

"Would I be asking you if you weren't?"

"No, I suppose not."

The path to Neuadd St Cenydd past the old stables was cobbled and slippery and in my silver evening shoes I had to cling to Charles for dear life. I could feel snow sliding over the uppers. Jack accompa-nied us at a distance of about six feet. He was an awkward boy. The walls of the lift were unaccountably mirror-lined and I looked wide-eyed at the strange reflection of two boys in duffels and bow-ties and a girl with a towering mass of Spanish ringlets, ash-white face and thick black eyelashes. Was that Gwendoline, then?

"Come into my parlour," invited Sinclair when we got to the top floor, and when I hesitated, "come *on,* woman, I'm not going to eat you."

It was a very small room, all bed, and I stood nervously inside the door as he produced from the bottom of the wardrobe a pair of thin-soled patent-leather shoes. I watched in fascination the removal of his chelsea-boots and the donning of his dancing shoes. "Why do you think people wear shoes, Berthold? Shoes which are made of tough, blind, silent leather. Yet everywhere else we cover ourselves with soft texture – with a fabric which talks, gossips and betrays secrets ... We wear shoes made of leather to hide our malformed five-ended stumps ...." I had conscientiously read the English translation of *Der Abstecher* before going to the German Society's production the previous term. Perhaps

153

Walser … I stood back for Sinclair to pass me in the doorway. He paused, put out his hand to touch my cheek and then changed his mind. He winked at me.

"Too early for a bit of the old slap and tickle. Won't be a sec."

I found his vulgarity exciting. He went past me into the corridor and I could hear him whistling as he tapped on another door and opened it. He returned almost immediately.

"Jack says to go ahead, he'll catch us up."

So, we summoned the lift, dropped eight floors, and went back down the slippery path to Union.

The Ball, which was being held in the Refectory, was well under way by the time we arrived. The room was smoky and dense with couples trying to do the new dance, the shake. Just inside the door there was a crowd of unattached boys drinking beer. (They must have gate-crashed, since the 'double' ticket for the Ball was by no means cheap.) As Sinclair and I entered, hand in hand, there was a barrage of wolf-whistles. I nearly died.

"Hey, Charlie, does your mother know you're out?" Sinclair went scarlet but he grinned and gave the ruffians a thumbs-up sign with his right hand. I pretended icily not to notice.

"Let's go and say hullo to Benny," he said, too jovially.

He led me over to a long table covered with a floor-length white cloth and set out with glasses and bottles. He greeted the barman like an old friend because Benny was also the St Cenydd porter.

"What are you drinking, darling? Gin and orange?"

I was pining for gin and orange.

"Okay, now let's find the others," he said, scanning the room. "I think I can see old Kevin over there."

A gigantic mesh hung in loops over the low ceiling, and the profusion of anchors, creels, and lobster-pots decorating the walls suggested that the theme was strictly nautical. Themes don't have to be relevant to anything, I thought, rather crabbily. Coloured lights, crowding the nets like treasures of the deep, threw ever-changing blue, green, and yellow beams on to the faces below. Holding our glasses and holding hands, Sinclair and I inched around the floor, trying not to get mixed up with the violently shaking dancers. We found Kevin sitting alone at a table littered with half-empty glasses and overflowing ash-trays. He was slouched over his beer, looking mournful.

"Not dancing, Kev?"

Kevin scarcely responded and Sinclair made no further effort to communicate with him. I was preoccupied with my own drink for I could taste only orange and I was vaguely wondering why people made such a fuss about alcoholic drinks when they were practically indistinguishable from ordinary fruit-juices. Sinclair was resting his left arm along the back of my chair but he too seemed preoccupied, watching the dancing with an expression that was almost petulant. The warmth and nearness that had been growing between us earlier in the evening had somehow evaporated. As usual, we seemed to have nothing to say to each other. The dance finished, there was some desultory clapping from the floor and some students whom I didn't know returned to their drinks at our table. I was introduced, but obviously Len, Diana, Chris and Barb, were not particular friends of Charles's, and I did not pay them much attention. I tried hard not to recognise the dreariness and listlessness that was creeping over me: it was delightful to be sitting next to Charles, but I wondered restlessly if we were going to sit there all evening, neither speaking nor dancing. Another dance began and still we sat there. I began to take the blame for being such an unexciting partner but I was much too intimidated by him to try being more brilliant. We sipped steadily. I watched the dancing enviously. I could see Jenny Gall and Keith Dent going through some professional looking motions. They were doing a Latin-American dance and each held a hand on one slim hip and whirled the other hand in the smoky air.

"God," said Charles.

He was not referring to Keith and Jenny. From the dense crowd in the middle of the floor emerged Jackie Davies and her partner. She was wearing a red dress with shoe-string shoulder straps. One of the straps had snapped and she was stepping undeterred through the Spanish rhythms, using the hand that should have twirled in the air to hold up the bodice of her dress. Her partner was a blond and handsome German whom I recognised as Berthold of *The Detour*. He was showing no emotion whatsoever and went thudding pedantically through the dance-steps. They danced nearer to our table and during one fancy spin which defeated Jackie's light skirt she caught Charles's eye. She waved, then grabbed her bodice again. Charles wiped imaginary sweat off his brow. Jackie and Herr Hetzel of the German Department drifted back into the crowd. Charles made no comment, but in a sidelong glance I saw that he was smiling into his drink.

It would be impossible for me to try narrating all the events of the evening with any sort of moment-by-moment clarity. I drank an awful lot of gin and smoked one cigarette after another. I did not become incoherent but there was a sharp cold feeling in my head, and reality, precise and brilliantly coloured, seemed miniature, at a vast distance from the centre of my brain. Superimposed on the deafening music provided by the Decibels in hunting pink with white cravats (like Dave Clark) and club-cut fringes (like the Beatles) and the procession of ever-changing coloured lights, one or two incidents stand out with clarity.

I did dance with Charles – once. The Decibels were giving us "She loves you, yeah, yeah, yeah" with a great deal of drumming. Giving myself to the compulsive rhythm of the drums and the electric guitars, and jerking my hips from side to side (for the shake was new and people still preferred the twist) as I had watched others do, I found that it was quite an easy dance after all. I felt elated and held my wrists tightly against my hips and felt with great satisfaction my circular skirt spiral and unspiral around my legs. I tried to feel charitable about Charles's uncouth style of dancing: he seemed to lie back and work his arms at his sides as if he were running a marathon in twinkling patent shoes. "But it's you she's thinking o-o-of – She loves you, yeah, yeah, yeah ..." A flushed young man suddenly elbowed Charles out of the way and began gyrating in front of me. He too was singing "yeah, yeah, yeah". I stopped dead and there was Charles obediently retreating from battle to join a group of boys at the edge of the floor. Jack Rowe was among them. They were lolling with laughter. I gave my new partner a look of hauteur ("drunk", I thought, morally offended). The dance finished, and Charles walked me back to our table without offering to dance again.

"What on *earth* did he think he was up to?" I demanded. Charles merely shrugged.

I was thoroughly upset by the incident. I felt humiliated. It was as if Charles Sinclair's easy success with his tutor had encouraged some of his friends to think that she was fair game for any kind of horseplay. I even went so far as to imagine that they were trying to pass me from hand to hand and I felt cheapened and insulted. Then, when we had nearly reached our table, we ran into a small man with sleek black hair, a triangular olive face, and an expression of some superiority. Charles introduced us.

"Gwendoline, darling, have you met our Warden, Dr Ferranti? This is Miss Vivyan, sir."

I had, of course, been vaguely aware of his existence, but I had never spoken to him before. His black eyes bored gimlet holes through my hot brain.

"Mr Batcup's protegée, I take it? I trust you are enjoying yourself, Miss Vivyan?"

It seemed to me, as I tried desperately to comport myself with proper dignity, that this was a statement not a question and that he managed to convey through an unimpeachably suave manner, merely by the tilt of his eyebrows, utter contempt – for the pair of us. But he behaved as if he owed it to Jasper Batcup to at least ask me whether I were not researching into the eighteenth century. *Hymnology* he had heard. I said well *partly*. And he said *extraordinary*. Having thus done his duty he excused himself and a few minutes later I saw through the crowd that he was deep in conversation with a huge African student resplendent in golden robes and astrakhan cap. Dr Luigi Ferranti, reputedly so brilliant, had had so little time for me – and none at all for Charles. I felt depressed because although I was in love with Charles Sinclair, I still wanted to be bracketed with the academic élite of the college. Later in the evening I saw Ferranti dancing with Jacqueline Davies, a sight that merely underlined my dissatisfaction with my lot. It did not help matters that Charles was paying me comparatively little attention. If only he would look at me, smile at me, talk to me, I thought, Ferranti could go to hell a phrase that was incredibly bold for such a fastidious spirit as mine.

Then there was the incident involving Clara Stacey, an assistant lecturer in the English Department. Phineas Larkin led Maggie Morgan over to our table. She was wearing a sleeveless lurex dress that hung like a sparkling pink cylinder around her bony body. Her brown arms, bent at acute angles, hugged her drink to her chest as she seethed with suppressed gossip. The toes of her winkle-pickers went on and on. I felt that Sinclair ought to have stood up as they approached.

"Charles, darling, I must tell you the latest."

She looked at me, in doubt for a split second.

"I'm sure Miss Vivyan won't mind, will you? After all, you're practically one of us." She took a deep breath, for dramatic effect. "We've just tripped over Clara Stacey on the floor of the Music Room practically being *undressed* by Greenslade."

She was breathy with excitement. Phineas winked at Sinclair over Maggie's shoulder and then raised his brows as high as they would go, disdaining his own action.

"Who's Greenslade?" asked Charles, rather taking the wind out of Maggie's sails.

"*Geology.*"

"Oho! I seeeee."

"I think you're all being most unfair."

My voice, small and tinkly, from a great distance outside myself.

Phineas Larkin coughed delicately behind his hand. Maggie looked nonplussed, hurt. I didn't look at Charles. My voice went on tinkling like a cow-bell on a distant alp.

"*Most* unfair. Just because she's a lecturer you can't expect her to suddenly forget she's a woman. She needs sex just as much as you lot do."

I was appalled. I had uttered the word sex. In public and not in a safe academic context. I failed to see why everyone was so tickled. Three faces, miles away from me, grotesque miniatures, grinning widely, all teeth. I could feel the tears welling up and Charles muttering, "Take it easy". I don't remember how the group dissolved itself.

Perhaps it was then that Charles suggested that we take a walk through Union to cool off. It was indeed stiflingly hot in the Refectory, and although my skull felt full of icy water, I could feel my face burning and my eyes like fireballs in round sockets. We edged out of the room leaving a devastated table behind us (Kevin had disappeared ages ago). We had to pass through a deafeningly narrow channel in front of the dais where the Decibels were thumping out 'Twist and Shout'. We were scarcely out of the room when Charles gripped my upper arm and quick-marched me off the beaten track, through the dimly-lit kitchens with the ghostly rows of cooking ranges and ovens and dully gleaming formica and stainless-steel surfaces, then out into the dark corridors at the back of Union, and eventually up a short flight of steps which I knew, from the miniature bird's-eye view of college in my brain, led to the familiar mezzanine landing outside the postgraduate common-room. Without any preamble, he pushed my shoulders against the lintel of the door and as his face came down towards mine in the dim light, I shuddered with distaste. But it was one of the big experiences of my life. One or two of my previous boyfriends had occasionally dared to peck me on the mouth with soft ridged lips that I had immediately recoiled from. No one had ever kissed me as Sinclair kissed me against that door-post. Limp with astonishment, I let him kiss me. I thought, I must love him very much.

"I've been waiting all evening to do that," he murmured, looking down at me, his face disconcertingly close to mine.

I believed him implicitly, and immediately forgave him all his apparent boredom. This was the sign I had been waiting for. He must love me, as much as I loved him. When I had tried to imagine what his kisses would be like I had come nowhere near the truth. He *must* love me – perhaps even more intensely than I loved him.

I have no other recollections of the evening, except that Keith Dent took the old Citroën up the shallow northern slope of Bryn Mawr, driving gingerly because although there had been no more snow, the minor roads were white and glassy. I sat in the back with Charles. Snogging was another new word in my vocabulary. I was deposited in Pantygwydr Terrace at half-past one in the morning. Charles excused himself from coming indoors with me as he wanted a lift back to college. So I stood in the snow, waving them off along the palely luminous roadway with the squiggles of tyre tracks crossing and recrossing all over the place.

from *That Watery Glass* (1973)

Jen Wilson
Zen and the Art of Thelonius Monk

To Miss Gyles, music mistress

Swansea 1960 ...
And did I ever tell you about when ...
On no, of course not, I'd left school by then.
It must have been that Young Conservative
that booked our Tempos band
into the Salisbury Club down on Walter Road
the night the piano got jammed
on the bend in the stairs,
the last flight up to the clubroom near the top of the stairs.
The boys in the band cursed and swore
'why can't you ****ing well play the flute
instead of the ****ing piano
like other ****ing people do?'
'Aw, c'mon boys, get a grip, mun
I know you really think I'm hip
in my silver lamé box jacket
and matching skirt with a slit'
as I stood on the stairs with my hand on my hip
covered by black fishnet tights
and stilletoed shoes with the winkle-picker tips.
They finally got the piano up the last few feet
and into the clubroom where the scrubbed Young Conservatives
meet every week,
in their tweedy sports jackets and sensible shoes
and the girls with tight perms, rows of pearls and black
patent leather shoes.
'Oh jolly good' they cry, 'here comes the band
we expect it's too late to give you a hand',
and 'oh its a gel who tinkles the eighty-eights what fun'

they cry from their gin
and tonics.
We grit our teeth and think of the money,
and as soon as I start playing ... there's something funny ...
Oh no! NOT AGAIN,
it's the dreaded Spew.
He's doctored the piano like he did once before
at the Community Centre near the beach last summer.
You see, poor old Spew suffered a mild affliction.
In the key of C only could he perform compositions,
and when he'd be backing his rock 'n' roll band
he had the piano tuned a tone down
to comply with the boys who blew in B/flat.
So it was my turn to rave and curse that night
as I transposed all our tunes in my head all night
while I kept the beat
with my strong left hand
and forever cursed Spew the previous piano man
who'd altered the pitch of the piano in the
Conservative Club.
'Spew, YOU SWINE, I'll kill you I will,
just wait till get my hands on you.'
And the boys in the band just grinned and said
'Keep your knickers on kid, you're doin' awright.'
Spew's a bank manager now somebody said.
Respectable.
Are you sure it's the same bloke? He's not right in the head.
But for all his faults I'll give him his due,
his piano playing was something to hear.
He sat astride the stool his head thrown back
his 'Roll Over Beethoven' and 'High School Hop'
were an absolute master of the genre.
Even though he could only play in the key of C ... for ever ...
And my liaison with the Young Conservative continued.
He said 'Care for a spin, Jenny' on Sunday afternoons,
and we lumped into his white Fiat 127 with the roll-top roof,
and sped down to Gower and stood on Three Cliffs.
And on the way back he said 'I've got something important
                                    to ask'.
So he stopped the car, his hand on my arm
the other across the back of my neck
and said

'Don't you think it's time you joined the Young Conservatives?'
I gasped out in horror my hand to my mouth.
'Oh I never thought it would come to this.'
And I shot out the door and ran like hell to the piano,
in the corner of my parents' front room.
And there I sang out four beats to the bar
'Gimmie a Pigfoot and a Bottle of Beer'
and
'Dirty No Good Man Blues' that I like to hear
Bessie Smith sing
on my record player.
Oh you cursed Conservative
with your Fiat 127
be gone with you
for ever and ever
Amen.
Is that what the Head wanted us to be?
Well-adjusted conservative gels?
Not me, who wore black tights and ankle boots
beneath the grey gymslip because she was
a beatnik,
and lowered the tone of the whole school.
And was hauled out of assembly one morning
by the Head in her billowing gown,
who roared from the platform
above my head,
'White ankle socks, my gel, must be worn
don't lower the decorum of this school'.
But Miss, I said, inside my head,
I only wanted to look cool, and keep warm at the same time
like those London girls at school this term
I'd seen on one of my little sojourns
to the jazz clubs of London Town.
And during the rest of my fourth year and into the fifth,
I could feel the noose tighten around my neck
until I knew I was choking to death.
And left.

from *On My Life* (1989)

Alan Perry
Live Wires

Albert I saw today
the eight year old scar
we made together
in lone Dyfatty Street,
healed thoroughly now

above it thrive
twelve storey flats
a children's park
swank tennis courts
sleek bowling green

and the town goes bustling by
while down below
the winding cable
runs silently and deep
humming in the dark

from *Live Wires* (1970)

John Pook
A View from Swansea

Each time that I come home it rains.
Clouds accumulate above the bay
like steam into high white swirls;
sea and low sky run into a palette of grey.

Your coast of Devon recedes then.
Details go first – white houses, greens
and mottled browns near Ilfracombe,
cars reflecting sunlight, the sheen

from off your cliffs, till only the silhouette
of pencilled coast survives the rain.
Then that goes too, drawn into the wet
wall of mist. We are cut off again.

When will it end, this longing to connect?
It is like watching the death of England
while for you in Devon the lights of Wales go out.
What countries, love, would I give to touch your hand!

from *That Cornish-Facing Door* (1975)

Michael Lenihan
Pennard Valley

The one that got away
Didn't come from here; the fibber who said so should
Be beaten about the brain (if any) with his rod,
Be trussed with cat-gut or slung from a passing ship
To the Bristol Channel, where, given he can swim,
If the headland did not, the fungus would get him.
    Nothing but the banshee
Lives here, and lots of titchy crabs fit only for gulls
(Infrequent guests but if you go to The Mumbles,
A pocket calculator will come in handy)
And though it's splashed through a couple of woody cwms
On its way to the bay – where some pinpoint the Booms,
    Though others disagree –
The sparkling Parkmill stretch of the pill might look so
But there's hardly a stray in a fishy mile or two
And the seaboard stretch is too muddy or so sandy
That only the stepping stones (a neat, professional job)
Support life: weeds, pied wagtails, the usual summer mob;
    It's pleasant anyway.
Should some foreign invasion force straggle ashore
One morning, at Threecliff Bay, they would do no more
Damage than the average family (who tip
The exigent seaside trash into the gorse bushes)
And, after trying on a few futile rushes
    Up the bramble-tight and
    Soft, slippy slopes of sand,
Defying their commanding officer with hoots
Of childish delight, they would kick off their boots
And spread out a picnic hamper in the ruined castle,
Filling flasks from the cool spring water which seeps
Down from the golf course. Parking space for the jeeps

Would be the main problem.
They would, thank God, get no further than South Gower
For even an Englishman – and there's none lower
In Plaid Cymru's notebook of undesirables –
Gets stuck, somehow, in the Graveyard of Ambition
And is put out to grass on this coastline where none
     Will recognise his name.
The same would happen to our tough invasion pards
Who'd, latching on, mail tons of picture post cards
Back to relations in the Fatherland; cables
Saying *Wish you were here!* or *Why don't you join us?*
Or *We are having fun with the Sandy Laners!*
     We are glad that we came!
We'd, all the same, have preferred them to stay at home
Or land somewhere else like Maidstone or Babbacombe:
We could then enjoy our walks without their hassle.
For where the pill murmurs is space to meditate,
Time to pray, while yellow hammer and lark create
     A roof of sound, bless them.

                                        Unpublished

Tony Curtis
Singleton

i
Three men in clown suits
are trying to fill an elephant with water
as the T.V. show dissolves.

An aquarium bubbles life to the delicate fish
moving each in its oblivion.

We are at such a height
that out over the town the coast
unfolds a string of lights
that maps the Bay's arms
as they pincer the dark sea.

ii
This hospital is a space-city
we shuttle to.

A thousand-lights house
in a suburb of our life.

iii
You shuffle to the window
and point out the edge of the campus.
I spent four years there.

All that time we watched
them build this place: ninth floor, tenth floor,
Accident Ward, Cancer Ward,

loud navvies racing dumper-trucks through the mud,
cranes swinging girders in the sky,
the drone of the big mixers.

iv
The fish slant and cruise
through the tepid water.
They pout and suck at the glass.

v
All the people here are dying. Carcinoma
of the throat, colon, brain.

You too, are dying.
Though they pepper with radium
the grid drawn on your shaven chest,
you are dying.

At the end of the hour
you rise, aching out of the armchair.
The arc of your back gives it away:
a year, a week, a day.

vi
These visits we kiss full-lipped.
It must be twenty-five years –
so long since we did that,
or watched each other as carefully as this,
weighing out our words.

vii
The lift drops
like a flat stone through water.

I'm stranded.

The night air is ice at the back of my mouth.
I drive through one sour pool of light
after another.

from *Preparations* (1980)

Russell Celyn Jones
'damaged beyond repair'

[When aged twelve Mark Swain murdered his sister. Now an adult, married and with two children, he has a new identity as Ray Greenland. His half-sister, Celandine, turns up and blackmails him. Ray takes the children and flees to Oystermouth, the hometown of Tom, his probation officer, whose identity he now assumes.]

It is early evening as we walk away from the station through the town that *is* as Tom described – damaged beyond repair by the Luftwaffe and rebuilt by criminals. An ancient Wessex colony, former medieval frontier of fire and destruction, erstwhile smelting nexus of iron, lead, zinc, nickel, copper and magnesium.

In the heavy, weeping air, Eliot pauses on the pavement. 'Is this is where you grew up, Dad?' His voice is full of incredulity.

In the distance an edge of the crescent-shaped sea glitters like silver. 'It gets prettier the further we get out of town. The beaches you'll enjoy, I think.'

'Where are we going to stay?' Eliot is concerned still.

'We'll find a bed and breakfast.' 'I wish you could drive, Dad. It would be much easier.'

In truth I want to walk to get a measure of this town, and as we wear down shoe leather I check off the real place against the blueprint I've held in my imagination for more than fifteen years. The children are good walkers, seasoned by our own Kent marshes, and make no further complaint as the High Street becomes Wind Street and then Chapel Street. There is a sort of lull in the life of the place, between the end of a working day and the muezzin calls of the nightclub-converted chapels that I see every few hundred metres. Large glass storefronts refract the red sky across the road that shimmers like a river or a pond, and makes me feel like I'm sailing my children through town rather than walking their little feet off.

We reach the entrance to the docks and from inside I hear a familiar sound of marine engines charging up ships' batteries. Tankers setting keel for open sea are oracles of light playing upon the oily water. We are on several borders at once, between heavy industry to the east – gasworks, oil refinery – and the golden beaches to the west; between night and day; between good and evil. I find the Regency Port Authority, Customs House and Chamber of Commerce in the vicinity where a future probation officer attended a nursery beneath a top-floor brothel.

A footbridge takes us across a sluggish river. On the other side is a blue prison singing out of tune and a virginally white law court. The arched stone gateway into a well-groomed park gives me such a powerful *déjà vu* I steer the children inside. Along the winding avenue of ash trees I hear their footfalls on the soft macadam. The rustling of encroaching foliage dampens them into silence. They are walking scared, while I seek out the tranquillity in all this regimented order.

We sit on a bench, and as the light continues to fade I put my arms around the children, pulling them closer. Eliot produces his Top Trumps and shares the pack with Flora, using my lap as the deck. But this game, which you win and lose on the basis of supercar performance statistics, fails to distract them. Still disorientated, they watch instead a platoon of park-keepers fan out of three separate doors in a green octagonal hut. Even Flora and Eliot recognise, by their stride, that they are going home, even if we cannot. Their work here is all done, their achievements displayed in the flowerbeds bordered with chain loops, in grass verges edged with a spirit level, in the straitjackets that constrain the sycamore saplings and in the stream swept clean of algae that runs silently into a glistening pond. A bowling green with a military haircut seems incongruously lush against the dead white lawns dried by weeks of unconscionable heat.

The humidity is ominous as a plague even at this time of evening as I make a move. Walking back the way we came, the children are stunned into an even deeper silence by the vague outlines of trees bordering the undulated path, by blue hydrangea-covered walls and by the eyes of nocturnal animals staring at us from down by the pond. The little wind there is racks the foliage and makes a sound of water running on corrugated tin.

We follow the road west between school playing fields and golf links, with sand dunes opposite. A disused railway line runs alongside the dark pulsating sea. Telegraph wires cut the sky into shreds. Beyond the

Territorial Army hall is Tom's old school, Emanuel. The buildings scattered around a grass arena fill me with such deep longing, I ignore my children's need to be settled somewhere for the night and steer them into the grounds. But the school has been abandoned and left to rot. All that remains of this Christian school, that took the children of missionaries as boarders, are three grey, pebbledashed schoolhouses called Bethel, Sharon and Galilee. Pillars crumble with age, windows are broken, the lawns are waist deep and weeds grow up the sides of the walls. The science laboratory I locate in a single-storey prefab building. Putting my eyes to a window I can just make out the shape of maple worktops with their sinks and taps and Bunsen burner gas fittings. A presence of the chemistry teacher, that sexual predator who kissed the sixth-form girl in his car, moves between the benches in a white coat.

I can't stop myself from saying, 'This is the old science lab. In the summer term, kids raced out of here at four with hands burning from chemicals and plunged them into the sea.' They display little interest, looking through dusty panes into nothing with sorrowful, bleary eyes. 'We'll be at the sea tomorrow. Now let's find an inn for us to stay.'

It's another epoch before we find such a place – the Seaview guesthouse in a terrace along the front. The landlady has a vacancy in a 'family room' with one double bed and a single. Decorated with flock wallpaper that curls at the cornices, the room feels ghosted by a thoususand former guests. A smell of mothballs clings to the air. Net curtains lift in the breeze over the open window. As I rifle through our bag, I realise I've forgotten to pack toothbrushes and toothpaste and pyjamas for the children in my rush to be away. Too tired to complain, they take off their clothes and go to bed in their underwear. They fall asleep instantly in the double bed.

I plug my mobile phone into the electricity supply and lie on the single bed. The phone, which has been off all day, suddenly jams with voicemail and text messages from their mother. I can't afford to know what they say and instead listen to the kids sighing in their sleep, to the starched duvet cover rustling in the dark. Eliot kicks his leg free, which lands across Flora's belly. She moans, turns to face the wall. The same question keeps droning in my head. What do I hope to find beside the sea, the closest you can get to another world?

Beyond the window, stars fall out of the sky. Everything out there is in eternal conference. The past, present and future coexist simultaneously. I seem to have reached a point where my personal time is going round and round on a loop. There can be no new surprises, no new experience for me. My wristwatch synchronises with the dead seconds. The true realisation I've been fighting for so long is I belong alone in the world. My children are simply visiting me. Plagued by this thought, even they seem to vanish into the night. I can no longer hear them sleep. They do not move in their bed, become like dishes in a rack, or friezes on the wall of a prehistoric cave.

Will this hot summer night never end? I grow listless upon the bed. My head pounds and my mouth is dry. I close my eyes and think of winter but my imagination fails me. I open my eyes and the furnishings shift, move and multiply. The room begets new rooms to resemble a doll's house, with my children asleep in the nursery [...]

From a chemist near the square I buy three toothbrushes and toothpaste before finding a bus whose destination chimes with one of my borrowed memories. We ride in the top front seat and twenty minutes later land at a beach. With the hold-all slung over my shoulder, I go down to the sand with a child's hand in each of mine. To any observer we may look like a happy family, rather than a father hanging on to his children by his finger-tips. What I *don't* feel in this Neverland is my old fear of someone approaching to ask me to help them remember where they've seen me before. A child actor ... An old school friend ... The slackening of that terror allows me to promenade the children gaily along the beach. A crescent of green beach huts facing the sea is fronted by manicured lawns and palm trees. This is order on the ground. I've never seen a place so benign. We've hit it at the right time too, in summer on a school day, the sort of day when truant boys are playing in the surf when they should be in a science lesson. The beach is cut in two sections by a large rock where boys are leaping off into the sea, as they have done for all time. Also on the sand is a clapboard café called The Surfside where the kid called Janway Davis once smuggled out money from the till inside ice-cream cornets. I notch that up for a lunch venue before leaving it to our stern.

Where the huts end the cliffs begin. It is wilder here, with ferns and thorn bushes hanging over the footpath. We walk before the wind with the sea to port, and at the headland watch the swell sweeping round the point. These swells with hard-muscled backs swing into the bay one end to the other. I am a river man out of my depth, but so excited I request to them that my ashes be scattered on this headland overlooking the bay.

They both protest. Eliot in particular seems worried that I'm going to die at all. Not now, he's implying, not when Mum's not here at least. I have not talked to Lily for twenty-four hours, the longest silence we've ever sustained.

We sit on the white grass. Flora makes daisy chains while Eliot prises stones out of the ground to throw into the sea. Both are slightly perturbed by the moaning of air forced by the swell through a blowhold in the rocks. Nothing could be simpler than this, inhaling ozone rising off the sea, and I want the children to feel my pleasure. If I really had grown up here the sea would run in my veins, whatever my final destination on the earth.

They seem to take pleasure from wasting time. Wasting time in such a spot is consuming time well, as healthy as meditation.

Or are they simply taking stock?

They *are* unusually pensive. I can hardly expect anything else. Maybe time is rushing through their heads after all, as they consider an uncertain future. It begins to worry me, and I start to crave their conversation as a vital sign. I point to the flashes in the sea where guillemots have dived, to sails on the horizon and to the sun breaking through cloud to shine like a torch upon the water. All this does is create minimal sounds and gestures back.

What they really want to do, I discover, is eat, and within thirty minutes we are back on the beach, sitting around an oval plastic table on the patio of The Surfside, gorging on fried egg, beans and chips and drinking Coca Cola. It's a number one hit in a number one venue with a view of the sea and the day begins to look like a winner.

from *Ten Seconds from the Sun (2005)*

Val Warner
By St Paul's Parish Church, Sketty

The evening's grey, and green and grey again.
Sweeping the grass, rain's given over to
the evening, grey and green. Daily, I skirt
the swollen spring. Tonight, bells scale the air
above the green hill's sodden emptiness
– silver torrents down muddy, bygone ways,
where blackbirds brazenly chime in.

Grey as a rock against the green, the grey,
the church hunches a kind of leaden grace
scaling the mind's eye, for some passers-by.
Bells wash over me, romantically,
closer to tears in midsummer's lush light.
They tempt with tongues of fire our mortal souls.
They tempt with tongues, promising the moon.
Hugging the grey eminence of the hills

above the bay, the church nestles beneath
the higher hills, hills risen to the sky.
Eye can't go by the shaky structure, lost
in clouds. Behind a Gothic screen of firs,
the way beyond stays quiet as ever,
apart from Sunday's queue of worshippers'

Japanese saloons, chrome fig-leafed by leaves
blowing in the wind, the rushing, mighty wind
across the wide skyscape of Swansea Bay.
Bonnets and boots get plastered in the fall.
Hell's keys are sycamore. Who sweeps a road,
as for by-laws, makes that and th' action fine.
Everyman can give tongue, too, to a piece

of her mind on our quality of life.
The church, these days, rises from its graveyard
with handfuls of cut flowers, compost soon.
Is its bed-rock, Welsh disestablishment?
The church, these days, takes care of certain souls.
Do they cross over green to bells, with scales
falling away, like this soil underfoot?

from *P.N. Review* (1984)

Nigel Jenkins
Chain Harrows

Diesel taints the sweet stench
of grass and scabbed manure,
Steel's rush, permitting only
tink of stone, drags hanks of couch

from stale pasture: they loll
in the crosswind, a whispered hay.
Third gear work, this: enigma
to Gower's newer eyes, peering

from the roads at little more than
some kind of lawn effect.
The bed reversed for cleaner ground,
I speed in top, dung shrapnel

sketting the air. Glancing back
to keep aligned, I catch
within the harrows' dance a frenzy
of bone – the skeleton burst

of rabbit or lamb. Shards litter
a region of bruised grass
like the spray of feathers
where a fox has killed.

from *Acts of Union: Selected Poems 1974-1989* (1990)

Beach huts, Gŵyr

Locked and padlocked,
foundationed on sand
where extremities meet

they huddle from winds
they can no more weather.
Planks rot, nails twist free:

they cannot bend
as the marram bends.

And there are hands here
re-enrooting the marram.
It whispers round their walls
binding together
the inarticulate sands, one
layer fixed, the
next one building.

And where these huts,
bloated with memory, spill

new seed shall root
and the marram wither.
To what grasses then, what
flowers take hold
there's no language yet

can lend a name.
Winds rattle their timbers:
they laugh a lot,
they are very frightened.
The lilting marram bends.

from *Acts of Union: Selected Poems 1974-1989* (1990)

Alan Perry
Nocturnes, Swansea Bay

1.
side by side
beneath an arch –
two shadows in the dark:
Flotsam and Jetsam,
sitting on cold wet stone
each nursing a bottle

Rain finely falls
Dream traffic passes ...
the man gets up, goes
and throws
an empty at the sea.
She watches hopelessly.
He misses.

2.
lamp-lit waves
rippling in
as in a dream
– the past rolled ever forward

killing time
I find
a piece of driftwood, recognise at once
its dark black knot of face
its smooth forbearance
its frozen scream

from *Poetry Wales* (1990)

Peter Thabit Jones
Gower Delivery

For the last hot hour or more,
I have been carrying boxes
To the top step, the ninth step,
Of the front door of this exclusive,
Seaside, mock Miami Beach hotel.
Once again, up into the rancid
Back of my van; checking cold boxes
Of scampi, cod, mixed vegetables,
Plaice, hake, French fries and slabs of meat,
Against the journey-crumpled,
Delivery-note. The frozen foods
Thawing in the furnace of the van.
Once more, I struggle back up the
Crunching, gravel path. A woman
Guest, as desirable as an iced lager,
Smiles from a high, sun-demanding balcony.
Two bold children, their ice-cream cones dripping
In the mischievous heat, hurry
Down the quaking path to the crowded
Beach: the dead sky shrouds sea and sand.
Back to my sea-blue van – with the painted,
Smiling fish and short-haired, apple-cheeked
Butchers on its doors. The sun has gone mad!
I guzzle the last sour drops
Of lukewarm Coca Cola in my can,
Wipe my wet brow in my shirt-sleeves
And stoop down to re-tie a limp shoelace.
Glancing up at the balcony,
I find my golden Eve has gone.
Then the front door opens and she comes out,
Her tanned body testing her bikini's strength.
Smiling, she moves to the car park
And gets into a dark red sportscar.
I return to the burning hotel,
For a man's unruly signature.

from *Visitors* (1986)

John Powell Ward
Evening Bathers

A creamy warm Atlantic thins
And washes up the cockles. Where
The August sun goes down and near
A nervous mother tiny boys
Adore the swirlings round their knees;
Stick-insects, laughing skeletons.

A surfer leans his thighs to guide
The pink foams to a beaching place.
A girl stares at the fishing-rod
Wedged in the sand. Bent from a catch
The curling tendril makes a snatch
At air. Before a rock's blue face

Last families are cricketing,
Ball sailing like a red-beaked gull
To be caught. The sea's rolled shavings steel
Themselves to come on in. Along
The hedgerow of each blossoming wave
The surfer rides, we divers dive

Under the saline drift for words
Down in a luminous green weed.
Philologies crash overhead
Above our continental shelf
And waist-deep fathers stare amazed
At orange and the sky itself

To see come catapulting in
The surfer's black cap like a seal.
The evening bathers feel so real
In their mauve caravans tonight.
They watch the huge tomato sun
Drop bouncing on its trampoline.

from *The Clearing* (1984)

William Virgil Davis
Landscape (Gower)

How old the dark has become,
standing silent in these fields while
horses weave through each other's shadows.
They have come like warm rain
and run over the hills in the moonlight
and stood so long alone no one
impatient would ever notice them there.

When the wind and the winter return
the horses will still be here,
their silhouettes outlined in the pale moonlight,
standing still and silent on these hills
or stamping, splattering snow in small spills,
the whole scene turning slowly into landscape
like our own earliest memories.

from *The New Criterion* (1987)

Living Away

memories of the Gower coast of Wales

1.
The landscape, from the upstairs window,
could keep me busy all morning. The
rolling hills waved away through history
as far as we could see. A herd of Holsteins,
like statues, grazed on the same small hill
beyond our neighbour's barn, one wall
in need of repair, the whole roof fallen in.
A dozen wild ponies roamed the moors,
entered open gates, ate roses in the gardens.

We couldn't see the sea, just over the cliff,
but the wind drove in from it, bringing
the regular rain and the blown birds.
They floated over the moors like lazy kites.
When the tide turned, they'd swoop down
to the beach to search the sand, find what the sea
stranded.

My study window looked out
from the back of the house, to the east. I liked
the late afternoons best, sitting in shadow,
watching, as if on lookout, trying to notice
and name the most minute changes in wind
and weather, in this place where everything
interrupted itself.

2.

Nothing was nearer
than one kilometer: grocery, school, post
office, the little village library – our only
outside world. One evening, without warning,
a red setter who entered opened doors,
wandered into our living room. We couldn't
find where he was from, and kept him.
We named him *Lost*. Often, he would be gone
for days at a time, and finally disappeared for good.

With only the sea for steady company,
everything adjusted to it. This rhythm
was easily learned. On days when it didn't rain,
we'd take the short steep trail to the small
private beach, a ten minutes' walk from our
front gate. Our son would climb the cliff
to the ruined castle, then swoop down on us,
waving his flag, flashing his wooden sword,
shouting *surrender, surrender or die.*

3.
Too soon, it was time to leave. This place,
now, was more than the land of our name;
it had grown into our bones like blood,
like life itself. Still, we knew we had to go,
and so we packed our bags, turned our backs,
and went. We knew we could never return,
except, again and again, in memory.

from *The Sewanee Review* (1995)

William Greenway
Pwll Du

Through caves of oak and beech, I walk a mile
above the stream that sinks and wanders
underground through limestone for a while

before it surges from the hill
into the clear, blue air of beach
and merges with the sea, now still.

The path, too, bursts into sun and rain
from out of moldy leaves and gloom of wood,
to cliffs where you can breathe again.

And there below is the quiet bay
where the weekend cottages once were pubs
when the quarry worked in golden days

and money brought men here. Now dogs
chase the creamy surf for sticks,
while lovers lie by driftwood logs,

and the old continually watch the tide
to see what washes up, as if
for consolation from the other side.

Above the beach, below the hill, alone,
is a grave of men, their only monument
a ragged ring of quarry stone

laid beneath the bracken of this cape.
The others never found, just sixty-eight
lie within a giant footstep shape

because one afternoon, against their will
they disappeared from Swansea streets
to live an hour at sea until

the ship in sea wrack struck the rocks.
The crew survived, but left them there below
in chains, their feet in stocks.

The transcript of the trial effaced the dead,
no mention made of men impressed;
the ship alone was lost, the record said.

Sometimes there is no metaphor,
analogy, or rhyme,
and reason winks its semaphore

at fog "shrouding" the mast,
waves "clawing" at the ship.
No elegy could hope to last

as long as lines of stones,
the want of name on every one
as elegant, articulate as bones.

And yet I say, *As bones,* as if I doubt
the things I see and feel
and cannot find them real without

another name, as ships are called
Endeavor, Self Reliant, Hope,
as if the words forestalled

the salted eyes and stolen breath,
the water at our feet, our waist,
rising like the certainty of death.

Never proper sailors like the rest
who lived or died at sea,
their signatures upon a manifest,

these men were on no list of any kind –
picked at random, stones were gathered,
aligned, and left behind.

I etch on each the names, like metaphor:
Water Filling His Mouth,
Forgotten, and *Forevermore.*

from *Simmer Dim* (1999)

Rowan Williams
Oystermouth Cemetery

Grass lap; the stone keels jar,
scratch quietly in the rippling soil.
The little lettered masts dip slowly
in a little breeze, the anchors here
are very deep among the shells.

Not till the gusty day
when a last angel tramples down
into the mud his dry foot hissing,
down to the clogged forgotten shingle,
till the bay boils and shakes,

Not till that day shall the cords snap
and all the little craft float stray
on unfamiliar tides, to lay their freight
on new warm shores, on those strange islands
where their tropic Easter landfall is.

from *The Poems of Rowan Williams* (2002)

David Hughes
Swonzee Boy See?

Sorrite livin up ere
bi farout like f ew wanoo gerrin t town.
Yea I knowzits u city
burile olliz call it town.

I wuz born downer Sandfields see,
down by werra Soshull is now
– eza joke forew.

Ayve done some fancy work round air, avenay?
Sorl been tarted up like
roun byer Lehjha un South Dock.
Ew doan see flats like at up Blineymice.
Meenmy brother ewsed t dive inner dock
– few tryed it now ewed crack ew ed onner yot.

180

I been in at Marrytime Museyum.
Ayve got bit vunole Mumbles train air.
I remember at wen I wozer kid.
Ewsed t put apenees onner line
forrer trains to go overum
soze ayde ged as big as pennys –
try um inner chewing gum machines see?

Awler famly ewsed t go downer Bracelet inner summer
on at ole train –
evenee ole man.
Ew could mover seats
soze ew coudall sitagether.

Ay still maker lotter fuss bout at train
ewed think it wuzy ony thing ut ad been taken from air.

from *Planet* (1986)

Jeremy Hughes
Swansea Boy

Dai Rees me
Swansea boy
Sketty
sixteen next birthday
mitched in arcades down the Mumbles
and making a raise here and there
dwellings
creepers sometimes
but motors is my real game
Cosworths
BMs
Porsches
a Lotus once
and a Mini GT too
nippy as fuck them
but I'm here for dope
you know
everyone does it
briefs and all
they've been to college

they knows the score
one minute they're defending
next they're skinning a deck
it's not bad see
should be legal
this place'd be a lot quieter
it sorts you out
the boys tries and gets it in all ways
off visits mainly
come through plugged they do
or have it kissed to them
and some have it in their hands
cos the screws don't check them on a rub
mad it is
drives you up the wall this place
be a lot quieter if legal
it sorts you out see
and I wouldn't be here
planted it they did
cos they wanted me off the streets
cos they couldn't get me on the rest.

from *New Welsh Review,* 31 (Winter 1995-96)

Neil Rosser
Swansea Jack

I was born in an industrial town down by the edge of the sea,
We talk with an accent and nobody much likes the likes of we;
Copper's stained the earth, and coal dust's altered many a voice.

Nothing moves in or out of here, nothing's ever new,
And if you're a local boy, well, nasty words are few.
Harden every consonant, that's how some talk round here,
And hold the slack tight, and hey mush, where you off to there.

Swansea Jack, Swansea Jack, Swansea Jack, yeah, Swansea Boy.

from *Cerddi Abertawe a'r Cwm* (2002), ed. Heini Gruffudd
translated by Grahame Davies

Jo Mazelis
Too Perfect

The man and the woman were standing side by side at the marina, studying the new housing development on the other side of the water. He had been expressing surprise tinged with disgust at the sight of the red brick buildings with their gabled windows and arches and as he put it "post modern gee-gaws". While she, having no knowledge of what had stood there before and no great opinion on architecture, said nothing.

Then into the silence that hovered between them he suddenly offered "Do you mind?" and before he had finished asking, took her hand in his. In reply she gave a squeeze of assent, noting as she did how large and warm and smooth his hand was.

To a passerby it would have looked like nothing out of the ordinary. He or she, on seeing this man and woman by the water's edge, would assume that this hand-holding was a commonplace event for them. But it wasn't. This was the first, the only time of any real physical contact between them.

Later, still awkwardly holding hands, each now afraid that letting go might signal some end to that which had not yet even begun, they made their way to the old Town Hall, once the home of commerce and council and now a centre for literature. This was the purpose of their trip, the reason why at seven that morning, she had stood at the window of her bedsit in Cambrian Street, Aberystwyth, waiting for the tin-soldier red of his Citröen to emerge around the corner.

Each had expressed an interest in visiting the Centre and had behaved as if they were the only two people in the world with such a desire. That was why, uncharacteristically, he hadn't suggested the trip to the other members of his tutorial group. It was also the reason why Claire had omitted to tell any of her friends, why she had agreed to wake Ginny that morning at ten o'clock, despite the fact that she and Dr. Terrence Stevenson would probably be enjoying coffee and toast together in Swansea by then.

Terry, as he was known to colleagues and students alike, was a large man, over six feet, with large bones and large appetites, which now as he neared fifty expressed itself in his frame. He had once been lithe and muscular but his body had thickened with age. He blamed too many years at a desk, the expansion of his mind at the expense of an expanding behind. But he dressed well enough, choosing dark tailored jackets and corduroy or chino slacks, as well as the odd devilish tie, which was about as subversive as he got. In colder weather, as on this grey October day, he wore his favourite black Abercrombie overcoat of cashmere and wool mix. The coat hung well from the shoulders and had the effect of tapering his body, disguising its imperfections with a veneer of pownful authority and masculinity.

Claire thought he looked like one of the Kray twins in this coat of his, and to her that signalled a sort of dangerous sexuality. She could not help but imagine herself engulfed in that coat, held willing captive in its soft folds.

Next to him, she looked tiny, even less than her five feet and a half inch. Claire had very long hair, grown in excess to compensate perhaps for her lack of height. It hung down, straight and sleek to her bottom and a great deal of her time was taken up with this hair: washing, combing and plaiting it before she went to bed each night. Most of the time she wore it loose and her gestures, the movement of her head, body and hands were all done in such a way as to accommodate her river of hair. When eating, for example, she would hold the fork in one hand while with the other she held her hair away from the plate. She was very proud of her hair and if asked which part of herself she liked the most, that, would be what she would choose. Her last boyfriend, whom she had met at the Freshers' Dance at college and dated for almost three years, had loved her hair; had sometimes spread it over her naked body, Lady Godiva style when they made love; had once even made the pretence of tying himself to her by it.

Claire's body was like a boy's: flat chested and slim hipped. And today she was dressed like a boy too, with jeans and heavy black lace-up boots and a white shirt and a man's tweed jacket two sizes too big. Through both her right eyebrow and right nostril she wore tiny silver rings and her eyes and lips were exaggerated with make up in shades of reddish brown. She seldom smiled, but when she did her entire face was transformed into something not quite wholly beautiful, but something very like it.

They had trudged through an exhibition of artifacts relating to the town's one famous poet: the scribbled postcards, the crumpled snapshots, the yellowing newspaper clippings, all framed for posterity like the relics of some dead saint. Terry had begun by ducking and tutting yet more disapproval of the venture, disapproval he'd been nurturing and planning since he first heard of it, but with Claire by his side he found himself softening, growing acclimatised to her open-minded acceptance of all such endeavours.

They spoke in whispers, though the place was almost entirely deserted, this being after all a grey Tuesday in October, and around the back, beneath some engravings by Peter Blake they kissed their first kiss. It did not feel like the world's best kiss for either of them, but did well enough as an awkward, uncertain snatched preliminary to better things. Afterwards Claire had wanted to wipe her mouth with the back of her hand, not from disgust but just because the kiss was a little wet. His mouth had swallowed hers, had not measured out the size of her lips yet.

After the kiss they each felt like a conspirator in some deadly plot; what they would create that day felt as if it might be as deadly as Guy Fawkes' gunpowder, as bloody as any revolution.

The second kiss came as they sat in a deserted bar of the Pump House. The barman, a student, they decided, was propped against the far end of the counter, his head bent over a book. They took turns to guess what the book might be. Terry said it was a handbook about computing, and she thought it was a script of something like *Reservoir Dogs*.

The clock above the bar, a faux-nautical affair hung with nets and cork floats and plastic lobster and crab, read twelve-fifteen. They had the afternoon and the early evening to spend together. He was thinking about the Gower coast, a cliff walk, the lonely scream of wheeling gulls and the sea a grey squall bubbling under the wind. She was thinking about a hotel room, the luggage-less afternoon ascent in the lift to the en-suite room and the champagne, herself languishing on the sheets, feeling intolerably beautiful under his grateful gaze.

After that second kiss, which was prolonged, they wrenched themselves away and began to speak in a strange language of unfinished sentences and hesitant murmurings.

"Oh."

"Gosh."

"You know we..."

"I never..."

"Oh my..."

"We shouldn't..."

"I never thought..."

"Nor me..."

"I mean, I always thought that maybe..."

"Me too..."

Then they kissed again and the barman, who wasn't a student, raising his eyes briefly from his novel by Gorky, watched them with mild interest and thought they made an odd pair.

The odd pair finished their drinks: pints of real ale. She stubbed out her cigarette and they made their way towards the exit, his arm thrown protectively around her shoulders while his broad back wore her tiny arm, its fingers clutching the cloth, like a curious half belt.

The sky looked by now greyer and darker than before. To the West a blue-black curtain advanced, promising heavy rain and a wind blew up from the East, sending her hair on a frantic aerial dance. They ran across the empty square as raindrops as big as shillings began marking the paving stones with dark circles.

Then she half stumbled and he caught her and in catching her, gathered her to him and they kissed a fourth time, this the best, with the rain splashing their heads and water pouring down their faces.

When they had done with this, this their unspoken moment of willingness and promise and wilfulness, their pact to indulge in what they knew was an unwise thing, he quickly kissed the tip of her nose and then hand in hand they began to run again.

Under the covered walkway, they slowed down and shaking off the worst of the rain from their hair and clothes, barely noticed a man sranding close by. He was busy putting away a tripod and Terry muttered, "Afternoon" and the man, grinning broadly replied, "Thanks".

Naturally neither of them made much of this, assuming it to be yet another curious aspect of Welshness. A further example of the strange smiling politeness, the thanking of bus drivers and so on, the chatting to strangers which each of them had at first perceived as alien, but now despite their breeding, accepted and in part adopted.

Later that afternoon, in his car near a field in the north of Gower, with the day as dark as ever they almost made love. The next day, back in Aberystwyth, they did make love.

She had rung him from the payphone in the hall of her house when she was certain all the other students had gone out. His wife had answered the phone and she'd given her the prearranged message, which was that she'd "found the journal with the Lawrence article he'd wanted."

What happened that Wednesday was perhaps rather sad, though not necessarily inevitable. It became clear to both of them that what they sought was a fugitive moment; that there could be no more of this, the furtive opening of the front door, the climbing of the stairs, the single bed dishevelled and cramped under the sloping roof, his glances at his watch, her ears constantly straining for any sounds from down below. Both of them too tense for pleasure, but going through its rigours, him professionally, she dramatically.

Afterwards, when they had dressed again, they sat side by side on the bed like strangers in a doctor's waiting room, each thinking silently about how to end it, how to escape. She took his hand and held it on her lap, then began to speak.

"Your wife ..."

"Catherine..."

"She sounded..."

"Yes."

"Nice?"

"She is. I..."

"I don't..."

"I can't..."

"I think that..."

"Me too." He sighed. She understood his sigh to mean that he didn't want to leave and she sighed back at the thought that he might cancel his three o'clock lecture in order to stay. He had sighed because he was wondering how long he ought to stay to make it seem at least remotely respectable. He rested his eyes on the small wooden bookcase next to her bed. She had all the required texts as well as a rather unhealthy number of books by and about the American poet Sylvia Plath. This made him sigh again. She was trying very hard to imagine him back in his study, with the coffee cups on the window ledge and the view of the National Library and the letter trays overflowing with student essays and she sighed again because now that she'd seen him in his underwear that ordinary idea seemed impossible.

He stood suddenly, ready to go, but somehow his watch had become entangled with her hair and she gave a yelp of pain as he unthinkingly yanked at it, ripping the hair from her head. They both looked aghast at the tangled dumps sprouting from the metal bracelet of his watch. He pulled at them but they cut into his fingers and stretched and curled and slipped and clung until finally they snapped, leaving short tufts poking out here and there.

Tears had come to her eyes with the sudden pain. He looked at her and seeing this, with ill-disguised irritation as much at himself as with her, said "I'm sorry," then bluntly, "Why don't you get that cut?"

That would have been the end of the story, except that some moments, elusive as they may seem when lived, come back in other guises, unbidden. Theirs was a photograph, unfortunately a very good photograph of a young girl on tip toes, her long wet hair lifted wildly in the wind and a black-coated man bent over her, his hands delicately cupping her upturned face as their lips met. Rain glistened on their faces and shone in silvery puddles on the paving stones at their feet and behind them the sky was a black brooding mass of cloud.

It was a timeless image, a classic to be reproduced over and over, whose currency was love, truth and beauty. The people who bought the poster and the stationery range and the postcard assumed that it must have been posed, that it was really too perfect.

from *Diving Girls* (2002)

Lloyd Rees
Wind Street, 1998

Once, a thought ago,
there was sombre stone
of lofty, serious banks
and a shining post office,
quiet money and marble and chrome,
consorting with, at the twisted end,
a Labour club, a bookie's,
a dubious pub with ancient
made-up women, grisly men
and a fierce, salivating dog.

Once, a photograph ago,
trams rattled and curved
up from The Strand past
iron signs for liver salts
and doleful shires and drays
outside The Duke. Men
in hats and girls in gloves,
are frozen by the Rialto, their faces
blank with sepia acceptance
of how it would always be.

But nothing stays the same.
It's café bars with good new wood
and brass, and brasseries,
all Bud and Tex Mex.

The sepia's been coloured in,
adorned with navel rings
and shaven hair. Two bouncers
in heavy overcoats,
muscled like cartoon heroes,
stamp and snort the air.

All change is retribution
for the stubborn, stillborn past.
The young, E'd wild and happy,
half-know, don't care. They link

their arms and sing themselves.
But down the stubborn end
the Labour club's still there.

From *Swansea Poems* (2000)

Stevie Davies
'shafts of memory. . . awakened'

[Mara has returned to Swansea to take up a senior psychiatric post. She sees a TV archive film of the 1960s that features Francesca, her one-time best friend who committed suicide. The film triggers recollections of her Swansea upbringing.]

Menna will get hold of a copy of the whole tape for me: apparently they're doing a clear-out of an archive of local footage at BBC Wales, unearthing Sixties and Seventies stuff; interesting stuff, the guy she's spoken to reckons, though not all as spectacular as the material they showed yesterday. Stirring up a lot of memories round here, the guy says. Real honey pot, and more to come.

"Were you into drugs, mam?" she asked on the phone, cautiously inquisitive. "They all looked well out of it."

"I was more into, you know, political things. Moon goddesses and druids not my cup of tea."

"No, I don't suppose they were. I can't imagine it. Don't you think ... it's, well, time you spoke to the family again? Blood is blood, after all. They honestly couldn't have been nicer to me. Everyone asks after you."

"Well, I will: no, really, love, I will. Haven't had much time, Menna, what with setting up the unit here [...]"

All along the gossip-web, the tribe is doubtless back in touch, receivers nuzzling warm against elderly ears, lines buzzing with salacious or piteous shock.

– Did you see?

– See what?

– The girlie, our poor girlie. On TV.

– Not Francesca? But she's...so long gone.

– And for a moment her wraith would stand in the air like a wisp of smoke.

– A film with her on it. Singing.

– What was the programme then?

– About drugs.

189

– No! Drugs!

– Flower-power on the Gower, remember all that? Nearly died of shame.

– Well. There you are.

– Naked girls there were. Dancing!

– No one we knew, I hope. Well, they were quite a depraved bunch at one point, came down from the north of course.

–Tribe, they called themselves.

– Communards! I'll give you communards, I said. Never had to work for a living. Always had it easy, that's the thing. Not like in our time. Penny a day I got and Mama had it off me as soon as I was in the door. But these young ones, they thought money grew on trees.

– Remember the beardy one like a goat?

– Well, at least you can't smell them on a film.

–That's something.

– And look at Mara Evans now: big fish in the NHS, who'd have thought it, keeps herself to herself, mind. Better say reclusive rather than rude.

– Temper on her when a child, mind.

– Remember our girlie's eyes? Ah, God love her.

The recurrently warring Evanses, Menelauses and Thomases, inveterately fratricidal, occasionally litigious, hanker after one another terribly when they've stopped speaking and internal gossip sources dry up. They think of one another incessantly. Love each other warmly. Forget their differences. Lapse into a good-natured lull of uncertain longevity, passing round reminiscences like stale bara brith. Oh and what a relief it is to get back in touch, or even cross the threshold to where the teapot sits beneath its cosy.

In the street I bumped into a second cousin this morning: embarrassing that I could not remember her name, Becca, until she'd gone into the fishmonger's. But of course: Becca the Mouth. Where had I been? she wondered, without stopping to hear the answer. I remembered my mother casting up her eyes lamenting, *Oh what a talker! Does she ever stop? And gossip!* Becca said Uncle Tony had seen Jack. She tutted. Sitting outside the White Rose dressed as a Russian, with a fur cap and those flaps down over his ears. Looking skew-whiff, half-seas-over [...]

Whereas our relatives were joined by bonds of blood, we young ones were united by pure, elated, rebellious choice. *Inseparable they are, those lovelies*, our families said of us two girls when we were very small. We shared our dinner mathematically, to the last pea. Francesca and I would eat a banana starting at either end and working inwards. We were blonde and played up to the notion of being angels, false smiles rewarded by barley sugar or ice cream. Our egalitarian distribution was admired by all and praised by Uncle Pierce as a fine example of Socialism, by Uncle Tony as implying elect status, by our mothers as a sign of superior upbringing. We had our own private language before we acquired English or Welsh, which spooked some and charmed others.

I've no crumb of that language left on my tongue. The bananas I do remember and the ice creams: I licked, she licked; I licked, she licked. One bleated if the other suffered a bruised knee. But our touching sisterliness was policed by both parties, vigilantly mirroring eyes ensuring equality of distribution. Aaron we petted and occasionally slapped. He was one of three ductile Thomas boy-cousins, whose descent from the heights of Sketty brought our families out in their Sunday best. Annie was all gracious condescension, her boys the apple of her eye, especially Aaron, the gentle eldest. He bunched his mam's skirts in one fist, sucked the thumb of the other hand, and was not rebuked.

Eyebrows were raised in the gossiping wake of their reascent to Sketty. For whereas the Evans and Menelaus families had achieved a certain respectability, our means were modest. The Thomases owned a large house with four bedrooms, two bathrooms and what Aaron's mother was pleased to call 'land'. Annie was a queenly woman, who had married old money and extended invitations to 'Come over, dears, and eat a simple picnic in the grounds'. But what could you eat when you got there, the family puzzled, since it was all foreign food with spices that detonated coughing fits. [...]

I remember Frankie's father in the last winter of his life. Uncle David was out of puff, moved heavily, and stayed on a bench overlooking the bay at Caswell.

He waved, her dad, as we chased one another with bladderwrack. We waved. Then we climbed on the rocks, prising off limpets. We waved again. Higher and higher we climbed. Beyond the pools with their magical crabs and minutiae of shrimp. Above the barnacled limestone, till we had neared the cliff path, and, turning, looked down over the beach. There sat Francesca's dad, peaceful-looking, arms spread out to either side on the bench, wearing his old tweedy jacket. He looked straight out to sea, his corduroy cap on the bench beside him. His face seemed ashy pale. As I look back, I realise how wasted he must have been. I did not consciously see it then. I saw one of our dads, Francesca's and mine, eternal and dear. Ordinary.

We could not hear the labouring of his breath, the curdled lungs thick with tarry mucus. All our menfolk had coughs, many had emphysema. Their teeth were nicotined, their fingers stained. All

191

smoked as they talked, smoked as they drank, smoked as they washed the car. David didn't smell simply or predominantly of tobacco. He smelt of baking bread, of pastry and griddles, his baker's trade, though by then he must have given it up. And of smoke.

Francesea stood silent. Her thin arms dangled. The strap of one sandal had broken.

'My da,' she murmured.

In the grey sweep of the bay, he was a recessive figure. A grey man dissolving in a grey scene.

'My da's lungs is popped.'

'What?'

'My da's lungs. Popped.'

'Lungs can't pop.'

'My da's have.'

'If they'd of popped, he couldn't breathe.'

'He hardly can't.'

'He can so.'

'It's not the whole lungs. It's the baby pods in them. Your lungs are full of pods. Like seaweed. When you got what my da's got, your pods pop.'

He sat with his hands on his knees, looking concernedly over and up at us, shouting something, but the sound didn't carry. Francesca crouched on the peak of a rock-slab fiddling with her buckle. I considered popped pods. A chill went through me and I laid my palm over my own chest. Uncle David was beckoning now, in a rather frantic and uncoordinated way.

'He's calling us.'

'I'm not going back. It's not time.'

'We better...'

'It's *not* time.' She turned her back and began to climb again.

'But we haven't got a watch,' I protested. David was on his feet and looking helplessly across the bay. I stood still, between retreating daughter and panicked father. That beach must have looked immense to him, the rocks a fortress he couldn't even think of scaling.

'Uncle wants us.'

'Cowardy custard,' she threw over her shoulder. A stammer of rock fragments ricocheted from her climbing feet.

She dared me. Beyond that, she dared him. *Come and get me.* Beyond that, she was defying his death, his power to die, the steady haul of the line drawing him in. Frankie began to sing, a tuneless screeching that got into my fillings like paper on a comb. She refused to countenance the supremacy of the popped pods.

I obeyed their imperative. Shinned down and jumped the rock pools from bone to bone of the great limestone dinosaur whose innards held the tiny worlds of rockpool and caves. I ran to Uncle David.

'Good girl.' Though his voice was reedy and hoarse, he looked all right. Perhaps she had made it up about the pods. Frankie was full of lies and stories. 'Won't she come?'

I shook my head. But I knew she would come, now that I was with him, sitting here discussing ice creams beside the closed and rickety café. She would be angry that I stole her dad. Had him all to myself while she punished herself clambering about on boring rocks. I nestled in to him. Examined the buttons of his woolly waistcoat at close range. Heard tides surge in his chest.

Francesca came sauntering back over the sands, her skirt tucked up in her knickers, as if she didn't care. There was a clump of tar on her sandal. She shot me a vindictive look.

'You gave your old da a fright there,' he wheezed. 'Come when I call, my beauty girl. Next time.'

She whipped out a piece of bladderwrack, pinched a pod between her fingers and snapped one after another viciously in his face.

That is how I remember him, her lovely dad, who was also a little bit mine, and how it was not within the bounds of my limited comprehension that he'd gone, or where he'd gone. I sit at the window and try to focus her in the wake of his death. I know she looked for him, stopping dead and swivelling her neck, as if hearing his voice or catching his familiar smell. Tense and quivering she stood, her naturally pale face drained of blood. It was somehow violent, a shock to me, as if I'd heard the report of a gun but she'd been struck by the bullet.

from *Kith and Kin*, Chapter Two (2004)

Stephen Knight
At the Foot of Division Four

Ow footbawlTeem wares blackenwhite:
a angz a reds, a looks kuntrite
fuhlOozin, Homer N'weigh,
buhstill aisle go unwatchum-play
in Winter wenner Windsor blowin
9gaylz offaSee unthrowin
rubbish rowndee airmTee stanz,

blowin ice throo my airmTee ands.
John Toshack wozzer-marrNidjer-wenn
a roe-zupp 2 Division won.
Enner sighed wasFuller codjers
attee-endov Ayr Koreas;
e boreTum fuhPeenutz neigh played
foruh season. Nunnervumstaid,
uh-gnat wozzer long thymer go.
Now we backin Division Phaw!

Prap zitzer clymitt aura food
innease parts duzzEwe so muchgood
eye-dun-owe, buttie oldest laydee
inner Brittish Aisles livzbuymee,
inner Gnome. Givorrtayker year
ov breethin Saul tea Swornzee Heir
sheezer nundruden-nighn, unTV
filmzer birthdaze rare gullully.

Sheezlimp, tie-udd, uvairj Tubble:
ur riser bearLeigh vizzible
re-seedin inner-red: ur skinz
udared, crakt Riverbared nuthinz
swammerbuv frayJiz: wenner voyss
leex throo gapZinnerShrungkunFayce
shee sairz sodAwl turimEmber
(lyke pose cards senTin Dissember,

nuthin air Butter Sea nurry).
Air vreethin z'owld innis cuntree –
gray ills, gray trees Anna poe-stuh
s'been stuckon Neath stayshun frair-vuh:
iss flew-rare-sunt unrareLidjuss
wither quaresChunn inbiggLairtuzz,
aniss quaresChunn tare-riff-eyes me.
Where will YOU spend Eternity?
                                    (1987)

from *The Sandfields Baudelaire* (1996)

[from] Notes for a Poem Called 'Me Me Me'

When winds from the sea peel back the beach
  A wind from the sea tears down the beach

I'm trying
sentences
and phrases
in my head
Drifting off
thinking of
somewhere
Some things
never change

                  eyes and ears of sand
                       years of sand

In autumn, when winds assail the coast, sand reshapes
the dual carriageway: the grains abrade each tree
and every wall that faces out to sea:
dunes billow at the kerb: sand drapes
itself in grey, restless folds
on the empty roads

                  ★

Wild Frost? Coral Cloud? Or Mulberry Crush?
Your lipstick smudged on a tissue in my fist.

Apart from the ticking of the windscreen wipers,
your car is a fishtank filled with silence

till 'Everyone is well
but the wheels are out of alignment'.

Li's Garden is awash with drunks.
The muscles of your face have frozen shut.

While seagulls crap on the Crazy Golf Course,
the coast-line is blurred by advancing sand.

The trickle begins
'I hope that you're established
before I close my eyes for good'

at the promenade,
where the cenotaph runs with green.
My bag on the back seat slides from side to side.

Splashing
the dashboard, your voice is repeating
'Why did we move? ...' 'We can never go back ...'

The drive
from the station takes twenty minutes.
I smile like a synchronised swimmer ...

★

In the corners of rooms
  and in the cupboards of those rooms

furniture is piling up like photographs
  a houseful in a flat

nudging you both
  with the past

dried flowers, heads down, tied at the ankles
  hanging from the curtain rails

the plants that overflow their pots
  dragging their feet across the floor

the thick-set, whingeing drawer
  the tasselled lamp

and everywhere I look, a different clock
  the years of sand between us now

★

The wearing of flippers indoors
  is not allowed [...]

Sunday morning, the three of us out for a drive. Nursing the suspension, you ease the car along a pot-holed road to Sandy Lane, to the house where you first made a home together thirty-five years ago. Occasionally, I lurch to one side in the back seat, putting out a hand to steady myself.

I say 'house' but 'shack' would be more appropriate: *Golf View* is a beach hut built on the edge of Pennard links. In the photographs we have, my brother – who must be under five – sits on a tricycle on the veranda, staring into the lens. My grandparents look benignly down at him. Since then, the veranda has been enclosed and my brother's eyes are not as blue.

On the short walk there, you remark on the changes since 1953. Surprisingly few, it seems. Several huts have been cleared and there are circles of scorched earth through which, I like to believe, blades of grass will push. A pair of goats are tethered to a gatepost and there's a dog imprisoned in a makeshift garden. "Write a poem about this," my father suggests awkwardly. Poetry embarrasses him.

We talk about an odd mixture of subjects; mostly things arising from our visit. Mortgages, for one; and past mistakes. There are crumbs of information about my father's parents: how they lost everything in the Depression – sold their silver, their furniture, everything – and moved to London, where my father grew up. In later years, my grandmother would point out the house in Swansea where she knew her sideboard was.

Peering through the window of *Golf View* you think you recognise a mirror. If anything does come back to you, standing before that bright green shack with the glass-paper roof, you keep it to yourselves. You are, both of you, ageing like sand. I barely remember your profiles.

We leave, lurching back the way we came. It's autumn and things are going to sleep. I put out a hand to steady myself.

*

Overlooking
the sounds of the sea

at the bottom
of Mary Twill Lane

the whitewashed
Home For The Blind

is hard to the touch
all year round

The clocks
are turned back in October

Winter
is a cleaner smell

The pier and lighthouse
stammer all night

for tankers
moaning in the bay

like ghosts
like the Braille warning

stamped
on a bottle of bleach [...]

from Flowering Limbs (1993)

Double Writing

Sea View, Water's Edge, Atlantis,
lugubrious Guest Houses welcome the tide

after dark, from the opposite side of the road.
Their windows are lit with VACANCIES.

At closing time, Covelli's chips do a roaring trade
though his name has flaked from the side of the building.

Tighter than fists in the gaps in wooden benches,
pages of the local paper soak in vinegar.

Wind sizzles through trees
while, from the promenade, waves reach for the last bus

back into town. Ticking over in the back seat,
somebody sleeps it off. His thumb is in his mouth.

The timetable never works
and graffiti spreads through the shelter like wires –

refinements of a thick, black autograph
above the spray of glass, below the one-armed clock.

In West Cross garages, drums, guitars and microphones
huddle together, waiting to be famous.

Things go quiet. Things are unplugged.
Cutlery is laid out for the morning.

from *Flowering Limbs* (1993)

Penny Windsor
Heroines

We are the terraced women
piled row upon row on the sagging, slipping
   hillsides of our lives
We tug reluctant children up slanting streets
the push chair wheels wedging in the ruts
breathless and bad tempered we shift the Tesco
   carrier bags from hand to hand
and stop to watch the town.

the hill tops creep away like children playing games
our other children shriek against the school yard rails
'there's Mandy's mum, John's mum, Dave's mum,
   Kate's mum, Ceri's mother, Tracey's mummy'
we wave with hands scarred by groceries and too
   much washing up
catching echoes as we pass of old wild games

after lunch, more bread and butter, tea
we dress in blue and white and pink and white
   checked overalls
and do the house and scrub the porch and
   sweep the street
and clean all the little terraces
up and down and up and down and up and down the hill

later, before the end-of-school bell rings
all the babies are asleep
Mandy's mum joins Ceri's mum across the street
running to avoid the rain
and Dave's mum and John's mum – the others too –
    stop for tea
and briefly we are wild women
girls with secrets, travellers, engineers,
    courtesans, and stars of fiction, films
plotting our escape like jail birds
terraced, tescoed prisoners rising from the
    household dust
like heroines.

from *The Bright Field* (1991)

Chris Bendon
Swansea

If I could make a poem, as joky, sturdy,
flagrant or encyclopaedic as the streets of this city,
I would.

Secretive too; where is the cathedral?
I can only search high and
low, past Deco cafés, bistros, white Edwardiana
rhetorical against the late sky,
neon strips where life as it can be
is lived vicariously, I vicariously assume,
by insiders
until I come to the close sad streets of
– I almost said home. This, I say,
is where I'd live.

There's the tracks, the fencing
                the historical sea,
all seen through these rows of knowing curtains
qualifying the light of day in rooms entitled,
like volumes: Tredegar, Merlin, Elmwood,
even Timbuktu, Bali Hai;

rooms whose credit's confined to a visitor's stare
and those who live there in a limited way
(apart from grants for glazing or occasional bay windows)
– all too cramped and all in line

but in no guidebook or any known poem
except the obvious rhyme of the streets'
own making, certainly not mine.

I know. I like their squat defiance of logics,
their wit, their litmus tests of love.
And spoke to one who could recall
the night raids of years ago. Walked through
flashback corners of his mind,
streets coming to full stops or piles of bricks.
My mother died in just such a place;
of all ways to go, perhaps the best. Home.

I generalise, quite rightly;
repeat myself in shop windows,
am sunned indulgently.

I change a vowel and then a tense.
At last bump into you, owl-like in your glasses;
– can't understand much, a tourist without a guide.

from *The Urgency of Identity* (1995)

Nigel Jenkins
Swansea Haiku

tide in, skiers out
– dollar signs carved
from shore to shore

above the pines
Bonny Tyler's palace
outshines the moon

she introduces
her baby to his shadow:
he waves, it waves back

two men on the bus –
their noses declare them
father and son

caught
on the anti-theft t.v. –
can that balding scruffy pate
be mine?

in the dead hallway
a whiff of scent: beauty has passed
either in or out

quick march down High Street,
new strimmer at the slope:
a man with a lawn

and after the rain, more drizzle:
this weather melts no jellyfish

just once, down all these
aircooled aisles, the tasty stench
of human sweat

smacking lushly ashore
from the bay long becalmed
: the vanished ferry's wake

from *New Welsh Review* (1995)

Tony Conran
Hiatus in Swansea

1.
In this city-scape of flesh
Cells twinkle,
Change shape
Like neon adverts.
Slots in their chemistry
Communicate.
Yes. No. Yes. No.
Oxidation. Reduction. Oxidation.
Pushed into admittance
Like a sluice-gate.

Like skyscrapers the bones stand.
Brain-work. The pull of the heart.
The cleansing of blood. The breath.
It all seems so much in order –
Dangers dealt with
By key, by signature,
By telltale and anti-body.

The structure moves into its future.
Fantasy
Enlivens its motions.
Work sparks out from its coils.

2.
But in the dusk, a row of shopfronts, gaptooth,
Dawdled me down like a wino
To the convenience of grass –

Open space where nothing
Might not happen
But fuses won't blow.

The castle didn't rate
– Or not much – before
I sat down on its tump
Plastic bags awry
Sprawling on the manky laund of it.

3.
Even within talkshot
It seemed ignorable. As I'd say,
'That's a very little castle.'

Now upon the sloping lawn
For the first time
I attend to it.

It is not very happy
But it is not small.

4.
Under sentence
The past exerts itself,
Resists shrinkage.

Though continually it slips,
Lets go of its space
(– How small these ancients are! –)
Yet here is a castle.
Dinosaur ribs
Elbowing out from the rock.

It takes all the energy that went into
Castles – dinosaurs –
Even to salvage this much being big
Where neither key nor signature
Scavenge, nor tell-tale nor anti-body
Diminish to the dust ...

Even to stay put
As the structure moves into its future –

It takes the Earl's energy –
Tyrannosaurus rex –
Even to dawdle you down like a wino
Onto its sloping laund.

from *Castles* (1993)

Jonathan Mallalieu
The Church

I

Jack saw the pink house from the beach. Waking from a nap, he thought he dreamed the stucco walls and twelve sash-windows, savaged roof and central door. Though he daily traipsed from Newton to Blackpill, he had not noticed it before.

On the beach he piled sandcastles half-heartedly to pass the time. In contest with the sea, he re-sculpted the bay. The sea won over Jack, the city council won over the sea. Each autumn, bulldozers nosed the retreating sand back to the waves. And so it was that a man, a city and the sea came to be at war.

Besieged, he patrolled the bay. Napping on a different dune each day, his dreams of guerrillas thrusting petrol bombs under his canvas coat awoke him regularly at four. Mockery from passers-by did nothing to dent his war effort. He was a lone partisan against the city council, a terrorist in hiding from the law. In a daily concession to civilisation, he walked along the Oystermouth Road and into the White Rose for opening at five.

That afternoon, he paused to consider the unthinkable. He would alter the pattern of a life's monotony. He would adventure.

He tramped up and over the dune and verge. Perpendicular to his habitual trudge, he walked thirty paces. And by the high flint wall, he pissed a claim on wall and house and yard.

He had plans, he had faith in plans.

Having urinated at each corner of the derelict, he ventured over the border wall. He approached from the back. Avoiding the twelve-eyed glare of the mansion, unobserved by all save you and I, he trespassed.

The garden frothed to fill the walled plot. As he valiantly adventured, snapped grass-stems and broken elderflower sent up a pungent incense to his nose.

His nose, not bald, sipped the air, wary for antagonists. He sniffed for assailants. He had once been set upon by brigands who stripped boots and cap and coat. Muggers regularly turned him over, as he slept, to see what lay beneath. Thugs booted his behind as he waddled on a curving course from the bar to the bay. The city and even the dogs were his enemies.

Jack was not naïve about the imperfectibility of man.

The house had been bombed. Its eyes blown outwards, its roof scattered about the plot, it had rotted since the war.

A single ordnance dropped from a scarpering craft landed smack-bang in the upstairs loo. It tore balustrades and cornices to shards. It whipped the busts and statues to a moment's fission and left them mouldering on the lawn.

Beneath boots, he ground the nose of Apollo to dust. He stomped to a window. Peering through, he appreciated the total ruin.

Adventurous ivy had populated the premises. The spine of the plant had rent a gash in the wall. The house had been sliced into estranged halves, a cheese cleft by the wire of the plant.

Jack gained a purchase with his boot-toe on the stalk. He hauled himself aloft. He mounted step by step, handhold by handhold, up the sturdy plant. From the vantage of the roof he viewed the bay.

Five miles distant, the cement cubes blurred. A gust blew meringues of sputum from the waves. It flicked a lick of brylcreemed hair from Jack's nosy scalp.

As a rule, he frequented only the city's older districts. Those which bombers had gutted and architects had rebuilt held for him no magic. In his tramp from bed to bed, he elected to nose in only magically ancient worlds.

A sudden blast of wind as from a detonated device threatened to put a stop to both this tale and Jack's ambitions for the house. The gust nearly swept boots and their occupant from the ledge.

He was weary. He dismounted, not without caution.

Once down from the clouds, he rested in a grove of rhododendron and speculated on property in the air.

His voyage had tired him. Like all men of a certain age, he was anxious for a place of rest, a home to lease for his confinement.

He did not rush to secure property. He spent decades making notes on all sea-facing houses in these parts. Mother taught him well: the business of speculation was nine parts dozing, one part haste. Accordingly, following her death, he dozed for twenty-one hours and forty minutes each day. Most prudently, he divided the two hours twenty minutes haste between his afternoon constitutional and the stampede to his bed.

He had never owned property, not having capital. He had not inherited wealth, having thriftless forebears. He received a modest income from the state which with farsightedness he invested in his potential as a seer.

While dozing in the shading shrub, Jack foresaw the renovation of the house, how with his skills in architecture, painting and design, the shell might live with him in momentary rejuvenation, a flame coaxed reluctant from a dying coal.

He pulled up the coatsleeve from his one forearm. Mysteriously, his other had been misplaced in the trauma of birth. He set about a hasty start to his life's task.

Sixteen minutes remained before the landlord of the White Rose threw open his double doors and welcomed in the world. And Jack's appetite was greater than his ambition.

It drove him from his Eden as autumn gloom arose, evaporated from the hocks. He clambered over flints and in a half-run fled to where pump-handles drew half a quart of ale to his glass.

II

Jack discovered that through astute management of resources he could pay his way in the White Rose each morning and evening of the week.

To his inventor's mind this discovery was as great a leap forward as the devising of the wheel. It eased his passage from snooze to snooze and, as such, he preached, possessed all the ingredients of entrepreneurial genius.

Afternoons busily taken up dozing, wandering and speculating left only nine hours of night to organise. These could be obliterated in sleep, the location for which remained his bugbear.

He devoted his life to the solution of this puzzle.

Appetites for food, alcohol and sleep forced him into the exploiter's arms. To eat and drink and doze he must pay good money to a snitch. Pickpockets thieved his hoarded wealth, trumped up as landladies, barmen and waiters.

Life was a slow coming-to-terms with this reality. He made savings, he was no squanderer. Fleecing the feckless for drinks, shoplifting loaves and frozen fish, begging from the foolish pedestrian, flitting from lodgings, sleeping in the comfort of Oystermouth bus-shelter – these economies preserved monies for his great invention.

He was by necessity an early riser. His tormentors awoke him at dawn. Officious bus conductors commanded he move to less salubrious surrounds.

Big Barney Bucks sympathised but, with the incomprehension of the housed, could only offer poor advice to his mate.

Jacko, he slurred, I always said you should get yourself a place, haven't I? Haven't I?

Jack said that he had got himself a place.

He stared mournfully at the vastness of his mate whose generous contours gave him the look of a man jammed in a council bin, his head shivering with conversation, his arms like lagged pipes reaching to a neck a half-pint of ale with each swig.

Barney, Jack said, in hope of cutting short the flow of bad advice –
I have found meself a place – down road, biggish, nice – it needs a little
doing up.

How you got that, then? Sold your arse?

Just renting – just renting.

Rentboy! Barney spluttered, victoriously repeating the wit so it
should not escape the note of all. All ignored him. Jack continued to
apologise for finding a property despite his sermons against owner-
ship.

Barney, I need some advice.

Barney Bucks, plumber, master builder, tax evader and oracle was
placed in his element. He laid his arms about his sides, having no alternative.

His expertise covered all continents of the construction world, his
globe of a body all sites of renovation in the town. He could lay twenty
bricks a minute in a cool climate. He could plane square a twelve-foot
length of four-by-two without geometrical aids. He had built more
than one hundred houses in the vicinity, tombstones to his having
been.

To Jack's description of his designs, Barney whistled by inhaling
several litres of air through clammed lips. Shaking his head, he dismissed ideas to roof the house with old slates, fit new floors, leave old
beams be, paint over sodden plaster, frame glass in ancient slats. His
scepticism was complete.

S'pose you could, he began sadly, you could – at a pinch – strip
walls – start again – you'd bring the whole lot on your head – not
worth putting a penny in a derelict...

Again he inhaled. He was a black-capped judge passing sentence.
It was a solemn moment. Jack fled to refill tankards at the bar. On his
turn, Barney's head was still shaking in mournful half-revolutions.

Knew this bloke once. Never guess what he had planned – build a
detached three-up two-down slap bang in the middle of that there
beach! – that there beach there! Course, council wouldn't have it –
imagine! mid the boats and surfers – tides each morning and evening
– a home! Imagine raising three kids and a wife in that! – Wouldn't rate
his chances of them or the house staying – and look: the lot vanished
by morning!

Barney giggled, or rather he vibrated as a laugh exploded deep in
the core of him.

Jack sipped beer and wondered at the man who conceived such a plot.
He toyed with asking his name. He envied the imagination that saw no
barriers to where man might build himself a hut, that did not bow to

the gods of the common-as-muck mob, to common sense, to common law.

He vowed to press on, to ignore doubters' voices. At worst, he would become a story told by Barney Bucks in the White Rose bar. He offered his oracle a pistachio nut.

III

He moved his kitbag from a hole in the hills above Langland and stowed it in the hut at the end of the garden.

After clearing the ivy from within, he hacked with a stolen axe and clippers at the great stalk which clutched the back of the house.

With a scythe, he harvested grasses and elderflowers, convolvulus and dock. A lawn emerged. He broke into a gardener's lock-up in Newton Road and borrowed a mower. In bleak gloom, he brushed stripes on to the vast patch. Beneath the tangle of runners, briars and clematis he discovered paths, flagged stones testifying to an earlier civilisation. He pruned and cleaned, then in sudden glee hopped from stone to stone about his land.

Under cascaded ceilings, upper floors and ornament he found a tessellated floor, the marbles pure and unbroken. A layer of earthy debris concealed black and white squares from the damp.

Clearing this mosaic floor cost several days' labour. He put aside his mother's dictum on the division of his time. Mothers could not be obeyed in matters archaeological. Were she here, she would put up a fight. In her absence, he could alter the rules. Obedience to a dead goddess resurrects that divinity, restores her rule, relieves the obedient of the terror of making up their mind.

In courageous autonomy, Jack found a new serenity. He worked for six days without ceasing, save for sleep and recuperation in the White Rose bar. In the solitude of his walled plot he reconstructed earth. Safe from the sea and the city council, his pyramids remained in rockeries and castles, unobserved.

On the sixth day, having wheeled, in a barrow, all the rubble from the house and made of it a hummock at the foot of the lawns, he set to puttying paned glass into the sash-frames.

Smoothing paste along the crumbling bevels he fell to dreaming, mixing the tiled floors and moulding walls with the ghosted reflections of garden shrubs and path.

His eyes looked at themselves, traced the scorelines and crow's-feet, the gape of astonished mouth. As the light caught them, his few teeth mirrored cream, his ears eclipsed the distant wall. The silhouette of head was crowned with the swell of slickered silver hairs, and in the depths of the glass he swore he saw his double, a miniature resting on the garden wall.

He turned to scan swiftly the boundary. With terror, he feared he might be being watched. A cloud obliterated the sun, shadows dulled outlines. He laid the trowel and putty on the earth.

Wiping hands on thighs he patrolled. It was vital he convince himself not a soul was watching.

Even in the highest mood, Jack could not suffer for long the scrutiny of crowds. He lay on the sand for hours with closed eyes or sat entombed within a public loo just to stop being for a while.

Now here in this sterilised enclave it was more vital than ever to ensure he went unseen. If he could be without being seen, so much infliction would be relieved him.

He built up flints where they had fallen on his entry. With gates lashed more firmly together, house and garden were made impregnable.

He concluded his circuit and warily sat to lunch.

While working at a second-storey window he heard a voice:

Wha'choo doing that for?

He pretended not to hear, then grew fearful his unresponse would draw the curious close. He turned.

A brown figure insolently sat on the wall. Its head lolled to its chest, its arms splayed to support it. Legs without knee-joints pointed large feet at the mocked.

Jack stared boldly, then turned to work.

Don't want to go doing that, you don't!

The heat of the sun drew sweat to Jack's brow, the glass shone vivid blue. He slaved on.

House is finished, it is – di'n't nobody tell you?

A bird screeched in terror from the shrub. Jack turned, instinctive. The figure picked at stones, scattering fragmented flint to the soil.

Oi!

What!

Stop!

Why?

I said so!

S'not yours!

Tis!

How?

Jack had broken his silence, he clenched teeth in regret. Mockers, scoffers and cynics had distracted him all his life. Opening dialogue legitimised criticism. He would say no more.

But Jack was an impressionable man. He had no character to speak

of, but what he had was chiefly formed from the jabs of the imperti-
nent. He reeled.

You don't want to go doing that, mister – house is falling down –
nobody worked that house for fifty years – you's behind the time! Ha!
Bin ripped off, you have!

In the glass Jack could see the figure rise and tread the length of the
wall. It paused, turned, then balanced along another perimeter. Closer
to him, it leered, intent on seeing what was being done.

Go away! Jack whispered the stones.

He dropped inside the house to a scaffold made from stolen irons.
He sweated vigorously. The onlooker had rattled him. He thought
murder, but remembered mother's opinions on the matter. It would
not do to bloody his hands in this his hermitage.

He moved to other windows to peer at his tormentor.

The brown figure scampered along the wall, stopped, looked up for
several moments, scrutinising the house, then ran again.

Jack scuttled about, vainly searching for a weapon. He had not
expected attack. He toyed with the axe, rejected it and crouched to
view the figure. The sun peeped for a better look from behind a cloud.

It seemed to be a man by the crop of russet beard which frothed from
the duffle-coat hood. And it could not be older than he, it had an agility
he had not enjoyed for decades. It jumped fearlessly along the wall's
crown, never venturing into the plot, searching for a view in the windows.

Jack grew agitated, racing from peephole to peephole. He feared it
would actually venture further into the property, confront him,
assault, or worse, rape his handiwork. It was most certainly an agent
from the council, sent to terrorise him. He lost forever his serenity, the
work had been seen.

The figure vanished. Jack spent the evening searching the gardens
to determine it was gone, that it was not infesting the plants, that it was
not hidden in one of the crab-apple trees.

That night he avoided the White Rose, staying instead to fortify the
premises, to line the tops of the wall with shards of glass, to board up
lower windows, to secure the doors. He stole a ladder, entered a first-
floor window and hauled up the steps behind him. He was at last
permitted sleep.

IV

The rains came with autumn.

To shield his work, he stole a vast tarpaulin from a lorry park. He
bore it on his shoulders to the house. With ropes he slung it like a tent

out of view below the ribs of shattered roof.

He sealed its edges with an ingenious guttering. The great sail of ceiling flapped in the storms, as if with flapping it might lift the house airborne or drive it out across the prom and on to waves that boiled in the bay.

The house resisted flight or launching. Jack worked dry and gloomy in the ark to the rattle of the roof. The rains sluiced along guttering and fell to the beds.

The lighting was the key, the way to perfect the illusion. He occupied days with wiring a set of fourteen lamps, carefully shaded to conceal the green canvas ceiling. The circuit was connected to the mains on the tenth day. The cavernous hold of the house blazed yellow.

He slung blackouts at every window. As if bombers might again cause catastrophe and render his world a shell, he flicked on lights only when each pane was shielded by a veil.

Desire to perfect the closed interior drove him. Taking Barney's counsel he stripped the rotten plaster from all walls. The labour cost him many exhausting hours, the obsession his evenings in the bar.

He was neither young nor old, nor ever had been, but the toll of labours such as these hastened ageing in his insufficient limbs. His arms grew muscular but scarred. His hair, ungreased, flowed thinly upwards in a cloud of silver; his eyes, reddened by the oyster's itch of dust, saw less well the vaulted ceiling and instead scrutinised the beauties of the floor.

Weeping at the hopelessness of ever plastering all four walls alone, he wished for sons, three sons with whom he might share the insane labours of his muddled mind.

But his numerous deformities dissuaded any woman from consenting to his plaints. No girl let him mount her to dispose of his cumbersome virginity. His chance to rear sons died with his youth when, one girl seeming inclined, he had refused, thinking another might respond. To refuse a hinted possibility is to refuse the woman, and no others ever offered Jack a hint.

He waited, life-perpetuating optimism hoping for a chance. But his only company for decades took the form of Barney Bucks, a certain Mickey Bocks and a rapist, Mr Charlie Bick.

The three visited Charlie in his lodgings at the city jail – where he passed much of his not unhappy adult life, doling out observations on the female sex to Barney, Jack and Mickey Bocks.

Knowing him to be of an impressionable cast, Charlie suggested to Jack that he simply grab a woman and ignore her finer feelings on the matter. Jack failed ever to let this ideal become an act. His admiration for his mother, added to his own dread of brigands, fiends and thugs, made rape an inadmissible crime against himself.

Jack was exiled from the sexual world. As his appetites were most highly developed, this testifies to a resilience of character I had not thought he possessed.

Barney, Mick and Charlie wasted no time telling him of the difficulty of woman-handling. But with soft affection for his mother, Jack recalled a time when a woman had shown more fascination for his soul than all the men he had ever known.

And in a moment of extreme fright, he remembered that he had no friend in the world, that he had forgotten the years of his solitude, that aloneness only pained him when he looked back over its many years.

He suddenly wanted to befriend his antagonist. The brown-coated figure appeared every evening in the arbour, materialised from the tawny alders then faded to a cone or leaves awaiting bonfire.

It was insanity, to want an association with his scoffer. And yet if they could come to some agreement or better, familiarity, the dream might be realised.

Jack had not stopped ruminating on the figure since its first appearance. He loathed it, he adored it, he wanted only to murder it, he wanted it to become a friend. While labouring he feared it would bring the house crumbling about his ears.

Worry at this end drove him harder, as if by creating his inner vision he would quash the ambitions of his twin.

Jack has, his doctors tell me, always suffered from delusions of oppression. They insist he is a free man, to his disbelief. He is free to do just as he wishes, he has no enemies. He begs to disagree. He knows of the evil in man.

He hung white sheets over the blistered walls, great shrouds through which the pale light of unshuttered windows made oblong murals. The cosmetics were almost complete.

To furnish the palace, he exceeded himself. On two nocturnal raids, he burgled antique shops. Four studded Regency chairs, a huge vase and a Persian rug were smuggled into the cathedral of the house.

In disturbed solitude, he sat enthroned, bored by completion, smoking a cigar butt, farting inaudibly to himself for want of company.

V

He looked over what he had created.

With parts of it he was not displeased. He paid particular attention to the stone outside the rear door on which he had intended of a night to dry his boots.

He felt, however, considerable distress at the shoddiness of the prior artificer's work. Poor beams, inept plastering and a lazy choice of window woods excited his disdain.

And closer inspection of his own incautious stringing of the roof, his hurried wiring, his rush to fortify the lower floors, his forgetfulness where kitchens and servants' quarters were concerned – all these brought on a fit which left him shivering on the floor.

He despised his workmanship. He loathed his impatience. But most of all he regretted his wish to see his reverie made real in wood and stone.

That was the folly. To have presumed his vision might be duplicated in stiff, resistant elements, that was idiocy – a child's hope at recreating for his mother an illusion that had gripped his mind.

He took a hold on drifting sheets and strapped the hemp of it about his wrist. He repeated the distracted action about his stump. He would hang for a while.

Murmuring regret to his half-hearing ears, he let himself become suspended on the veils.

He kicked his feet and shrieked without enthusiasm, part hoping some invader would burst in and laugh. Then he fell.

A small fire was started by the explosion of fourteen lanterns. On striking the tiles, they disintegrated, the heated coils igniting oiled canvas, cotton and Jack's hairs.

For some time he thrashed about beneath the descended roof in a Samsonian struggle with the cloth.

Emerging, he found the ropes and wires and sheets of his most temporary world about his feet. Deprived of his silver hair and the uppermost layer of facial skin, he howled and bawled as if his shrieks would make his melodrama great.

No one wept, no one stirred with empathy. No one visited to calm his noise, nor to bathe his wounds. The curious were blocked by sealed gates and barricaded doors. The echoed squeals set off a sympathetic howling among local hounds. A while passed and neighbours grew relieved at the quiet.

Much later, on discovering the hidden ladder, Jack clambered from the charred but largely unchanged house. From without, it remained as it had been, a shell mocking interior decorators.

He expended much excess energy by many times kicking an inner wall. It remained intact, unlike the larger of his ten toenails.

The mutilation of his face and hand was aggravated by an over-eager mounting of the wall. Forgetting his farsighted installation of sharded glass, he rent the blistered palms and chin as with a slap he hauled himself aloft.

Without a bed, he slunk to the beach and, with much emotion, reunited himself with the sand. He burrowed a shallow grave and with the excavations built a modest pyramid to mark his presence. He laid his bruised decrepit body in the pit and buried all but a hooded head in beach.

And as he slept, the muddied waves corroded the contents of his kitbag, his mother's photograph and his spare boots. Gnawing gently at his tomb, waves ate round his ankles, under arms and behind his neck. In his first good wash for weeks, the sea lapped at his lugholes and plucked the wax from nose and eye and ear. He dreamed, smiling.

Totally immersed, the baptist failed to see the dove descending to the flooded beach.

from *The Prince of Wales and Stories* (1993)

Don Rodgers
Tycoch

I saw, when you said it, a house on a hill
as red as a dragon, holding in thrall
the anglicized semis and estates, that blenched
at the mighty name of 'Tycoch', like vassals
cowering before its mythic magnificence.
But when I got on the bus in the Quadrant,

the driver couldn't understand my accent,
and asked me: "Is it Tea Coke you meant?"
Thus I discovered our new home was called
after colonial beverages. Nodding my assent,
I repeated after the teacher: "Coke and Tea";
and tendered him an inexact image of the Queen.

from *Multiverse* (2000)

Alun Richards
Someone Out There

The cry was at the back of the throat, like an animal's, hardly human. It couldn't shape a word. There was not a recognisable syllable, but it came from within; despair, terror, and exhaustion too. An awful sound. Truly awful. And then half-choked sobs, like footsteps between one abyss and another. It was the sobs that made it human, that told you: *"There's someone out there...A Person...There...Somewhere...But where?"*

First the dawn, one of those early mornings you could hardly see because of the mist rolling in, the siren on the lighthouse moaning at intervals – one sharp, one long – and all along the sea front every noise was somehow enclosed by the mist as if everything was happening inside a paper bag. Drop a key and the clang was hollow, muffled, and across the road a high spring tide sucked against the sea wall, its lapping also muted like someone slapping a child a long way off. Everything was close, yet everything seemed distant and even the battery hum of Maxie Keefer's milk float might have been out in the Bay, not just around the corner. You could hear it but you couldn't see it and you didn't know where it was coming from. (Later, the woman's first cry was like that, lost, disembodied, enclosed; somewhere out there ...)

From my bedroom window I could see the masts and halliards of the sailing dinghies chained to the Hard opposite but the wall obscured their foredecks and that too was eerie because the masts looked as if they were hanging down, not standing up. This is what mist does when it's that thick, but it wasn't cold or really damp like a winter mist, and, I suppose, from a visitor's point of view, in the few yards you could see, in front of you, everything looked normal. You were in your own little world, just you and nobody else; cut off, enclosed.

At least, that's what I suppose the woman felt. I hadn't seen her then and I never saw the child. There was a boarding house next door but one, but it was going down, 'no class at all', and although they did a few bookings, it was mostly casuals. But the woman was a booking because of the child, we later learned. She had been there before. Only she couldn't tell anybody. She was one of those unfortunates who have no roof to their mouths, my mother said. But this was later, all later. At the time nobody knew in which boarding house she was staying. There were nineteen dotted along the front.

So... at six o'clock there was just me hanging out of the window, the sea lapping across the road and the hum of Maxie Keefer's milk float. I knew Maxie was chancing it because he wasn't sixteen and didn't have a licence. Sid Fairfax, the real driver, got himself dropped off at a widow's he knew, Maxie'd do half the round, then pick Sid up again, Sid giving himself a spell most mornings. There was a lot of gossip about that, but Maxie handled it in a very diplomatic way.

"Where's Sid?" people said in that knowing way.

"Suh-Suh-Suh-Sid likes his greens," Maxie'd say with his cheery stammer, that half-melon grin creasing up his pinched face, the basin-cut hair style falling over his ears, his fingers checking the list to remember his orange juices and creams where the bonus was. That, and no more. He was always on the move and he was willing. He wasn't very bright, not three ha'pence short of a shilling, just not very quick on the uptake. In school, the woodwork master had a nail cabinet, three drawers, all different sizes of nails, tacks, bolts. If they got mixed up, he'd empty the lot on the floor, then send for Maxie to sort them out.

"Job for you, Maxie!"

"I'll huh-huh-huh-have a go!" Maxie said. Happy as a sandboy doing that, sitting cross-legged on the floor. He spelt no trouble for anyone. They didn't seem to notice the sores on his legs, his thinness, the years he went without proper meals. You notice people who complain. Maxie just had a go. He wasn't from the village outside. But he came every day.

That morning I heard the hum of the milk float, then it stopped. I couldn't hear any footsteps at all, then the cry came, the first one. You won't believe it, but there'd been a fox on the mudflats that summer. We'd had bracken fires everywhere and they said the fox was short of prey and had come right down the cliffs, patrolled the beach, then went out on the mud, waited, sprung, and caught a seagull. You've got to be fast to do that. The fox was fast. It had never happened before, not in living memory. But it happened. There were feathers everywhere, and pad marks on the beach, and the scrape of his brush. And it had been seen, a dog fox, long legs. And so, hearing the sound, I mixed it up in my mind. I didn't know if a fox howled like wolves did. I wasn't a country person. And the sound was so unnatural, I mean.

So I paid no attention. I dismissed it. I heard it first and I dismissed it! There was no sign of the mist lifting so I pushed up the window and went back into my bedroom. Everyone was asleep so I got back into bed. Just lay there. Oh, the times I've thought about that! I heard it and I did nothing. Nothing! I just went back to bed. And I could've been a hero! But I went back to bed.

The next thing I heard was Maxie running, his daps flapping – he always had a loose sole and the laces were too long – then voices, the splash and the shout, and the woman again.

I went to the window. But you still couldn't see. It was further along from us. And the mist was getting thicker. I thought I'd dress. Might as well. I put on a matloe's jumper, crewe neck, the wool hard. You could brush mackerel scales off it, but it itched. So I took it off, found something else, then shoes, down the stairs, unlocked the front door, put the clip back. They wouldn't let me have a key of my own. I had to ask always. That hurt. Then I went out.

I still couldn't see anything happening. The mist was thickening. I crossed the road, climbed over the wall on to the Hard. The tide was high, up to the top of the sea wall, and in the water below me you could see a mess of flotsam, a semi-circle of it, weed, timber wedges, a twisted bundle of lobster twine and netting. The tide was beginning to run now but the rime was still there, close by the steps, enough to put you off swimming. because it looked so dirty. But further down ...

I heard the woman again, moaning now, a deep moaning in the chest, but it seemed a long way off to walk. I was curious, but half-scared. I thought, sometimes people on holidays fight. Couples, I mean. They get in the pub and have real up-and-downers. The women were worse than the men, my mother said. The thing to do was keep away. For a second, I thought it might be one of those.

I went on, still peering in the mist. Then I saw her with her back to me, thin, roundshouldered, an old black overcoat down to her ankles, her hair in a turban like the factory girls. She was reaching down over the sea wall to receive something, breathing now in short convulsive gulps as if she'd had a fit. Then there was Maxie, coming up the wall like a seal, soaking, his hair plastered, his clothes clinging to him. You could see the line of his underpants through his sopping trousers.

It looked like he was handing her a bundle. The woman seized it, turned and ran away, her back to me. Maxie was halfkneeling, laying across the top of the sea wall like a bent sack. He had no breath. He was panting – great sobs, looking at the stones, his eyes frantic, staring, as if he'd thought he'd never see them again. I could hear the woman hurrying away, scolding, but never finishing the words.

"Yaw ... yaw ... yaw ... yaw ..." all in the back of her throat.

And then she was gone and I could hear the fog siren and Maxie's gulping.

I remember going up to him and keeping away because he was so wet. There was stuff coming out of his mouth too. He didn't see me. I thought: "Look at the state of him – he'll cop it!" I bent over him.

"Maxie ..."

He looked up. He still couldn't get his breath back. You could practically see his ribs through his shirt, all moving. He looked for her. She was gone. Then he said:

"She was talkin' to me."

"What?"

"She was talkin' to me, the little girl. Under the water. She was sittin' on the sand talkin' to me. Under the water. Down there ..."

The bundle was a little girl.

"Did she fall in?" He didn't know. He'd heard the woman, saw this shape in the mist, went over. The woman kept pointing to the sea but he couldn't see anything. It was flat calm, nothing to see. But the woman caught hold of him, tugging, groaning. She was so fierce she tore his shirt.

"Down there, Missus?"

She kept nodding, dribbling.

"She couldn't speak proper," Maxie said.

So he went in. Dived. At first, he couldn't see anything. The tide moved the child down. It was no more than a few yards from the wall, but it was a big tide, seven foot of water and the child sitting down there, talking to him, a little girl, her hair swirling around as if in the wind. But it was under the water.

He couldn't understand that.

"She must've been nearly drownded", he said.

It didn't seem possible. It didn't seem to have happened. We went back over the road to the milk float. We didn't know what to do.

"Nearly drownded. Definite," Maxie said.

There was nobody about. Nobody you could ask. We just stood there. You couldn't see a soul. Then we heard a motorbike. It was Bunty, one of the lifeboat boys, coming off shift in the docks. Maxie wandered into the middle of the road, stopped him. He could see by the state of Maxie something was wrong. We explained. The woman had just picked the child up and run off. There was something wrong with her. "Mental, like. Definite. She couldn't talk. Just, like – gruntin'," Maxie said. The child wasn't talking either. "Nearly drownded." What to do?

Anything like this happens, you're glad when someone takes over, and Bunty was the boy for taking over. In minutes, he had them all there, police, coastguard, and just about everybody else out on the street. And very soon that picture was in everybody's mind, the little girl sitting on the sea bed, talking under the water.

What they did, they turned out the boarding houses. *Was there a woman with a child ?* I don't know when they realised – who put it together, I mean – that the woman wasn't quite right in the head. It was her own child, but she'd stolen it from foster-parents, come down for the weekend to where she'd been before. Somebody told us this later – *came down to where she was happy once.*

They found the woman and the child, cuddling up in bed. She was pretending nothing had happened. The curtains were pulled. It was warm in there in the dark. It hadn't happened. It was all right.

But it wasn't. They did artificial respiration in the bedroom. No good. Then the ambulance, hospital. No good.

And that was the end of it. There was a lot of talk after, bits and pieces of information, what people thought they knew.

"Wasn't it awful? A little child like that? And the intelligence of the woman? I mean, I ask you ..."

First, Maxie was in big trouble. And Sid Fairfax. Maxie'd left the switch on in the milk float. The battery went flat. By the time Sid had left his widow and come looking for Maxie, the Boss had come down from the depot in another float, saying that both of them were going to get the bullet. The rumours had got back to him, he said. And look at the state on Maxie! "Was that any way to make deliveries of a pasteurized product?"

It was Bunty who spoke up. And the Police; and, in the end, Maxie got a medal. *"Although not a good swimmer, acting on his own initiative, he did not hesitate the moment he realised a life was in danger."* And that was that.

But when the mist is thick, I hear the woman's voice still. It is as if all the world's pain is echoed in it.

"There's someone out there. A Person ... There ... Somewhere ... But where?"

And Maxie: "I'll huh-huh-huh-have a go!"

from *Mama's Baby (Papa's Maybe)* (1999)

Tudur Hallam
Bryn Road

From our house in Swansea town
on the town side there's a sports ground
a stadium. From my study,
nice and quiet, I can see
the men, their faces a white hue,
like wives, a close-knit crew
in the stand, the screech of their call
as you hear them beg for the ball:

220

is as wild as any hen-night
one hell of a shout. "You All White?"

And it's the sound of *hwyl*, St Helen's;
where the shocked faces of men
watch Gibbs, as wide as his field,
crash the defence, make them yield,
release with his pass – out to Garin –
the team for the distant tryline,
and the afternoon crowd aflame,
the clamorous, clinching cup game.
Their heaven, young or old,
on the North Bank, is their world.

This is the stadium of the study – St Helen's,
which gives me my rugby,
though nothing but Llanelli
can gladden the heart of me.

Because there's constant *hiraeth*
in my captive inner life
for some street where the Stradey
still brightens the South for me,
and Wyatt and Matt and Moon
inspire me to devotion
a quickening song, like Quinnell,
a religion, a Ray Gravell.
What better team than Llanelli?
That's the stadium's thrill for me.

Yet all the same, look and see,
the piercing light of the enemy
studding my study's wall tonight.
Doesn't it blind my sight?
I'm an impediment, a foreign man,
a betrayal, two wringing hands,
am my heroes, am another,
am for the posts, am a blind watcher,
am far away, am Llanelli,
am strong, am weak, am Swan-sea.

But all the time in my study - I know well,
though exiled by Tawe
that they can't take Llanelli
tonight ever away from me.

from *Cerddi Abertawe a'r Cwm* (2002), ed. Heini Gruffudd
translated by Grahame Davies

Robert Minhinnick
Paradise Park

GOD. IT WAS COLDER THAN EUROPA. That little world in its
locket of ice. Over near Jamhal's a man was setting up a flower stall. You
didn't often see those at this time of year but he said hello which was fine.
Ignoring him was fine too and gave her a buzz because what does anyone
expect? Then she went past the blue blockhouse and there she was,
Sladie Beaver 9T9, in big letters at the back. Lady that was no way to
behave. Better dead than read. A few kids were hanging about but the
teams were already inside getting changed. For another grudge match.
For another world cup final on the park at the top of the world.

Strange to see the car burnt out. What was missing was the paint.
There was no colour anymore only the bare metal smoked and rusted.
And the roof so low because the tyres were gone. The wheels were still
there but all that was left around them was wire. Bunches of it like old
wreaths in the crem. And the mousetraps of the brakes. Where the seats
should be were the springs. And where the dash should be was an empty
space. All the rubber melted off the pedals. And on the floor the melted
plastic was like some kid's abortion left under a sheet. Three large chips.
Three minicods. Three gravies. Five bread rolls because he'll be starving after the match. Three large cokes. And something else. No it's gone.
There's definitely something else but it's gone. I'll come for them at five.
Yes, it is cold.

With her girl and her boy she goes to the library behind the security
fence and the librarian releases the door electronically. Thirty minutes
later they have the picturebooks in the shopping bag: a blue giant; an
artist's impression of *The Singularity*. Must be a hell of an artist. She
goes down Merlin and this time almost forgets to look, even though the
day is clear. But at the corner she points. There is the sea, white as a
steamiron's hotplate. Then between the houses her children glimpse the
three headed creature which is sometimes there in the ocean. Then the

thin line of silver like the ink for Christmas cards drawn along the shore. As far as you can see. As her mother said: You've got the views so make the most. On a clear day.

What you wear is who you are. Out of the metal bunker they come and it could be Inter, could be Real, because the kits are that good, yes immaculate, the keepers leaping like harlequins, clapping their gauntlets together in the cold, the captains gesturing already at phantasms that await down the touchline or across midfield, and the referee is in black as if black was neutral – but when was black ever neutral? – and no linesmen, it's not that important, the professionalism here is in the intent, in the ritualism that starts by standing naked in that blockhouse, tightening the strap under your scrotum, already shrunk-red and wrinkled as a peachstone, then pulling the shirt over your head, fingering its strange insubstantiability, and the number on it more exciting than your own name, for you are now 1 or 2 or 7 and you possess all the arcana of that number because you carry its spell out into the proving ground, you are branded with your number on Paradise Park, where the earth soon will be more pitted than the thin white daylight moon that rides the bay, by the fusillades of studs, that iron hail, by men chasing their own lives across a whitelimed field and making such a spectacle that other men will come to stare. In their black fleeces. Will come to judge. In their black balaclavas. Men turned loose with time to kill. Thinking that maybe this will be enough.

She pushes her breasts against the counter. Where her daughter with glittery eyelids is dangling her feet. Where her son is playing with the vinegar bulb which she always liked to hold herself. Because of its dimples, cold and prickly. So she picks it up. Too good for vinegar somehow. And there is the salt cellar she can remember the man in school said looked like the constellation of Orion. Like the Ford, remember. If you looked. If you really cared to look. If you stood out on Paradise Park on a winter night and looked over the bay. Weather and everything else permitting. Because he knew there was always a lot of everything else. Or turned the other way where there was less streetlight. To Polaris over the hills that rose blue as mosques from under the mist. And then to the left where the chemical works was brighter than Las Vegas. The fizzing ampullae of an industrial town. Behind them the flame from the steelworks leaning over in the wind. And that man had also said something like da da da the rag and bone shop of the heart. He had read that out. Well, sir, she'd said. That's not bad. But what about the litterbin of the mind? How the others had laughed. How their eyes had loved her then. What she didn't say was that teaching you to think wasn't teaching you to live. Sir. Like how were you supposed to know? Because now look at it all. Are you looking now? Sir?

It's the wind that wins. The wind that terrorises the hill. Low and hard, says 2, but when he launches the ball it blows back over his defence. The striker nips in but blasts wide. How his own side vilifies him, the young man in his armorial silks. Noone else volunteers so he must chase the ball across the mountaintop and into Paradise View. And how diffident he is, away from the white net. How polite with his huge hands open and empty, a little blood already over an eyebrow, the Paradise skidmarks down one leg. There are decorations in every window here, those electric candles beginning to show in the late afternoon. The ball's gone over the reservoir. Some kids get under the barbed wire and bring it back. He can hear 2, guttural behind him. Hard and low this time. Yeah, yeah, wait till tonight. There'll never be an end to it. But it's the wind that wins. It's playing them off the park.

Very dark now. Three weeks left and Christmas decorations in every house. Cartoon reindeer, aerosol snow. Walking away past Our Lady you can see right into the docks. Two ships berthed under the floodlights and the ferry coming back with every deck ablaze. A 13 crawling up the hill. She's got the rest of the groceries from Jamhal's and watches the man on the flower stall pulling polythene off the bunches. He snaps the stems, smashes the heads against the kerb. Big yellow dahlias bursting like belishas. She looks away from a private act. But it reminds her of the time that car went over the quarry. A boy from the special school had taken it. They called him Headshot because he drank vodka and white lightning that his dad bought for him in Victoria Wine. Only fourteen, which was impressive. He rolled the Astra down the the slope and the petrol tank exploded. Headshot was good with cars. Screwdriver in the keyhole, crowbar through the steering to snap the lock, then the applied science of hotwiring. Ninety seconds for a Vauxhall, Headshot used to say. A yellow ball of fire gathered itself in the air before bursting into streamers. The pylons behind had been hung with flame. Champagne supernova, like those Chinese poets saw, writing in the light of an exploding star that was brighter than moonlight. Everybody was cheering and then the smoke started coming up thick and black and there were sparks where the bracken had been set on fire and sparks falling out of the sky like tiny hatchlings that lay hissing and blinking on the road as if they might have been alive. She trod on one of the spitting things, a red spider that ran across the slabs. Headshot's greatest moment. Headshot, Headshot, the kids were chanting. King of the Hill.

The books are on the table and the children drawing with the glitter and silver ink. Cards for Nana. Cards for Miss. And in her own book one page open to a black tunnelmouth. In its centre an even blacker point. Where noone has ever been. Where noone will ever be. Darker than the rag and bone shop? Oh much darker. Because that black spot was where it was all happening. The Singularity. If she ever owned a club that's what she'd call it. Not the Zone, not the G-Spot, not even the Zodiac. The Singularity. Where it all ended up, time, space, the orange batter round the minicods. Nothing so grand it didn't get sorted out by ultimate gravity.

It's her turn this Saturday so she'll be going. Off the 13 down the Kingsway. Platinum discodiva top from Peacocks above the black split-sided and the black string and the platinum heels. A swab of Heliotrope behind each ear. And the snow blizzarding as the aerosols go to work and she'll never have been so cold as they crowd down Wind Street and into the Passage. She with her Stellas. Kath and Ceri with their Pils. But no chance will they be going anywhere near the football boys because sometimes you think if you hear that *Delilah* sung once more you'll puke your ring up. All over their nice clean chinos. Something singular tonight if you please. So maybe the meteors around the face. Maybe the aldebaran in the naval because it was still there despite the kids. Got to keep the stargazers happy

The show's scorching and he goes back to the folded packet of his clothes. So neat you could post it, says Gee, next up the bench. Someone's got an Adidas full of Grolschs and the first one goes down when he's still naked and scalded and if ever there was a cure for what you were sickening for or whatever was working you over from the inside because some bastard thing was always doing that then this is it and put this cold one on your balls says Gee because it's got to be as good as sex anytime and that's what you're supposed to do in saunas anyway you stupid twat don't look at me like that because I never done any uphill gardening in my life ever.

Or maybe it's his turn. So will he be going? In the bathroom he presses himself, hair moussed in twists, sticking up like sweetpapers, a bruise around the cut he got in the game, the proudest thing he'll wear all week. And him barearmed too but not feeling it. The anaesthetic kicking in. He'll stand at the bar with the hundreds, the thousands, the younger ones loud, the fortysomethings still blown from the park but keeping up, quieter, watching the dancefloor traffic, who's in, who's stuck at home, if there's a chance, because what's it all about anyway if you haven't got a chance, the dancefloor exhausts pumping out their dry ice, and there he'll be on the screens, on every screen, close up, famous, laughing. Hiya luv. For five seconds. Number 1.

You go.

No you go.
You go.
It's your turn.
You go.
I doanwannago.
Well I doanwannago either.
Okay no fucker goes.
Brilliant.

Get some kebabs. Get a video. Walk around by the park and realise
that this is high as you'll be. Counting the five pences in your pocket you
poured out of the Old El Paso jar. Forget the presents get some Stella.
Yeah Stella. And look at the city. That orange fog climbing up the hill.
Must be radioactive down there tonight. Kath and Ceri and Gee gone
down on the 13, snowspray on the bus windows and the flowerbloke's
black panicles stuck to its wheels. Then furthest away the ferry. The
ferry in the dark like a burning car falling ever so slowly over the rim of
the world. Yeah, insane down there tonight. Mad as the milky way.

from *To Babel and Back* (2005)

Mari George
Swansea Beach

August was listening intently...

But only you and I heard
the melodies of the waves
wrapping their necklace
about the beach
and giving a goodnight kiss
to the tourists.

August was listening intently...
for the peace,
for the chance to sweep the rubbish
and scour the beach,
and kick the Bud bottle of their anger...
for hearing nothing but
the clink of bottles
from the pubs

and the cough
of a fisherman.
August listening intently
to us two
listening to the last melodies
of our holiday camp beach.

from *Cerddi Abertawe a'r Cwm* (2002), ed. Heini Gruffudd
translated by Grahame Davies

Kathryn Gray
The Italians in the Rain

You could almost see them down the backstreets
as it bucketed on a Saturday night, the purr
of a Vespa, his right foot pressed on the kerb,
as he leans over, calls to a girl, and she parleys
a while, then hops on, wraps herself around him.
Or along the sea front, in the mirrors of Sidoli's
where a couple share a Neopolitan with one spoon,
the crest of biscuit between them, fight out
who gets the strawberry and who the chocolate.
You think it's just possible that she always knew
what he'd done with her best friend, and sister.
Quicker than the grabbed coat and clipped heels,
from Landore to Y Crwys, now you hear
the parked Fiats as they creak at the beauty spots,
slapped faces and the smashed bottles outside the bars.
And maybe you see there is a man who lifts up
the fryer with its welded batter or does the books
on a stool by the till, the packets of coffee on the shelves
behind him. There's a watercolour of St Mark's
or the Trevi fountain under the arrow to the toilets,
and as this rain shows no sign of stopping, he looks on
it all, gestures at two passers-by who try the door
a WE ARE CLOSED, returns to his work, forgets
                                                        where he is.

from *The Never-Never* (2004)

Driver

Where exactly on this road it was they dipped
their heads, got in and were driven away
to be back in bed - as they'd said - by eleven,
no witness could remember or agree, but as we go
along at about 70, and you turn the radio up,

I start to think of their laughter, their arms held out,
thumbs straining at the cars that passed them,
the way they might have pushed each other,
swayed, and then a Ford slowed, his face lowered,
he leaned over as the nearside window wound down.

One goes in the front and turns to her friend
again and again, and it could be any other night.
Knitted sleeves rub on the brown leatherette.
Here and there a stray fibre falls. He says nothing,
turns off just before the lights to Jersey Marine.

It is already behind us in the rear-view mirror.
And when we stop, the two of us slam the doors,
watch the boot of your car go around the corner,
it's then things occur: the coiled length of washing
line I saw, a blue sweater I left on the back seat.

from *The Never-Never* (2004)

Biographical Notes

Dannie Abse (b.1923), was born in Cardiff and educated at University College Cardiff and Westminster Hospital. He qualified as a doctor in 1950 and worked for many years as a specialist in a London chest clinic. *Selected Poems* (1994) was followed by *New and Collected Poems* (2003). Abse has published novels - notably *Ash on a Young Man's Sleeve* (1954) and *The Strange Case of Dr Simmonds & Dr Glas* (2002), the latter long-listed for the Booker Prize - autobiographical writings and plays. He has homes in London and Ogmore-by-Sea.

Graham Allen (b.1938), born in Swansea, was educated at the University of Wales, Swansea, and Cambridge. He was Senior Tutor and Vice-Warden of Coleg Harlech. He has written poetry (see *Out of the Dark*, (1974)) and stage and radio plays. In his retirement he has returned to live in Swansea.

Kingsley Amis (1922-95), was born in London. After St John's College, Oxford, and a short period at Leicester University, he lectured at University College Swansea for ten years from 1949 and retained strong links with the area. He was knighted in 1990. Amis wrote two volumes of poetry before his first novel, *Lucky Jim* (1954) made him famous. Of his many novels, *That Uncertain Feeling* (1955) and Booker Prize winning, *The Old Devils* (1986), have Swansea settings.

Martin Amis (b.1949), son of Kingsley Amis, was born in Oxford, brought up partly in Swansea and educated at Exeter College, Oxford. *The Rachel Papers* (1974) began a prolific prize-winning, controversial and continuing literary career mainly as a novelist.

John Arlott (1914-92), was born in Basingstoke. As a BBC Poetry Producer he was the friend of Dylan Thomas and other leading writers. He became the most famous of all radio cricket commentators, was *The Guardian's* cricket correspondent, and wrote numerous books, mainly on cricket and wine.

Chris Bendon (b.1950), was born in Leeds and educated at St David's University College, Lampeter. He is a widely published and prize-winning poet. His most recent volumes are *Jewry*, *Crossover* and *Novella: a Novel Poem*, all from Poetry Salzburg. He lives in Lampeter, Dyfed.

John Beynon (b. 1943), was born in Swansea and educated at the University of Wales, Swansea, and London University. His poems are in important Welsh anthologies. He is Professor of Cultural and Communication Studies at the University of Glamorgan.

Ruth Bidgood (b. 1922), was born in Seven Sisters, near Neath, and read English at Oxford University. After serving in the WRNS and working in London, she has, for many years, lived in mid-Wales. *New and Selected Poems* (2004) brings together much of her best work.

George Borrow (1803-81), was born in Norfolk. He was educated in Edinburgh and Norwich. He travelled widely, at times for the British and Foreign Bible Society. As well as *Wild Wales* (1862), his most famous book, his volumes include *Lavengro* (1851) and *The Romany Rye* (1857).

Thomas Bowdler (1754-1825) was an Edinburgh doctor who lived in Rhyddings House, Swansea from 1811 until his death. In 1818 he published his expurgated Shakespeare, the best-selling *Family Shakspeare*. Immortality followed when "to bowdlerise", meaning "to expurgate", entered the language. He is buried in Swansea's All Saints, Oystermouth, churchyard (the grave can no longer be found).

The author of *Memoir of the Late John Bowdler (with a note on Thomas Bowdler)* was Bowdler's nephew, the Reverend Thomas Bowdler (1782-1856).

Arthur Granville Bradley (1850-1943), was the son of the Dean of Westminster, and educated at Trinity College, Cambridge. He spent some years as a gentleman farmer in Virginia. Bradley was a frequent contributor to *Blackwood's Magazine* and *Macmillan's Magazine*. He was a prolific author, mainly of topographical and historical studies.

Tony Conran (b.1931), was born in India and educated at the University of Wales, Bangor. He is well-known as a critic (particularly *The Cost of Strangeness* (1982) and *Frontiers in Anglo-Welsh Poetry* (1997)) and as a poet. *The Penguin Book of Welsh Verse* (1967) made his reputation as a distinguished translator of Welsh language poetry.

Tony Curtis (b. 1946), was born in Carmarthen and educated at the University of Wales, Swansea, and Goddard College, Vermont. A widely published prize-winning poet (see *Selected Poems 1970-1985* (1986) and *Heaven's Gate* (2001)) he has also published short stories, criticism, a monograph on Dannie Abse, and edited anthologies. He is an authority on modern Welsh art (see *Welsh Painters Talking* (1997)). Tony Curtis is Professor of Poetry at the University of Glamorgan.

Dafydd y Coed (fl. late 14C), was probably from Llandovery. He was one of the last of the "Poets of the Gentry". His poem in praise of Hopkyn ap Tomas, of Kilvey, Swansea, is preserved in *The Red Book of Hergest*.

Stevie Davies (b. 1946) is from Swansea. Born into a forces family, her upbringing was peripatetic. Educated at the University of Manchester, she is best known as a prize-winning novelist (twice long listed for the Booker Prize, most recently with *The Element of Water* (2001)) who is also an historian, biographer, and critic. A Fellow of the Royal Society of Literature and a Fellow of the Welsh Academy, she is Director of Creative Writing at University of Wales, Swansea, and lives in Oystermouth.

William Virgil Davis (b. 1940), was born in Ohio, and educated at Ohio University. He lived for a period at Pennard, Gower. He has published fiction and literary criticism (notably on Robert Bly and R.S. Thomas) but is best known as a poet who has published widely in the USA and elsewhere. *One Way to Reconstruct the Scene* (1980) won the Yale Younger Poets Award. He is Professor of English and Writer-in-Residence at Baylor University, Texas.

Moira Dearnley (b. 1942), was born in Swansea and educated at the University of Wales, Swansea. She has published a novel - *That Watery Glass* (1973) - short stories, scholarly articles, a study of the eighteenth-century poet, Christopher Smart, a monograph on Margiad Evans, and *Distant Fields: Essays in Eighteenth Century Fictions of Wales* (2001).

Daniel Defoe (1660-1731), was born in London. The son of a butcher, he was educated at a Dissenting Academy. During a colourful life he failed in business, took part in Monmouth's rebellion, and became a government secret agent. His prolific literary career included savage pamphleteering, for which he was jailed and pilloried. As the author of *Robinson Crusoe* (1719) and *Moll Flanders* (1722) he was a major influence on the English novel.

Elizabeth Amy Dillwyn (1845-1935), was born in Swansea. She reviewed for *The Spectator* and wrote several novels of which the best known is *The Rebecca Rioter* (1880). Keenly interested in women's rights, she was one of the first women industrialists: after her father's death she managed the Dillwyn Spelter Works in Llansamlet, Swansea.

Maura Dooley (b. 1957), was born in Truro and educated at the Universities of York and Bristol. She lectures in Creative Writing at Goldsmiths College, University of London. She has worked as an arts administrator (for a time she directed the 1995 Swansea Year of Literature) but is best known as a poet (see *Kissing the Bone* (1996)) and *Sound Barrier: Poems 1982-2002* (2002)). She lives in London.

J.C. Evans (b. 1923), was born in Gorseinon and now lives in Three Crosses. He was educated at the University of Wales, Swansea, Birkbeck College, and the Open University. Until 1984 he lectured on Mathematics and Physics at what is now Swansea Institute. *The Survivor* (1990) and *Late Lamps* (1999) collect his best work.

Paul Ferris (b. 1929), was born and educated in Swansea and began work as a journalist on the *South Wales Evening Post*. He is the author of over a dozen novels, and an investigative journalist whose subjects have included the Church of England, the House of Northcliffe, and biographies of Richard Burton and Huw Wheldon. He is also an authority on Dylan Thomas, having edited Thomas's letters and written important biographies of Thomas and of his wife, Caitlin. Ferris has written regularly for *The Observer* and for television.

George Sutherland Fraser (1915-80), was born in Glasgow and educated at St Andrew's University. He began as a journalist but after war service lectured at Leicester University, becoming Reader in Poetry. His many publications include *The Modern Writer* and *His World* (1953, rev.1964). *Poems of G.S. Fraser* was published in 1981.

Samuel Clearstone Gamwell (d. 1896), was born in Swansea of poor parents. Whilst an apprentice printer he learned shorthand, French and Latin, and became a newspaper reporter. Known as "the cleverest pressman in South Wales" he became editor of *The Cambrian* newspaper, and wrote the *Official Guide and Handbook to Swansea and its District* (1880). As "Pierre Claire", his witty version of his middle name, he was a prolific composer of verse on local subjects.

Mari George (b.1973), is from Bridgend and was educated at University of Wales, Swansea. She works for BBC Cymru as an editor and script-writer, which includes writing for *Pobol y Cwm*. Her publications include a collection of poems, *Y Nos yn Dal yn fy Ngwallt*, and she is currently working on a travel book about Mexico. She appears regularly on *Talwrn y Beirdd*, the Radio Cymru poetry programme. She lives near Treharris.

Kathryn Gray (b. 1973), was born in Caerphilly and brought up in Swansea. She studied German and Medievalism at the Universities of Bristol and York. Her poetry has been widely published; she also reviews art, theatre and books. *The Never-Never* (2004), her first volume of poetry, was nominated for the T.S. Eliot Prize and the Forward Prize. She lives in London.

William Greenway (b. 1947) is of Welsh ancestry. He was born and bred in Georgia, USA, and educated at Georgia State University and Tulane University in New Orleans. He is now a professor of English at Youngstown State University, Ohio. Professor Greenway has published several collections of poetry, most recently *Ascending Order* (2003). His Welsh connections and an interest in Dylan Thomas have brought him to Wales (to Swansea in particular) on many occasions.

Bryn Griffiths (b. 1933), is from Swansea. He joined the Merchant Navy and also worked in London. He has published numerous volumes of poetry and edited the important anthology, *Welsh Voices* (1967). He lives in Australia.

Tudur Hallam (b.1975), was born in Morriston, Swansea, brought up in Ammanford, and educated at the University of Wales, Aberystwyth. He lectures in the Welsh Department at University of Wales, Swansea, and lives in Swansea's Brynmill.

Barbara Hardy (b.1924), was born and brought up in Swansea. After reading English at University College, London, she held chairs of English at Royal Holloway College and Birkbeck College, both in the University of London. She is a Fellow of the University of Wales, Swansea. Professor Hardy is an authority on the nineteenth-century novel. In her "retirement" she has written a volume of memoirs – *Swansea Girl* (1994) – a novel – *London Lovers* (1995) - *Dylan Thomas: An Original Language* (2000) and a volume of poetry. She divides her time between London and a cottage on Gower.

Ernest Howard Harris (1876-1961), was born and brought up in Swansea. He was a teacher in England and much-travelled in northern Europe. From 1919 to 1959 he published six volumes of poetry, English translations of Finnish poetry, and studies of the literatures of Friesland and Estonia.

Julia Ann Hatton ("Ann of Swansea") (1764-1838), was born in Worcester, the sister of Sarah Siddons. After a notorious early life she and her second husband ran the Swansea Bathing House from 1799 to 1806. When he died she ran a dancing school before devoting herself to writing poetry and novels, at which she was dreadfully prolific.

Peter Hellings (1921-95), was born in Swansea. After working for the GWR and war service in the RAF, he studied at the University of Wales, Swansea, and became a teacher in England. He published two volumes of poetry: *Firework Music* (1950) and *A Swansea Sketchbook* (1983).

David Hughes (b. 1947), was born in Bargoed but moved to Swansea, aged seven, when his father became Vicar of Oystermouth. He was educated at Trinity College, Carmarthen, and the University of Wales, Cardiff, and works for Swansea's social services. His poems and short stories have appeared in a number of magazines. He lives in Swansea.

Jeremy Hughes has worked as a lecturer in English. In 1995 he won first prize in *Poetry Wales's* thirtieth anniversary poetry competition. His poems have also appeared in *New Welsh Review* and *Rialto*. In 1996 he was living in Risca.

Nigel Jenkins (b. 1949), was born in Gower and educated at Essex University. He is a prize-winning poet (see *Acts of Union: Selected Poems 1974-1989*) and has also published a study of Welsh missionaries in India - *Gwalia in Khasia* (1996) - which was Welsh Book of the Year. He is the co-editor of a forthcoming *Encyclopaedia of Wales*.

David Jones (1895-1974), was born in Brockley, Kent. His father was from Flintshire. Jones studied art in London before and after serving on the Western Front as a private with the Royal Welsh Fusiliers. Apart from periods at Capel-y-Ffin with Eric Gill, after 1918 he lived alone in the London area, preoccupied with Welsh landscape and culture and with his own Welshness. He remains a painter of distinction. *In Parenthesis* (1937), The *Anathemata* (1952), and *The Sleeping Lord* (1974) have established him as a major modernist writer.

David James Jones ("Gwenallt") (1899-1968), was born in Alltwen in the Swansea Valley. He was educated at the University of Wales, Aberystwyth, and spent much of his later career as a lecturer in its department of Welsh. Gwenallt remains one of the most distinguished Welsh language poets, and a literary scholar and critic of importance.

Peter Thabit Jones (b. 1951) was born in Swansea (where he still lives) and educated at Swansea Institute. He is a prolific, widely-published and much-anthologised poet, writing for children and adults.

Russell Celyn Jones (b.1954), was born in Swansea and educated at the Universities of London and Iowa. He is a novelist and critic, a staff reviewer for *The Times*, was a Booker Prize judge in 2002, and is Professor of Creative Writing at Birkbeck College, University of London. His novels, several of which have Welsh settings, include *An Interference of Light* (1995) and *Ten Seconds from the Sun* (2005).

Sally Roberts Jones (b.1935), was born in London and educated at the University of Wales, Bangor. From 1967 she worked in Port Talbot as a reference librarian and founded Alun Books. Her many publications include four volumes of poetry, a study of Allen Raine, and much local history.

T. Harri Jones (1921-1965),was born at Cwm Brogau, Brecknockshire, and educated at University of Wales, Aberystwyth. He became a lecturer in English at the University of New South Wales. His *Collected Poems* were published in 1977. T. Harri Jones was found drowned in the sea near his Australian home.

Francis Kilvert (1840-1879), was born near Chippenham, Wiltshire and educated at Wadham College, Oxford. From 1865 to 1872 he was curate of Clyro, Radnorshire. His famous Diary covered the period from 1870 until his early death (from peritonitis). Only a comparatively small portion has survived, mainly in William Plomer's edition.

Stephen Knight (b. 1960), was born in Swansea and educated at Oxford University. His poetry has been published in leading British literary magazines and collected in three volumes. His novel, *Mr Schnitzel*, was Welsh Book of the Year for 2001. More recently he has published *Sardines* (2005), poems for children. In addition, he reviews for the *TLS* and tutors creative writing.

Walter Savage Landor (1775-1864), was born in Warwickshire. He was educated at Rugby and Trinity College, Oxford. His numerous writings include the epic poem, *Gebir* (1798), much lyric poetry and, in prose, *Imaginary Conversations of Literary Men and Statesmen* (1824-1829). During 1796-1797 he lived in Swansea with a young woman from Tenby and their illegitimate child. He is satirised by Dickens as Boythorn in *Bleak House*.
   Rose Aylmer (1780-1799), was the step-daughter of Landor's friend, Howell Price of Laugharne. Landor met her "walking on the burrows at Swansea". Three years later she went with an aunt to India and within six months died of cholera. Her death inspired Landor's most famous lyric, and the final lines of "Abertawy".

Michael Lenihan (b. 1949), was born in Nottingham and educated at Warwick University and University of Wales, Swansea. He is a former civil servant and local government employee. Since 1975 he has lived in the Swansea area, at present on Gower. His poetry has appeared in numerous magazines.

Saunders Lewis (1893-1985), was born in Wallesey, Cheshire, and educated at Liverpool University. From 1922 to 1937 he lectured in the Department of Welsh at University of Wales, Swansea. He was dismissed when, in 1936, he was convicted of arson on an RAF bombing school in North Wales. As a political activist and journalist he was a controversial figure. A prolific career as a scholar and as a creative writer - playwright, poet, and novelist - made him a dominant force in twentieth-century Welsh language literature.

Lewys Glyn Cothi (c. 1420-1489), was probably from Carmarthenshire. Little is known of him. Some two hundred and thirty of his poems have survived. Dafydd Johnston's definitive edition of his work was published in 1995.

Andrew Lycett (b. 1948), lives in North London. He read Modern History at Christ Church, Oxford. He has worked as a foreign correspondent in Africa and the Middle East. and is a regular book reviewer for national publications. Lycett is the distinguished biographer of Colonel Qadaffi, Ian Fleming, Rudyard Kipling, and Dylan Thomas.

Jonathan Mallalieu (b. 1966), was born in Medway Towns, Kent. He lived in Swansea and West Wales for ten years, and read English at University of Wales, Swansea. He has worked in the Far East as a teacher and musician. In the mid-1990s he was living and writing in Cumbria.

Mervyn Matthews (b. 1932), was born in Hafod, Swansea and witnessed first-hand the blitz on the town. He read Russian at Manchester University and has written several books on the Soviet Union, including *Privilege in the Soviet Union, Poverty in the Soviet Union, The Passport Society* and *Mila & Mervusya: A Russian Wedding*. Now retired from academic life, he lives and writes in London.

Jo Mazelis (b. 1956) is Swansea born and educated at Swansea Institute and University of Wales, Swansea. Her prize-winning and much-anthologised short stories are collected in *Diving Girls* (2002) and *Circle Games* (2005). She also works as a visual artist.

Robert Minhinnick (b. 1952), was born in Neath and now lives in Porthcawl. He is a Forward Prize-winning poet - *Selected Poems* (1999) - who also edits *Poetry Wales*. In 1993 his volume of essays, *Watching the Fire Eater*, was Welsh Book of the Year. His "Paradise Park" essay began life as the text accompanying a booklet of photographs of the Townhill area of Swansea, a troubled council-estate above the city now visually transformed by European Urban Regeneration funds. This anthology uses a revised version of "Paradise Park" from *To Babel and Back* (2005) winner of Welsh Book of the Year 2006.

Leslie Norris (1921-2006), was from Merthyr. He was educated at Coventry Teacher Training College and Southampton University. He was Humanities Research Professor of Creative Writing at Brigham Young University, Provo, Utah, and for many years until his death lived in nearby Orem. His work has won prestigious literary prizes, establishing him as one of the leading Welsh writers of the generation after Dylan Thomas. His *Collected Stories* and *Collected Poems* appeared in 1996. Norris also wrote poetry for children and translated Welsh language poetry and poems by Rilke. He was a Fellow of the Royal Society of Literature and a Fellow of the Welsh Academy.

John Ormond (1923-1990), was born in Dunvant, Swansea, as John Ormond Thomas. He was educated at the University of Wales, Swansea. After working for *Picture Post* he had a distinguished career with BBC Wales as a director and producer. *Requiem and Celebration* (1969) and *Definition of a Waterfall* (1973), established him one of the finest Welsh poets of his time.

Alan Perry (b. 1942), was born in Swansea, educated at Swansea College of Art, and has worked in Swansea as an art teacher. He is well known as a painter; his poetry and short stories have been widely published. *Music You Don't Normally Hear* (1998) collects interviews with the homeless, and has been adapted for the stage. *Dreaming from North to South: New and Selected Poems* (2006) includes work from over forty years of writing.

John Pook (b. 1942), was born in Neath and lived in Gowerton. After Queen's College, Cambridge, and University of Wales, Bangor, he became a teacher in Ruthin. He is best-known for his volume of poetry about Swansea, *That Cornish-Facing Door* (1975).

John Prichard (1916-1989), was born in Swansea. He was a member of the "Kardomah Circle" (which included Dylan Thomas and Vernon Watkins) during the 1930s. At that time he published stories and poems in Wales. After the war he lived in England and published little apart from one novel, *A Journey to the End of the Alphabet* (1951).

Denis F. Ratcliffe (1933-2004), was born in Gorseinon, brought up in the Mayhill area of Swansea, and educated at the University of Wales, Cardiff. He served in the RAF, and was for many years a chartered accountant and management consultant in London. Despite poor health he published two novels: *Second Chances* (1996) and *A Stranger at Home* (2004).

Lloyd Rees (b.1949), was born in London, brought up in Swansea, and educated at Sussex University and University of Wales, Swansea. He lectures in English and Creative Writing at Swansea Institute. His poems and short stories have won several literary prizes. He has published two novels and several volumes of poetry, and edited two volumes of student writing.

Alun Richards (1929-2004) was born in Pontypridd and educated at Monmouthshire Teachers' Training College, Caerleon, and, later, at University of Wales, Swansea (where, in 1985, he became an Honorary Fellow). He worked as a probation officer, teacher, Royal Navy seaman, and adult-education tutor. Following lucrative TV and film scriptwriting (most notably for the 1970s TV hit, *The Onedin Line*), he settled in Mumbles until his death. Via novels, short stories, plays, and a fine autobiography (*Days of Absence* (1986)) Richards remains one of the most important chroniclers of English-speaking South Wales. His Swansea writing includes *Ennal's Point* (1977), a novel about lifeboat men, and *Barque Whisper* (1979).

Don Rodgers (b. 1957), was born in London and educated at Lincoln College, Oxford. He has lived in South Wales since 1989 (currently in Neath) and is a prize-winning poet (see *Moontan* (1996)) who also writes fiction and drama. He is a qualified teacher of adult literacy.

Neil Rosser (b.1964), was born and brought up in Swansea. He was educated at University of Wales, Aberystwyth, and now lives in Carmarthenshire. Currently he is teaching in Cross Hands. He is well-known in Welsh language circles for his often satirical songs. Sain Records has brought out a number of his CDs; more recently he has formed his own record company.

Clement William Scott (1841-1904), was born in London. He was a playwright (using pseudonyms) and drama critic of the *Daily Telegraph* for thirty years from 1872, He also edited *The Theatre*. Scott was a drama critic of the old school, remembered now for his hostility to Ibsen and Shaw: he dismissed *Ghosts* as the work of "an egotist and a bungler".

Henry Skrine (1755-1803), was born in Warley, Somerset. He was educated at Christ College, Oxford, and called to the Bar in 1782. Thereafter he spent most of his life travelling throughout Britain.

David ("Dai") Smith (b. 1945), was born in Tonypandy. He was educated at Balliol, Columbia, and the University of Wales Swansea, becoming a lecturer at the last-named. Dai Smith held a Chair of History at Cardiff University, was Head of English Language Programmes at BBC Wales, and Pro Vice-Chancellor at the University of Glamorgan. He is Research Professor at CREW (Centre for Research into the English Language and Literature of Wales) at University of Wales, Swansea.

Dylan Thomas (1914-1953), was born in Swansea. He was educated at Swansea Grammar School, worked briefly as a local journalist, then became a full-time writer. *18 Poems* (1934), *Twenty-five Poems* (1936), *The Map of Love* (1939), *Portrait of the Artist as a Young Dog* (1940), and *Deaths and Entrances* (1946), made him famous, and one of the most important English language poets of the twentieth century. *Collected Poems 1934-1952* (1952) was acclaimed. His "play for voices", *Under Milk Wood*, is widely read and performed. He was well known as a broadcaster; he also wrote film scripts. During his last three years he made successful reading-tours of North America. His heavy drinking and wild behaviour have made him a byword for bohemian living. He died in New York.

Edward Thomas (1878-1917), was born in London of Welsh parents, and educated at Lincoln College, Oxford. He often stayed with his father's relatives in the Swansea area. His prose includes *Beautiful Wales* (1905). His poetry was published posthumously, following his death at Arras on the Western Front. He is now established as an important twentieth-century writer.

Peter Thomas (b. 1939), was born in Manchester, but spent part of his childhood in the Swansea area. He was educated at the University of Wales, Cardiff, and New York State University. He was, until his retirement, for many years Professor of English at the University of New Brunswick, Canada. His publications include a monograph on Richard Hughes, and *Strangers from a Secret Land* (1986), a much-praised study of Welsh settlers in Canada.

William Thomas ("Islwyn") (1832-1878), was born in Ynysddu, Monmouthshire, and became a Calvinistic Methodist minister. Islwyn's major works are two long poems entitled "Y Storm", responses to the sudden death of his fiancee, Anne Bowen of Swansea. He later married Martha Davies, also of Swansea.

John Powell Ward (b. 1937), was born in Felixstowe and educated at the Universities of Toronto, Cambridge, and Wales. For many years he lectured at University of Wales, Swansea. He is a widely published, prize winning poet (see *Selected and New Poems* (2004)). John Ward's publications include studies of Raymond Williams, R.S. Thomas, English poetry, and Shakespeare. He is a former editor of *Poetry Wales* and the editor of Seren's "Borderlines" series.

Val Warner (b. 1946), was born in England and educated at Oxford University. She was Writer-in-Residence at the University of Wales, Swansea, 1977-1978. Her volumes of poetry include *Before Lunch* (1986) and *Tooting Idyll* (1998). She has translated Corbire, and edited Charlotte Mew, *Collected Poems and Prose* (1982).

Vernon Watkins (1906-1967), was born in Maesteg, but lived much of his life in Swansea. After Repton and Cambridge, from 1926 to 1966 he worked at Lloyds Bank, St Helen's Road, Swansea, and lived at Pennard, Gower. An occasional member of the "Kardomah circle", he was a close friend of Dylan Thomas. Faber published *The Ballad of the Mari Lwyd* (1941). Six further volumes of poetry followed during his lifetime, plus translations of Heine, all of which established him as one of the most important poets of his day. His *Collected Poems* appeared in 1986.

Harri Webb (1920-1994), was born in Swansea and educated at Magdalen College, Oxford. He was a bookseller in Cardiff, then a librarian in Dowlais and Mountain Ash. Though he wrote scripts for television, songs, ballads, and children's stories, he remains best known for his, at times, fiercely political poetry. *Collected Poems* was published in 1995.

John Wesley (1703-1791), was born in Lincolnshire. He was educated at Oxford, where, with his brother Charles and George Whitefield, he founded Methodism. Thereafter he made many preaching tours, and wrote thousands of sermons, as well as hymns and other improving works. His energy was amazing, his influence for good incalculable.

Gareth Williams (b. 1945), was born in Barry and educated at Balliol, LSE, and Chicago. He is Professor of History in the University of Glamorgan. As well as co-authoring *Fields of Praise* (1981) with Dai Smith, he has published much on modern Welsh history, with a particular emphasis on the history of sport.

Rowan Williams (b.1950), was born and brought up in Swansea and educated at Christ's College, Cambridge and Oxford University. He was Lady Margaret Professor of Divinity at Oxford, before becoming Bishop of Monmouth in 1992, Archbishop of Wales in 2000, and Archbishop of Canterbury in 2002. Apart from numerous books on theology and spirituality, he has published two volumes of poetry.

Waldo Williams (1904-71), was born in Haverfordwest. He was educated at University of Wales, Aberystwyth, and became a teacher in England and Wales. A life-long pacifist, like his parents, he was also a prominent member of Plaid Cymru. His high reputation as a poet is based mainly on *Dail Pren* (1956). Tony Conran has translated *The Peacemakers: Selected Poems* (1997).

Jen Wilson (b.1944), was born in Swansea where she has lived for most of her life. She has been a Tutor in Performing Arts at University of Wales, Swansea. Jen Wilson is Director of the thriving and important Swansea Women's Jazz Archive. She has published on local history. Though she regards herself as essentially a performer, playing jazz-piano in various bands, she has also written jazz settings of Dylan Thomas poems.

Penny Windsor (b.1946), was born in Cornwall and educated at Swansea Institute and University of Wales, Swansea. She has worked as a teacher, youth worker, and for the Citizen's Advice Bureau. She is widely known and published as a poet - *Dangerous Women* (1987) and *Like Oranges* (1989) - and performance poet. Penny Windsor lived in Swansea from 1968 to 2002. She now lives in Shepton Mallet, Somerset.

The editor, **James A. Davies**, was born in Llandeilo in 1939, and brought up in Tonyrefail, Tonypandy, and Pontypool. His family connections with Swansea go back many years; he has lived in the city since 1962. Jim Davies was educated at University of Wales, Swansea and was a Senior Lecturer in its Department of English, retiring in 1998. He has been visiting professor at Baylor University, Texas and Mellon Research Fellow at the University of Texas at Austin. His numerous books and articles on Victorian literature and Welsh Writing in English include *The Textual Life of Dickens's Characters* (1989), *Leslie Norris* (1991), *A Reference Companion to Dylan Thomas* (1998) and *Dylan Thomas's Swansea, Gower and Laugharne* (2000). He is a Fellow of the Welsh Academy.

Acknowledgements 2006

Whilst preparing this new, expanded edition, I am grateful to Peter Finch, Robert Minhinnick, M. Wynn Thomas and Fflur Dafydd, for help of various kinds, willingly given.

Particular thanks to Marilyn Jones, whose enthusiasm and indefatigable custodianship of the Swansea Collection in the city's Central Reference Library, lightened my task. I am grateful to Grahame Davies, who found time in a busy life to translate the three new Welsh language poems.

Mick Felton and his colleagues at Seren have, once again, demonstrated their efficiency and commitment.

Needless to say, I remain responsible for any errors.

James A. Davies

Acknowledgements 1996

For help of various kinds, willingly given, I am grateful to the following: John Alban, Elinor ap Howell, Dafydd Johnston, Marilyn Jones of the *Cambrian* Project, Lowri Lloyd, Glyn Pursglove, Robin Reeves, Robert Rhys, Sally Roberts-Jones, Peter Stead, Wynn Thomas, Leigh Verrill-Rhys.

I owe particular thanks to Tony Conran for translating all but one of the Welsh language poems, and for being so generous with his time and learning.

Mick Felton and his colleagues at Seren have expedited matters with their usual efficiency.

Needless to say, I alone am responsible for any errors.

James A. Davies

Publisher's Acknowledgements

Acknowledgements are due to the following for permission to reprint work in this anthology.

Dannie Abse: 'A Sea-Shell for Vernon Watkins' from *Way Out In the Centre* (Hutchinson, 1981) by permission of Shiel Land Associates. **Graham Allen**: 'Out of the Dark' from *Out of the Dark* (Triskele Press, 1974) by permission of the author. **Kingsley Amis:** 'Aberdarcy: the Main Square' from *A Look Around the Estate* (Hutchinson, 1967) copyright 1967 Kingsley Amis. Reprinted by kind permission of Jonathan Clowes Ltd, London, on behalf of the Kingsley Amis Literary Estate; extract from *That Uncertain Feeling* (Gollancz, 1955) by permission of Victor Gollancz Ltd. **Martin Amis:** 'Memories of a Swansea Childhood' from *Experience* (Jonathan Cape, 2001). Reprinted by permission of The Random House Group. **John Arlott**: 'Cricket at Swansea' from *The Cricketer's Companion* (Penguin, 1960), by permission of the Estate of John Arlott. **Chris Bendon**: 'Swansea' by permission of the author. **John Beynon**: 'An old lie out' by permission of the author. **Ruth Bidgood**: 'Catherine at Stouthall' from *The Fluent Moment* (Seren, 1996) by permission of the author. **Tony Conran**: 'Hiatus in Swansea' from *Castles* (Gomer, 1993) by permission of the author. **Tony Curtis**: 'Singleton' from *Preparations* (Gomer, 1980) by permission of the author. **Stevie Davies**: extract from *Kith and Kin* (Phoenix Press, 2004) by permission of Phoenix Press, a division of the Orion publishing group. **William Virgil Davis**: 'Landscape (Gower)' and 'Living Away' by permission of the author. **Moria Dearnley**: extract from *That Watery Glass* (Christopher Davis, 1973) by permission of the author. **Maura Dooley**: 'The Women of Mumbles Head' from *Sound Barrier Poems 1982-2002* (Bloodaxe 2002) by permission of Bloodaxe Books. **J.C. Evans**: 'Crofty Flats' from *The Survivor* (Swansea Poetry Workshop, 1990) by permission of the author. **Paul Ferris**: 'A Holiday Gone Wrong' from *Infidelity* (HarperCollins 1999). Reprinted by permission of HarperCollins Publishers Ltd. © Paul Ferris 1999. **G.S. Fraser**: 'Memories of Swansea' from *Poems of G.S. Fraser* (Leicester University Press, 1981) by permission of Leicester University Press. **Mari George**: 'Swansea Beach' from *Cerddi Abertawe a'r Cwm* (Gomer 2002) by permission of the author and Gomer Press. **Kathryn Gray**: 'The Italians in the Rain' and 'Driver' from *The Never-Never* (Seren 2004) by permission of the author. **William Greenway**: 'Pwll Du' from *Simmer Dim*, the University of Akron Press, © 1999 William Greenway. Reprinted by permission of the

University of Akron Press and the author. **Tudur Hallam**: 'Bryn Road' from *Cerddi Abertawe a'r Cwm* (Gomer 2002) by permission of the author and Gomer Press. **Barbara Hardy**: extract from *Swansea Girl* (Peter Owen, 1994) by permission of Peter Owen Ltd, London. 'Sweets' from *Severn Bridge: New and Selected Poems* (Shoestring, 2001) by permission of the author. **Peter Hellings**: 'A Local Habitation' from *A Swansea Sketchbook* (Ponte-fract Press, 1983) by permission of Manon Hellings. **David Hughes**: 'Swonzee Boy See?' by permission of the author. **Nigel Jenkins**: 'Chain harrows', 'Beach Huts, Gŵyr' from *Acts of Union: Selected Poems 1974-1989* (Gomer, 1990) and 'Swansea Haiku' by permission of Gomer Press. **David Jones**: extract from *The Sleeping Lord* (Faber, 1974) by permssion of Faber and Faber Ltd. **David James Jones**: 'Rugby' from *Eples* (Gomer, 1951), translated by Tony Conran, by permission of the translator and Gomer Press. **Peter Thabit Jones**: 'Gower Delivery' from *Visitors* (Poetry Wales Press, 1986) by permission of the author. **Russell C Jones**: 'Damaged Beyond Repair' from *Ten Seconds from the Sun* (Little, Brown 2005) by permission of Little, Brown Books. **Sally Roberts Jones**: 'Rhossili' from *Poems '69* (Gomer, 1969) by permission of the author. **T. Harri Jones**: 'Swansea' from *The Beast at the Door* (Rupert Hart-Davis, 1963) by permission of Gomer Press. **Stephen Knight**: 'At the Foot of Division Four' from *The Sandfields Baudelaire* (Smith/Doorstop, 1996) by permission of the author; extract from 'Notes for a Poem Called Me Me Me' and 'Double Writing' from *Flowering Limbs* (Bloodaxe, 1993) by permission of Bloodaxe Books. **Michael Lenihan**: 'Pennard Valley' (1995) by permission of the author. **Saunders Lewis**: extract from *Monica* (1930), translated by Meic Stephens, by permission of the translator and the Estate of Saunders Lewis. **Lowri Lloyd**: translation of 'In praise of Hopkin ap Thomas' by permission of the translator. **Andrew Lycett**: 'Swansea Grammar School in the 1920s' from *Dylan Thomas: A New Life* (Phoenix Press, 2003) by permission of Phoenix Press, a division of the Orion publishing group. **Jonathan Mallalieu**: 'The Church' from *The Prince of Wales and Stories* (Phoenix, 1993) by permission of Orion Books Ltd. **Mervyn Matthews**: 'Coal Trimming' from *Mervyn's Lot* (Seren, 2002) by permission of the author. **Jo Mazelis**: 'Too Perfect' from *Diving Girls* (Parthian 2002) by permission of the author and Parthian Books. **Robert Minhinnick**: 'Paradise Park' from *To Babel and Back* (Seren, 2005) by permission of the author. **Leslie Norris**: 'Percy Colclough and the Religious Girls' from *Collected Stories* (Seren, 1996) by permission of the author. **John Ormond**: 'Poem in February', extract from 'City in Fire and Snow' and 'Homage to a Folk Singer' by permission of Glenys Ormond. **Alan Perry**: 'Live Wires' from *Live Wires* (1970) and 'Nocturnes, Swansea' by permission of the author. **John Pook**: 'A view from Swansea' by permission of the author. **Denis F. Ratcliffe**: extract from *Second Chances* (Seren, 1996) by permission of the author. **Lloyd Rees**: 'Wind Street 1998' from *Swansea Poems* (Christopher Davies, 2000) by permission of the author. **Alun Richards**: 'Someone Out There' from *Mama's Baby (Papa's Maybe)* (Parthian 1999) by kind permission of Helen Richards and Parthian. **Don Rodgers**: 'Tycoch' by permission of the author. **Dylan Thomas**: 'Hunchback in the Park' 'I have longed to move away' 'Once it was the colour of saying' from *Collected Poems* (Dent, 1988); 'Reminiscences of Childhood (First Version)' from *The Broadcasts* (Dent, 1991) by permission of David Higham Associates. **Peter Thomas**: 'The Lascars' by permission of the author. **John Powell Ward**: 'Evening Bathers' from *The Clearing* (Poetry Wales Press, 1984) by permisssion of the author. **Val Warner**: 'By St. Paul's Parish Church, Sketty' by permission of the author. **Vernon Watkins**: 'Rhossili', 'Ode to Swansea', Bishopston Stream' and an aspect from 'The Broken Sea' by permission of Gwen Watkins. **Harri Webb**: 'That Summer' and 'In Gower' by permission of Meic Stephens. **Rowan Williams**: 'Oystermouth Cemetery' reproduced from *After Silent Centuries* (Perpetua Press: Oxford, 1994) by kind permission of the Archbishop of Canterbury, © Rowan Williams 1994 **Waldo Williams**: 'The Peacemakers' from *Dail Pren* (Gomer 1956) translated by Tony Conran, by permission of Gomer Press. **Jen Wilson**: 'Zen and the Art of Thelonius Monk' by permission of the author. **Penny Windsor**: 'Heroines' by permission of the author.

Extract from *Fields of Praise* (University of Wales Press 1980) by David Smith and Gareth Williams by permission of University of Wales Press.

Other titles from Seren you may enjoy

Christmas in Wales, **edited by Dewi Roberts** £6.95

Celebrate Christmas the Welsh way in the company of some of the country's leading writers, past and present. Among the many subjects drawn from stories, poems, diaries and letters are Christmas Mass, the Nativity Play, plum pudding and turkey, folk customs such as the Mari Lwyd, shopping, presents, frost and snow, and the post-Christmas blues. *Christmas in Wales* is the perfect literary companion to the festive season, a present that will be opened again and again ...

Letters from Wales, **edited by Joan Abse** £14.95

Ranging over eight centuries, this fascinating anthology of private and public correspondence, journals and diary entries provides an enthralling commentary on Wales. From Kings, Princes and Bishops to writers, artists and politicians; from the medieval machinations of Glyndwr and Hotspur to bitter industrial disputes; from Oliver Cromwell to Lloyd George, George Eliot to Dylan Thomas: a richly textured, entertaining and informative book emerges.

Love from Wales, **edited by Tony Curtis & Siân James** £6.95

The passionate nature of the Welsh finds full expression in *Love from Wales*, as selection of poetry and prose on the theme of love in a Celtic climate. Poet Tony Curtis and novelist Siân James have chosen from the works of Wales' most intense and romantic writers in an anthology ranging from the eleventh century to the present. Includes Dylan Thomas, Dannie Abse, Gillian Clarke, John Ormond, Alun Richards, Alun Lewis, R.S. Thomas, Vernon Watkins, Jean Earle, Gwyn Thomas, David Lloyd George, Dafydd ap Gwilym, Emyr Humphreys, Jean Rhys, Idris Davies, Alexander Cordell, and many more.

Swansea Girl, **Barbara Hardy** £8.99

Swansea Girl is a recollection of childhood and adolescence in the '20s, '30s and '40s, told with an attractive candour and made vivid by the author's remarkable eye for detail. Barbara Hardy groups her memories into themes and shows us how the lives of her parents were shaped by history, in particular by the two World Wars, the Wall Street Crash of 1929 and the '30s Depression. The emphasis of this appealing story is on family life, with its rich throng of relations, friends and languages, and their compelling influences.

Mervyn's Lot, **Mervyn Matthews** £7.95

Mervyn Matthews' childhood in the '30s, '40s and '50s was remarkable even by the standards of the time. Bombed out of his house during the Swansea blitz, he went to live with his maternal grandmother in the Hafod area of Swansea, was evacuated to west Wales and also spent a long period hospitalised. Against the backdrop of bombed-out Swansea and the beautiful Gower, and with a cast of friends, teachers, neighbours and his large family - Mervyn's Lot - this is a story by turns comic and poignant, and always true to the life of the times.

Kerry's Children, **Ellen Davis** £7.99

Ellen Davis was born in 1929 in the small German village of Hoof. Her Jewish family had lived there since 1760 but its peaceful existence was shattered when Hitler came to power and German Jews were persecuted.Ellen's autobiography tells the harrowing story of her childhood struggle to protect her younger brothers and sisters from the terrors of life in Nazi Germany and her escape to Swansea via the *Kindertransport*. This is also the moving story of Ellen's life in Britain, the difficulties of her first marriage and her love for her own Welsh children as she finds happiness in a new relationship. Meanwhile she continues to search for her German family and relatives in Australia, Israel and the US - a search which ends finally, heart-rendingly, in Riga in Latvia.

Second Chances, **Denis F. Ratcliffe** £6.95

Critically injured in a mysterious air crash, D. considers the question which has haunted his young life: "what am I doing here?" What he recalls is a disturbing story of a child's struggle for survival set against the backdrop of the deprivations of the Second World War, and the bombing of his hometown, Swansea. *Second Chances* is a gripping and authentic account of the pain of an unhappy childhood, and life in an industrial housing estate in Swansea during and after the war.

Available from bookshops or direct from www.seren-books.com